# Speaking of Language and Law

# OXFORD STUDIES IN LANGUAGE AND LAW

Oxford Studies in Language and Law includes scholarly analyses and descriptions of language evidence in civil and criminal law cases as well as language issues arising in the area of statutes, statutory interpretation, courtroom discourse, jury instructions, and historical changes in legal language.

# Speaking of Language and Law

CONVERSATIONS ON THE WORK
OF PETER TIERSMA

Edited By Lawrence M. Solan,
Janet Ainsworth,
and
Roger W. Shuy

OXFORD
UNIVERSITY PRESS

# OXFORD
UNIVERSITY PRESS

Oxford University Press is a department of the University of
Oxford. It furthers the University's objective of excellence in research,
scholarship, and education by publishing worldwide.

Oxford   New York
Auckland   Cape Town   Dar es Salaam   Hong Kong   Karachi
Kuala Lumpur   Madrid   Melbourne   Mexico City   Nairobi
New Delhi   Shanghai   Taipei   Toronto

With offices in
Argentina   Austria   Brazil   Chile   Czech Republic   France   Greece
Guatemala   Hungary   Italy   Japan   Poland   Portugal   Singapore
South Korea   Switzerland   Thailand   Turkey   Ukraine   Vietnam

Oxford is a registered trademark of Oxford University Press
in the UK and certain other countries.

Published in the United States of America by
Oxford University Press
198 Madison Avenue, New York, NY 10016

© Oxford University Press 2015

Library of Congress Cataloging-in-Publication Data
Speaking of language and law : conversations on the work of Peter Tiersma / edited by
Lawrence M. Solan, Janet Ainsworth, and Roger W. Shuy.
pages cm.—(Oxford studies in language and law)
Includes bibliographical references and index.
ISBN 978–0–19–933418–6 (hardcover : alk. paper)   1. Law—Language.   2. Tiersma, Peter
Meijes.   I. Tiersma, Peter Meijes, author.   II. Solan, Lawrence, 1952- editor.   III. Ainsworth,
Janet, editor.   IV. Shuy, Roger W., editor.
K213.S665 2015
340'.14—dc23
2014050058

9 8 7 6 5 4 3 2 1
Printed in the United States of America
on acid-free paper

For Peter, of course

Peter Tiersma

1952–2014

# TABLE OF CONTENTS

## Defaming

## PART IV **Interpreting Laws**

## PART V **Language and Criminal Justice**

## Crimes of Language

# PREFACE

Ceci n'est pas un Festschrift. Instead, to celebrate Peter Tiersma's distinguished career and many significant contributions to the study of law through language and the study of language through law, we have republished excerpts from some of his most important writings, and invited 32 scholars (including ourselves, we must concede) to write short essays that spring from Tiersma's work, and at the same time convey each author's views concerning some important aspect of the study of language and law. The result, we hope, is a book full of interesting pieces, each engaging in its own right, which together form a tribute to one of the great contributors to the study of language and law.

Indeed, it takes 32 scholars to provide meaningful commentary on Peter's work. One can never predict in advance that a particular individual will so shine, but once it happens, we can all learn much from looking back. We start with language. Peter was born in Friesland, in the north of the Netherlands in 1952. His first language was Frisian, his second Dutch. His family were dairy farmers, some of whom are still in California, where they moved when he was a child, after a brief stop in Wisconsin. Peter went to public school among many other immigrants, mostly Latinos, making English his third and Spanish his fourth languages. In college (Stanford), German became his fifth, with Latin a hobby.

Not surprisingly, Peter had become engaged not only in languages, but also language as a phenomenon, and earned a PhD in linguistics from the University of California at San Diego, where he focused on phonology and phonetics. He taught linguistics for a while, but soon decided that he would go into law, and enrolled in Boalt Hall School of Law at the University of California, Berkeley, where he earned a law degree. He then clerked for Stanley Mosk, a prominent justice on the Supreme Court of California, practiced law for a few years, and in 1990 accepted a position at Loyola Law School in Los Angeles, where he spent his entire academic life as a law professor, including many years with an endowed chair. He lived throughout these years with his wife Thea near Santa Barbara, from which he traveled weekly to Los Angeles to teach and engage in the life of his law school, until his premature death from cancer in April 2014.

As Peter began his teaching career, his scholarly research on language in legal settings was developing in earnest. Lawyers had contributed writings analyzing legal language, often criticizing "legalese" for being turgid and incomprehensible. However, this work by lawyers was impressionistic in nature, uninformed by research in linguistics and psychology on the nature of language and linguistic competences, and frequently marked by personal idiosyncratic preferences about legal usage. Meanwhile, linguists, anthropologists, and psychologists were beginning to engage in a systematic examination of language use in legal contexts. The focus of this work explored the ways in which language used for special, particularized purposes in situated contexts—such as the varieties of legal language—could shed light on the nature of language in social contexts more generally. Often, however, these researchers lacked a full understanding of the legal contexts in which legal language was embedded and failed to appreciate the instrumental complexity of legal language as used by legal actors. The time was ripe for a scholar who had training in both law and in linguistics to examine the many facets of legal doctrine and practice that involve language issues. That scholar was Peter Tiersma.

Right from the beginning of his legal academic career, Peter launched into writing a series of articles on the tacit linguistic assumptions embedded in many legal doctrines. Often using the theory of speech acts, these articles unpacked legal doctrine, demonstrating which elements correspond to the ways people actually communicate, and which ways do not. Linguistic theory and legal theory have different goals. The former seeks to account for how language works, the latter seeks to establish a system in which values such as the rule of law and the sense of justice prevail. Yet when a legal system incorporates rules of language into the rules of law, the two fields merge. It was at these points of coincidence that Peter began his explorations. They included the theory of contract formation, defamation, inferences we draw from a person's silence (so important in the law of evidence and the law of criminal procedure), the nature of consent, the interpretation of statutes, and the definition of crimes committed through language, such as perjury and threats. To these subjects Peter added the nature of legal language and its history, and a commitment to the goal of improving instructions to juries, which often remain incomprehensible to the average person even today.

In every one of these areas, Peter Tiersma became a leading scholar and has remained a leading legal scholar. Some of the work is recent, some now a quarter century old. All of it is influential in the literatures of different disciplines, especially law and linguistics, but also history, psychology, and philosophy. And, happily, Peter's books in particular are also accessible to the uninitiated. It should not be surprising, then, that this book contains contributions from people educated in law, linguistics, criminology, philosophy, anthropology, psychology, history, and medicine. All of these pieces are tributes to Peter Tiersma's excellent contributions.

All are good reads.

We had intended this book to be a living tribute to a great scholar. Sadly, that was not to be. We hope only that the excerpts and new contributions stand as a testament both to the vitality of the inquiry into questions of language and law, and to Peter Tiersma's contributions to it.

LMS

JA

RWS

March 2015

# ACKNOWLEDGMENTS

The chapters containing excerpts of Peter Tiersma's work have been previously published and are reprinted here with the kind permission of Peter Tiersma and the original publishers:

Chapter 1. A History of the Languages of Law. *Oxford Handbook of Language and Law* (P. Tiersma and L. Solan, eds) 13–26 (2012), 19-26.

Chapters 2 and 46. *Legal Language*, University of Chicago Press (Copyright 1999 by The University of Chicago), 95–100, 233–40.

Chapters 3, 10, and 30. *Parchment, Paper, Pixels*, University of Chicago Press (Copyright 2010 by The University of Chicago), 75–82, 134–147, 169–176.

Chapter 4. Some Myths about Legal Language, *Journal of Law, Culture and Humanities* 2: 9–50 (2006), 44–50, with permission granted by Sage Publications.

Chapter 11. Reassessing Unilateral Contracts, *U.C. Davis Law Review* 26:1–86 (1992), 24–34.

Chapter 16. The Language of Silence, *Rutgers Law Review* 48:1–99 (1995), 11–12, 74–80.

Chapter 17. Nonverbal Communication and the Freedom of "Speech," *Wisconsin Law Review* 1993: 1525–1569 (1993), 1569–75.

Chapter 21. The Language of Consent in Rape Law, in Janet Cotterill (ed.), *The Language of Sexual Crime*, 83–103, Palgrave Macmillan (2007), 83–103. Reproduced with permission of Palgrave Macmillan. The full published version of this publication is available from http://www.palgraveconnect.com/pc/doifinder/10.1057/9780230592780.

Chapter 26. The Language of Defamation, *Texas Law Review* 66:303–350 (1987), 314–22.

Chapter 31. The Textualization of Precedent, *Notre Dame Law Review* 82:1187–1278 (2007), 1187–89, 1257–62. Reprinted with permission. © Notre Dame Law Review, University of Notre Dame.

Chapter 35. The Language of Perjury: "Literal Truth," Ambiguity and the False Statement Requirement, *Southern California Law Review* 63:373–431 (1990), 409–14.

Chapter 36. *Speaking of Crime: The Language of Criminal Justice* (Lawrence M. Solan and Peter M. Tiersma), University of Chicago Press (Copyright 2005 by The University of Chicago), 198–204.

Chapter 40. The Judge as Linguist, *Loyola of Los Angeles Law Review* 27: 269–84 (1993), 279–83.

Chapter 45. The Rocky Road to Legal Reform, *Brooklyn Law Review* 66: 1081–1119 (2001), 1082–88.

The excerpts are as originally published apart from minimal editing to references and allusions to earlier parts of the works excerpted, to ensure that the selections chosen are fully accessible to readers.

We wish to express our gratitude to our editor at Oxford University Press, Hallie Stebbins, who has helped to make this somewhat complicated project seem easy.

Our thanks also go to Sara Thompson, Francesca Ciarrocchi and Alejandra Vargas for their valuable work as research and editorial assistants, and to Lorraine McDonald for her excellent assistance with the manuscript.

Finally, in a volume in which scholars are "talking about" the writings of Peter Tiersma, the obvious person to acknowledge is Peter Tiersma himself, for without his many books and articles on language and law, this book could not exist. Peter also worked with us to select the excerpts included in this volume in an effort to include the most representative of his thoughts about each substantive area. However, the identity of the contributors, all of whom have been marvelously cooperative and supportive of this project, and the substance of their contributions, remained the editors' secret until the book was completed, and the contents shared with Peter

# CONTRIBUTORS

**Janet Ainsworth,** John D. Eshelman  Professor of Law, Seattle University School of Law.

**Susan Berk-Seligson**  Research Professor of Spanish Linguistics, Department of Spanish and Portuguese, Vanderbilt University.

**Brian H. Bix,** Frederick W. Thomas  Professor of Law and Philosophy, University of Minnesota Law School.

**Ronald R. Butters**  Professor Emeritus, English Department, Duke University.

**John M. Conley**  William Rand Kenan Jr. Professor of Law, University of North Carolina School of Law.

**Malcolm Coulthard**  Emeritus Professor of Forensic Linguistics, Aston University. Visiting Professor, Federal University of Santa Catarina, Brazil.

**Sidney W. DeLong,** William C. Oltman  Professor of Teaching Excellence, Seattle University School of Law.

**Bethany K. Dumas**  Professor Emerita, Department of English, University of Tennessee.

**Susan Ehrlich**  Professor, Department of Languages, Literatures and Linguistics, York University.

**Edward Finegan**  Professor of Linguistics and Law, Emeritus, University of Southern California Gould School of Law.

**Philip Gaines,** Department Head  Department of English, Montana State University.

**Tim Grant**  Professor, Centre for Forensic Linguistics, Aston University.

**Peter Goodrich**  Professor of Law, Director, Program in Law and Humanities, Benjamin N. Cardozo School of Law.

**Chris Heffer**  Senior Lecturer in Linguistics, Cardiff University.

**Jeffrey P. Kaplan**  Professor of Linguistics, Department of Linguistics & Oriental Languages, San Diego State University.

**Hannes Kniffka**  Professor Emeritus, General Linguistics, Bonn University.

**Krzysztof Kredens**  Director of Undergraduate Programmes in English Language, Deputy Director of the Centre for Forensic Linguistics, Aston University.

**Richard A. Leo**  Hamill Family Chair Professor of Law and Social Psychology and Dean's Circle Research Scholar, University San Francisco School of Law.

**Laurie L. Levenson**  Professor of Law, David W. Burcham Chair in Ethical Advocacy, Loyola Law School, Los Angeles.

**Jeffrey M. Lipshaw**  Professor of Law, Suffolk University Law School.

**Meizhen Liao**  Director, Institute of Linguistics, Professor of Linguistics and English, Dean of the School of Foreign Languages, Central China Normal University.

**Nancy S. Marder**  Professor of Law, Director of the Justice John Paul Stevens Jury Center, and Co-Director of the Institute for Law and the Humanities, Chicago-Kent College of Law, Illinois Institute of Technology.

**Gregory M. Matoesian**  Professor, Department of Criminology, Law and Justice, the University of Illinois at Chicago.

**Elizabeth Mertz**  John and Rylla Bosshard Professor of Law, University of Wisconsin Law School.

**Frank S. Ravitch**  Professor of Law & Walter H. Stowers Chair of Law and Religion, Michigan State University College of Law.

**Frances Rock**  Senior Lecturer, Cardiff School of English, Communication & Philosophy, Cardiff University.

**Frederick Schauer**  David and Mary Harrison Distinguished Professor of Law, the University of Virginia School of Law.

**Roger W. Shuy**  Distinguished Research Professor of Linguistics, Emeritus, Department of Linguistics, Georgetown University.

**Lawrence M. Solan**  Don Forchelli Professor of Law and Director of the Center for the Study of Law, Language and Cognition, Brooklyn Law School.

**Dr. Kerrie Spaul**  General Practitioner, Newbold Verdon Medical Practice, Leicestershire, UK.

**Dieter Stein** Professor of English Language and Linguistics, Heinrich-Heine-University Düsseldorf.

**Dru Stevenson** Professor of Law, Helen and Harry Hutchens Research Professor, and Baker Institute Scholar at the Rice University James A. Baker III Institute for Public Policy, South Texas College of Law.

**Gail Stygall** Professor, Department of English, University of Washington.

# Speaking of Language and Law

PART I

# Legal Language and Its History

1

# On the Origins of Legal English*
Peter M. Tiersma

The other major legal system in the world today is common law. It arose in England and by force of conquest was imposed on Wales and Ireland (Scotland retains to this day a type of civil law). Via the legacy of the British empire, the common law and English legal language currently hold sway in dozens of countries throughout the world.

## Celts, Romans, Anglo-Saxons, and Danes

Although the British Isles have been inhabited for many thousands of years, the first people to have left historical traces are the Celts. Most of what we know about their legal system comes from Wales and Ireland. Although Welsh and Gaelic are still spoken in the British Isles, Celtic law and its language have largely disappeared.

Somewhat over two thousand years ago, the Romans under Julius Caesar conquered what is now England. Roman law would surely have applied to its citizens who were living there. Yet it would have had limited influence on the lives of the Celtic population, and it seems to have disappeared after the Romans left the island in the fifth century to defend their disintegrating empire. The Romans did leave behind a linguistic legacy, but it consists mostly of place names and a few words of Latin origin, none of them particularly legal (Mellinkoff 1963: 36–9).

The Roman retreat left a power vacuum of sorts, which the Angles, Saxons, and other Germanic warriors and settlers from the continent quickly exploited. They conquered most of the territory of what is now England.

* Excerpt from Peter M. Tiersma, A History of the Languages of Law, in Peter M. Tiersma and Lawrence M. Solan (eds.), *The Oxford Handbook of Language and Law* 13, 19-26 (2012).

Their related languages eventually merged into one, which we now refer to as Anglo-Saxon, or Old English.

The Anglo-Saxons were not literate at the time and their law was entirely customary. Legal decisions were often made by a type of popular assembly, sometimes called *moots*. If someone injured or killed someone else, the victim or his clan were entitled to take revenge on the perpetrator, but in most cases he could save his head or hide by paying compensation. The amount depended on the severity of the injury and the status of the victim.

Oaths were often used to decide cases. The words of the oath were fixed and had to be recited verbatim, without stammering, or the person would lose his case. Other types of legal transactions, like wills and transfers of land, also relied on reciting exact verbal formulas. Use of these formulas, which often contained poetic devices as an aid to memory, indicated that the transaction was legally binding. Thus, "to have and to hold" was part of the formula used to transfer land. This alliterative phrase is still encountered in many deeds (Tiersma 1999: 9–16). Interestingly, oaths retain a talismanic quality even today. After US Chief Justice Roberts made a verbal slip in administering the oath of office to President Obama in early 2009, he repeated the ceremony the next day to ensure that it was valid.[1]

Around the year 600, Christian missionaries arrived in England. In addition to religion, they brought with them (or re-introduced) literacy and the Latin language. Soon thereafter, the first written English laws appear. Several of the Anglo-Saxon kings issued codes of law, and some private legal transactions (wills and transfers of land) were also memorialized in writing. Many of these texts were drafted in Latin, but others were in Old English. They functioned primarily as records of customs or oral transactions (Tiersma 2010).

Vikings, mostly from what is now Denmark, raided the British Isles during much of the ninth and tenth centuries. Some of them later settled in England, especially in an area of northeastern England called the *Danelaw* (because it was governed by Danish law). The Scandinavians eventually merged with the Anglo-Saxon population, but their language left behind distinct traces in English. Most notable in the legal sphere are the words *gift, loan, sale, trust*, and the word *law* itself, originally meaning "that which is laid down" (Tiersma 1999: 17).

By far the most significant invasion was yet to come, however. In 1066 William, Duke of Normandy, who claimed the English throne, crossed the channel and defeated the English defenders, an event now known as the Norman Conquest. English ceased to function as a written legal language, although it remained the spoken language of most ordinary people. The rulers of England were now men who spoke a type of French, and their written legal transactions were almost invariably in Latin.

By the end of the thirteenth century, statutes written in Latin started to become common. Royal courts were established and a class of professional lawyers emerged. French was still spoken by the upper nobility at this time, so it stands to reason that oral proceedings in the royal courts would be in that language. Also, the language of written statutes shifted from Latin to French at around 1300, and remained so until it was replaced by English at the end of the fifteenth century.

Thus, at the time when the centralized English court system and the legal profession arose, French was the primary language in which the law was expressed. Of course, French has had a lasting impact on English in general, but this is even more so in the legal sphere. Words relating to courts and trials are almost entirely of French origin: *action, appeal, attorney, bailiff, bar, claim, complaint, counsel*, and *court* are but a few examples. Just about every area of the common law is full of French terminology, as attested by words for basic legal categories like *agreement, assault, easement, estate, felony, lease, license, misdemeanor, mortgage, property, slander, tort*, and *trespass*. French word order (noun+adjective) is apparent in terms like *attorney general, condition precedent, letters patent*, and *notary public*.

French was used as a legal language until roughly the seventeenth century, long after it ceased to be a spoken language in England. Reports of cases were in French for most of this period. This is important because the common law is based in large part on case law, or *precedent*. The legal principle that a judge uses to decide a case must generally be followed in later cases that present the same issue. These precedents can be found in case reports, and for hundreds of years those reports were written in French. Thus, many of the most important principles in the common law were first articulated in French. Moreover, almost all legal literature was written in that language.

Although English lawyers were not normally educated in Latin, they would nonetheless have had some knowledge of it. Maxims or sayings about the law were usually in Latin, as in *de minimis non curat lex* ("the law is not concerned with trifles"), *caveat emptor* ("let the buyer beware"), and *expressio unius est exclusio alterius* ("the expression of one thing is the exclusion of the other"). Writs (orders from the king or judge to a sheriff or lower court) were in Latin, and even today many retain Latin names, including the writs of *certiorari, habeas corpus*, and *mandamus*. Records of court cases were maintained in Latin until the early eighteenth century, which explains its widespread use for terminology found in case names (*versus, in personam, in rem, in propria persona*, etc.) (Tiersma 1999: 19–34).

Although both Latin and French were and continue to be widely used in the civil law, as we discussed above, there is less overlap with the common law than one might expect. Some French terms used in English legal language, such as *agreement, crime, arrest*, and *misdemeanor*, are not used in French legal language or have a different meaning (Mattila 2006: 231–2). Moreover,

Mattila reports that, roughly speaking, only around one-fourth of the Latin terms and maxims in a sample of German legal dictionaries are found in dictionaries of legal English. This suggests that most of the Latin used by the civil and common law systems is unique to each (Mattila 2002). A study of Latinisms used in the United States and Spain reached a similar conclusion (Balteiro and Campos-Pardillos 2010).

## The Rise of English

The profession's continued use of French, long after it ceased to be a spoken language in England, was not always appreciated by the public. Critics suggested that lawyers wished to hide the law, thereby securing their monopoly on legal services. Lawyers responded that Law French (the distinctive dialect of French used by the English legal profession) was far more precise than English. Moreover, if the law were expressed in English, ordinary people might try to act as their own lawyers and, failing to properly understand the law, would "fall into destruction," in the words of Sir Edward Coke (Tiersma 1999: 28–9).

As early as 1362, a statute—written in French!—required that all court pleading be in English, so that "every Man ... may the better govern himself without offending of the Law." In 1650 Parliament, during the Commonwealth, passed another law requiring that all books of law be only in English. The statute was repealed when the monarchy was restored ten years later. By this time, however, Law French was moribund. Its use in legal proceedings, along with Latin, was finally abolished in 1731 (Tiersma 1999: 35–6).

Documents previously written in French or Latin now had to be composed in English. Rather than translating them into idiomatic English, however, lawyers and clerks tended to favor a very literal, word-for-word, translation. Medieval deeds often began with the words *sciant omnes ...*, which was translated as "know all men ..." This phrase has been copied verbatim countless times since then. The criminal law concept of *malice afore-thought* is a direct translation of the Law French phrase *malice prepense*, preserving the French word order.

Moreover, many terms were not translated into English at all. These words and phrases were almost all technical terms that had acquired a specific legal meaning, making it difficult to find an exact English equivalent. Unlike those who developed the German legal system, which took great pains to "Germanize" foreign terms (Mattila 2006: 169), English lawyers mostly incorporated French terms without change. Of course, the English language is renowned for borrowing foreign words, and French and Latin especially have been a major source for such borrowing. In the legal arena, some of these originally foreign words have entered ordinary speech, such as *court, judge, jury, plaintiff,* and *defendant.* Others, however, are completely unknown outside the profession (consider *tortfeasor* or *profit a prendre*), and their foreign origin makes it hard for people to even guess at their meaning.

In the last several decades a movement has thus arisen advocating for plain English (see Adler 2012). Proponents in essence argue that although all legal texts have officially been in the vernacular since 1731, the law is actually expressed in a type of English, often called *legalese,* that deviates in some important ways from ordinary language. Lawyers continue to hide the law, they suggest, but in place of Law French they now use obscure and convoluted English.

The legal system has not been impervious to these criticisms. Much anachronistic terminology has been replaced by more modern equivalents. The Law French term *cestui que trust* is being supplanted by the more common word *beneficiary.* The phrase *Cometh now plaintiff,* which was once used to introduce a pleading, has been modernized as *Comes now plaintiff* or simply *Plaintiff alleges as follows.* Most drafters are content nowadays to write *John Smith* in place of *the aforesaid John Smith.* Such changes have been especially common in consumer documents, including insurance policies and various types of disclosure forms.

There has also been a movement, which has met with some success, to make instructions to jurors more comprehensible (see Marder 2012). Still, the instructions of many jurisdictions are not exactly models of clarity, especially when it comes to the politically charged area of death penalty law. Part of the problem is that the language of instructions is often copied directly from statutes, which were never meant to be understood by jurors, but which judges resist translating into ordinary speech for fear of being reversed by a court of appeals (Tiersma 1999: 211–40).

Thus, while there has been much improvement in the language of the law during the past decades, much remains to be accomplished.

## Legal English Around the World

Just as the civil law of Europe migrated to many parts of the world via colonialism, the common law and its language spread throughout the former British empire. Some of these countries are mostly English-speaking today, including Canada, the United States, Australia, and New Zealand. Others, like Pakistan, India, Nigeria, and Malaysia, have retained English legal language even though most of the population speaks indigenous languages for most purposes.

The American colonies rejected many things British when they won their independence. Yet they retained the common law system, including the notion of precedent. Despite reservations by some prominent Americans, most notably Thomas Jefferson, they also continued to use the legal language associated with that system. Thus, modern English lawyers can understand American lawyers fairly well, and vice versa. Yet in some important respects the British and American legal systems have diverged, producing what are arguably differing dialects of legal English (Tiersma 1999: 43–7). In contrast to the United States, countries such as Canada, Australia, and New Zealand broke away from the United Kingdom much later, and as a result their legal languages are closer to that of England.

In former British colonies where English is not widely spoken, it is common for lower court proceedings to be in native languages. Yet English is often used in the higher courts, as in India and Pakistan. The English used in these courts can be surprisingly conservative at times. Many former British colonies have high courts consisting of a chief justice and several *puisne* (associate or junior) judges.[2] *Puisne* comes from the Law French *puis* "after" and *ne* "born," and thus referred originally to a younger child (Baker 1990: 177).

As might be expected, the English used in higher courts is generally imbued with some local flavor. Thus, Indian courts take cognizance of customary law in some situations, which will generally be expressed in local languages. And Islamic law is applied to family matters of Indian Muslims, which leads to the use of much Arabic terminology in this area (Mattila 2006: 248–9).

One would expect that in many of these countries, local languages will gradually replace English. To some extent this has started to happen in Malaysia, for instance, where high court judgments may currently be written not just in English, but also in *Bahasa Malaysia*. Of course, the same happened in England itself, where the local language (English) eventually supplanted Law French.

### The Globalization of Legal Language?

If legal systems are increasingly influencing each other, will legal language likewise be subject to globalization? One consequence of globalization on the law has been a growing need to translate from one legal language into another.

Another aspect of globalization is the creation of international alliances or confederations, such as the European Union. Curiously, as the nations of Europe create a common legal superstructure, they have discovered that despite their shared civil law tradition, it can be problematic to translate from one legal language into another. This is an important issue in the EU, which has around two dozen official languages (see McAuliffe 2012; Gotti 2009).

Vocabulary relating to new institutions or novel legal concepts usually does not present difficulties. For example, EU institutions and legal rules may be generally referred to by the French term *acquis communautaire* (used not only in French, but sometimes also in Dutch and English), by a direct translation (Italian *conquiste comunitarie* or *acquis comunitario*), or by a neologism (German *gemein-schaftlicher Besitzstand*) (Mattila 2006: 120–1).

Yet in most cases EU law—for instance, directives of the Commission or decisions of the Court of Justice—is originally formulated in French or English and then translated into the other official languages using the existing legal terminology of those languages. As observed by Šarčević 2012, legal terms in one language cannot always be translated exactly into another. The meaning of *delict* in the civil law is not entirely the same as *tort* in the common law. Thus, a law or regulation, intended to be uniform throughout the EU, may acquire subtle differences in meaning via the process of translation.

One solution would be to have one official language, which could be used to draft a single authoritative version of all EU legal texts. Some have suggested that International English could carry out this function (Ferreri 2006). However, the EU seems firmly committed to the principle of multiple official languages, which inevitably requires translation.

A more likely approach is to build a corpus of common or uniform legal terminology with precise definitions that can be used in all national languages. At one time Latin terms fulfilled this function throughout much of Europe, but despite its historical importance, it is probably no longer a serious contender. Creating an entirely new vocabulary, on the analogy of invented languages like Esperanto, might also be a possibility, but it likewise seems improbable. Perhaps a more attractive notion is taking a certain number of legal terms from each EU language in order to create one common legal lexicon. Because of the great structural disparity of the major language families, this may also not be practical.

Using the vocabulary of an existing language may be the only feasible option. At one time French provided much legal terminology that could be used internationally, but today the most obvious choice is English. There is, in fact, a serious movement to create a common EU legal vocabulary using English as the basis, but it would have to be a type of international legal English that is not burdened by common law precedent.[3]

Whether the EU will embrace the use of international legal English, if only to standardize its legal terminology, is uncertain, as is the question of how widespread legal English will become in the rest of the world. In any event, predictions about the future go beyond the scope of this chapter, which is historical. No doubt a later edition of this *Handbook* will be able to answer these questions after the future has become history.[4]

## Notes

1. http://www.abajournal.com/news/article/did_roberts_oath_change_cause_obama_ stumble/ (visited August 3, 2010).
2. See the constitution of Kenya, ch. IV, pt. 1, § 60.
3. See http://www.juridicainternational.eu/the-launch-of-the-draft-common-frame-of-reference?id=10521. See also Von Bar et al. (2009); Pozzo and Jacometti (2006).
4. I would like to thank Heikki Mattila of the University of Lapland and Barbara Pozzo of the University of Insubria for their assistance.

## References

Adler, Mark (2012) The Plain Language Movement, in Peter M. Tiersma and Lawrence M. Solan (eds), *The Oxford Handbook of Language and Law.*

Baker, John Hamilton (1990) *Manual of Law French* (2nd edn) Aldershot: Scolar Press.

Balteiro, Isabel and Miguel Angel Campos-Pardillos (2010) A Comparative Study of Latinisms in Court Opinions in the United States and Spain, *International Journal of Speech Language and the Law* 17:95–118.

Bar, Christian von, Eric Clive, Hans Schulte-Nölke, et al. (eds) (2009) *Principles, Definitions and Model Rules of European Private Law. Draft Common Frame of Reference (DCFR) Interim Outline Edition.* Munich, Sellier.

Ferreri, Silva (2006) Communicating in an International Context, in Barbara Pozzo and Valentina Jacometi (eds), *Multilingualism and the Harmonisation of European Law.* Alphen aan den Rijn: Kluwer Law International, 33–44.

Gotti, Maurizio (2009) Globalizing Trends in Legal Discourse, in Frances Olsen, Alexander Lorz, and Dieter Stein (eds), *Translation Issues in Language and Law.* Düsseldorf: Düsseldorf University Press.

Marder, Nancy S. (2012) Instructing the Jury, in Peter M. Tiersma and Lawrence M. Solan (eds), *The Oxford Handbook of Language and Law.*

Matilla, Heikki E. S. (2006) *Comparative Legal Linguistics* (trans Christopher Goddard). Aldershot: Ashgate.

McAuliffe, Karen (2012) Language and Law in the European Union: The Multilingual Jurisprudence of the ECJ, in Peter M. Tiersma and Lawrence M. Solan (eds), *The Oxford Handbook of Language and Law.*

Mellinkoff, David (1963) *The Language of the Law.* Boston and Toronto: Little, Brown and Co.

Pozzo, Barbara and Valentina Jacometti (eds) (2006) *Multilingualism and the Harmonisation of European Private Law.* Alphen aan den Rijn: Kluwer Law International.

Šarčević, Susan (2012) Challenges to the Legal Translator, in Peter M. Tiersma and Lawrence M. Solan (eds), *The Oxford Handbook of Language and Law.*

Tiersma, Peter M. (1999) *Legal Language.* Chicago and London: University of Chicago Press.

——— (2010) *Parchment, Paper, Pixels: Law and the Technologies of Communication.* Chicago: University of Chicago Press.

2

# Why is Legal Language So Conservative?*

Peter M. Tiersma

As we have seen, the legal lexicon has many obsolescent or obsolete English words and grammatical constructions, as well as outdated Latin and French terms.[1] It is very evident that these outdated words and constructions do absolutely nothing to enhance communication; in many cases they impede it by introducing ambiguity or lowering comprehension. So why do these anachronisms persist?

One reason for conservative or archaic language is that it is considered more formed than everyday speech. Language continually changes. Most people today combine *data* with a singular verb (*the data is convincing*), use *input* as a verb (*I inputted some data into the computer*), and readily employ new and useful coinages like *prioritize and finalize*. Yet many writers avoid these innovations in formal prose until the winds of change prove irresistible. Formal and archaic language are thus closely related. As we discuss in somewhat greater detail below, because legal language often strives toward great formality, it naturally gravitates toward archaic language.

It is worth comparing legal language to another major area in which language is very conservative: religion. The Roman Catholic Church clung to Latin as the language of religion for well over a millennium after it died out as a vernacular. In the same way, Jews have maintained Hebrew, and Hindus retain Sanskrit as sacred languages. Some religions have experienced "plain language" movements, just as with the law. The best known is the Protestant Reformation; one of Martin Luther's major reforms was to translate the Bible into German so that ordinary believers could read and understand it. The King James version of the Bible was similarly motivated. Curiously enough, however, the natural tendency toward linguistic conservatism quickly

---

* Excerpt from Peter M. Tiersma, *Legal Language* 95–100 (1999).     **11**

reasserted itself among many Protestants, who cherish the language of the King James Bible as if God spoke Elizabethan English.

Much of this linguistic conservatism derives from an attribute that most major religions share with the law: a veneration of authoritative texts. Many Christians, for example, regard the Bible as divinely inspired, believing that every word was dictated by God Himself. When every syllable in a text is holy, translating it into another language can be problematic, or at a minimum would produce something less reliable or authentic than the original. The same is true for updating the text to more modern language.

Just as the Bible or the Koran is the authoritative source of religion for believers, documents like statutes, constitutions, and judicial opinions are the main sources of law for the legal profession. These sources are obviously not sacred in a religious sense, although many American lawyers show great reverence for the United States Constitution. Yet they are clearly regarded as authoritative. It would be almost unthinkable to establish a commission of scholars to rewrite the Constitution in more modern English, even though certain parts of it have become difficult for citizens to understand. Not surprisingly, therefore, the archaic vocabulary and grammar of authoritative older texts continues to exert great influence on contemporary legal language.

A related reason for not modernizing archaic legal texts is that specific words and phrases may have received authoritative interpretations over the years. Rewriting statutes and constitutions could wreak havoc with decades of court decisions that have clarified what those texts mean and how they are to be applied. This does not mean that legal texts cannot be modernized, but it does inspire caution.

Two further reasons for the conservatism of legal language are safety and convenience. In the legal sphere, the safest course of action is almost always to reuse the same worn phrasing time and again. As we will see later, jury instructions are often very difficult for jurors to comprehend. But judges keep reading the same tired instructions to the jury because it is safe. To paraphrase the instructions in more modern terms might invite a reversal by a higher court because of some perceived change in meaning. Likewise, if lawyers learn that a particular format and phrasing in a complaint has passed judicial scrutiny in the past, they will be extremely reluctant to deviate in the future. If it worked before, it should work again.

Not only is it deemed safer, but it is far more convenient and economical to keep recirculating the same forms. Over the years, law firms build up collections of documents that were drafted in the past and can serve as samples for the future. Moreover, published collections (form books) are available commercially. The result is that stilted language that may have been written decades or centuries ago is continually reincarnated, virtually without change, in modern legal documents.

Archaic language also seems particularly authoritative, perhaps even majestic. Using antiquated terminology bestows a sense of timelessness on the legal system, as something that has lasted through the centuries and is therefore deserving of great respect. Witness the British enactment clause. Somehow language that has withstood the test of time seems more potent and valuable than innovative phrasing. Few people know how much a *score* is these days, but the *four score and seven years* of Abraham Lincoln's Gettysburg Address has a ring to it that *eighty-seven years* clearly lacks.

Although lawyers are reluctant to admit it, archaic language also happens to help justify the profession's monopoly, an age-old theme. Clients confronted with an impenetrable legal document have no choice but to seek the advice of a lawyer as interpreter, just as medieval clients sought out lawyers to translate Law French. Whether this is as strong a factor as in centuries past is hard to say. The law has become so complex in recent years that it would be foolhardy for most people to represent themselves in a complicated legal matter, even if legal language were as straightforward as could be. Still, many lawyers show little inclination to encourage self-helpers by modernizing legal vocabulary and making the law more accessible to the general public.

## Linguistic Creativity

### NEW WINE IN NEW BOTTLES

Although there is plenty of archaic usage in legal contexts, the point should not be exaggerated. Lawrence Friedman has observed that most legal vocabulary is not especially ancient: "spendthrift trust" is only about one hundred years old, and "zoning" is very recent.[2] In fact, it is easy to add examples of innovative legal terminology to Friedman's list, some of very recent vintage. The development of securities law during the past half-century or so required the creation of a whole new vocabulary, including terms such as *antitrust, blue sky laws, poison pill, predatory pricing*, and *tying arrangement*, to name just a few. Innovations in the law of contracts, torts, and damages has led to the coining of neologisms like *cramdown, hedonic damages, lost volume seller, palimony, sexual harassment, toxic tort*, and *wrongful birth*. Lawyers now *Shepardize* cases and make sure the police have properly *Mirandized* their clients.

Even as lawyers create new vocabulary for novel areas of practice, old terms tend to die out with the obsolescence of the legal concepts to which they refer. Terminology relating to feudal property law has become obsolete along with feudalism itself. Words or phrases like *demesne, fee tail, fief, scutage, seisin*, and *subinfeudation*, to name just a few, have passed from the legal lexicon into the history books. Conversely, legal terms generally retain their vitality as long as the concepts to which they refer remain current. Much property terminology, such as the hoary Law French terms *chattel, fee simple, easement, estate,* or *reverter,* have proven quite durable. As long as the concept remains part of the law, the corresponding words are unlikely to disappear. Though these words may be ancient, they are not obsolete.


### ASYLEES, ESCAPEES, AND TIPPEES

Another example of linguistic innovation in legal language is the frequent addition of the suffix *-ee* to a verb, primarily to indicate the human object of an action. As discussed previously, this trait ultimately derives from Law French. Although the process itself has a long history, words formed in this matter can be very creative.

Otto Jespersen notes that although the process began with legal language, it spread into ordinary speech. He cites examples such as *lovee, gazee, staree, cursee, laughee, flirtee, floggee, wishee,* and *callee,* all attested in various literary writings.[3] Yet today, ordinary language has retained only a few of these terms, virtually all derived from legal usage: *employee, referee,* and *trustee,* for instance. In legal language, on the other hand, the process is still quite vibrant.

Many *-ee* forms function as direct objects to refer to the person who is acted upon: *acquittee, arrestee, conscriptee, detainee, expellee, inauguree, indictee, invitee,* and *shelteree* are some examples. If *V* represents the verb, these words have the meaning "the person who is *V*-ed." Each can be paraphrased as a person who is acquitted, arrested, or conscripted.

Formations with *-ee* can also refer to the indirect object of an action ("the person to whom something is *V*-ed"): *albcatee, covenantee, grantee, indorsee, lessee, patentee, payee, pledgee, referee,* and *trustee.* Here, the paraphrase must include the preposition *to:* someone *to whom* something is allocated, covenanted, and so on.

Other formations are more idiosyncratic: *asylee* (someone who seeks asylum, not the person who is "asyled"); *condemnee* (someone whose property has been condemned, not someone who has been condemned); *discriminatee* (a person discriminated against); *escapee* (someone who escapes, not the person who is escaped from); *tippee* (a person who is tipped off); *abortee* (a woman who has an abortion, not the aborted fetus); *optionee* (a person against whose interests someone else has an option).

All of these forms are attested in Bryan Garner's *Dictionary of Modern Legal Usage,* though they vary in acceptability, even within the profession. Yet they illustrate that while some legal language may be archaic, other usage is extremely innovative.

Frequently, *-ee* words come in matched pairs: *mortgagor/mortgagee, trustor/trustee, bailor/bailee, employer/employee,* and so forth. The *-or* word typically indicates the actor, and hence has more of an active sense, while the *-ee* word refers to the recipient of the action, and thus has more of a passive sense. For example, the *mortgagor* is the person who mortgages property (i.e., the borrower of a loan), just as the *lessor* is the person who leases real estate to someone else (i.e., the landlady). In contrast, the *mortgagee* is the person to whom the property is mortgaged (i.e., the bank), and the *lessee* is the person to whom real estate is leased (i.e., the tenant). Obviously, a drawback to these sets of words is that people—including lawyers sometimes—find it hard to remember which is which. Just who is the *lessor* and who is the *lessee*?

Despite some stylistically questionable formations, words created with *-ee* are very functional. Being able to refer to the *assignee*, instead of having to say *the person to whom an obligation has been assigned*, promotes an economy of expression that justifies retaining this means of word formation. Of course, these words are mainly useful when they fill a lexical gap (as in *assignee*, for which there is no term in ordinary language). When ordinary English has a word for a concept, there is no need to create neologisms. Thus, the more common term *tenant* is preferable to *lessee*, especially when dealing with nonlawyers.

Occasionally the French *-ee* form (originally a past participle) is replaced by the English equivalent, as in *the insured*. In ordinary English such words typically have generic or collective reference and take a plural verb: *the insured are quite lucky these days.*[4] In legal usage, by contrast, *the insured* functions as a singular noun that refers to an individual (*the insured is required to give notice of any claim within 10 days*). In fact, legal usage allows such words to be pluralized (*the insureds*), and they can even be used as possessives. One case not too long ago commented on *an insured's right to rely on the provisions of this policy.*[5] Although they derive from past participles, therefore, these words now act as regular nouns. Other past participles that lawyers use as ordinary nouns include *the accused, the deceased*, and *the condemned*.

Legal language is an odd mixture of very archaic features, on the one hand, and quite innovative usage, on the other. To some it may seem rather schizophrenic. But perhaps this is no more odd than seeing conservatively dressed lawyers in a baroque courtroom, advancing highly creative and pathbreaking arguments about privacy on the World Wide Web.

### Notes

1. See also David Mellinkoff, *The Language of the Law* 12–16 (1963).

2. Lawrence M. Friedman, *Law and Its Language*, 33 Geo. Wash. L. Rev. 563, 565 (1964).

3. Otto Jespersen, *Growth and Structure of the English Language* 103 (10th ed. 1982).

4. See Randolph Quirk et al., *A Comprehensive Grammar of the English Language*, §7.24 at 421 (1985).

5. *Cook v. Equitable Life Assurance Society,* 428 N.E.2d 110, 114 (Ind. Ct. App. 1981).

3

# Writing the Law in England*

## Peter M. Tiersma

The earliest inhabitants of England to leave substantial traces in the history books were the Celtic Britons. Because they were illiterate at this time, we know little about their legal system, but it appears to have been largely regulated by custom.

During the Roman occupation of Britain, from roughly ad 50 to around 400, Latin was used for administrative and legal purposes. Latin, of course, was a written language in this period. The Roman administration of Britain (which included judicial officers) would likely have been done in accordance with a written statute, called a *lex provinciae*, which laid down some basic principles on how the province was to be governed.[1] But whatever legislation might have been in effect in Britain largely disappeared when the Romans left the British Isles. For the most part, written laws seem to have departed with them.

### Lawmaking in Anglo-Saxon Times

By around ad 500 Germanic tribes who had come from the continent controlled much of what is now England, organizing themselves administratively into several small kingdoms. Like the other Germanic tribes of the time, the Anglo-Saxons, as they came to be known, were largely illiterate. As far as we know they did not have written laws.

This situation began to change with the arrival of Christian missionaries around ad 600. As we have previously mentioned, Christianity reintroduced the Latin language and, more importantly for our purposes, the practice of literacy.[2] Not long thereafter, the first written English laws appeared, those of

* Excerpt from Peter M. Tiersma, *Parchment, Paper, Pixels* 138–47 (2010).

King Æthelberht of Kent. Other codes of Anglo-Saxon law followed. These compilations of law were in the Anglo-Saxon language, also known as Old English.[3]

It is generally accepted that these early English legal codes, which were usually issued in the name of a certain king, were not legislation in the modern sense. Like the Code of Hammurabi, they were written records of laws or customs that already existed in some sense, not attempts to impose new rules or change existing law. That is certainly true of the laws of King Æthelberht, which are little more than lists of compensation to victims for various offenses, such as the following:

> Gif man mannan ofslæhð, medume leodgeld C scillinga gebete.
>
> [If a person kills someone, let him pay an ordinary person-price, 100 shillings.][4]

Writing down laws in the king's name no doubt imbued them with a certain authority that they might not have had before. And it is possible that in the process of recording existing law, innovations slipped in. But on the whole, Æthelberht's code is best described as a compilation of existing law or custom rather than as legislation by the king and his council. As Patrick Wormald has remarked, most of what Æthelberht put into writing was "established" rather than "innovatory."[5]

Subsequent Anglo-Saxon compilations of law contain provisions that suggest grander ambitions. Several of Æthelberht's successors issued codes of their own, sometimes adding new laws. For example, they inserted provisions to deal with the increasing influence of the church and to funnel more money into their treasuries. Moreover, the language of these later laws is syntactically more complex and the content more abstract.[6] Wormald concludes, "Law was now *made* as well as *recorded* in writing."[7]

While it is arguable that Æthelberht's laws were nothing more than custom written down, these later innovations would almost certainly qualify as law by most standards. In such cases, the king (often with the assistance or consent of spiritual and secular advisors) acted much like a modern legislator.

King Alfred, whose code is the longest set of Anglo-Saxon laws, proceeded a step further in this direction by sometimes using the first person (*we settad*, meaning "we fix" or "we set down"), as when fixing the peace for a consecrated church.[8] This strongly suggests that he viewed himself as a lawmaker. Additional evidence comes from a comment by Alfred that after commanding that the laws be written down, he showed them to his wise men, who agreed to observe them.[9]

Similarly, King Ine of the West Saxons insisted in his code that his officials and subjects obey his decrees.[10] And King Edgar's Wihtbordesstan code reveals additional evidence of a developing awareness of the rule of law. It provided that multiple copies should be made and that they should be sent "in all directions" so that the law should be known to rich and poor alike.[11]

The notion that it is possible to explicitly create or modify rules governing human behavior, which resembles the modern concept of lawmaking, was clearly beginning to emerge. What is less clear is the process by which such laws were enacted, mainly because the historical record is so sparse. Alfred's code states that he gathered together rules from synod books and the laws of other kings. He rejected some, kept others, and had them written down.[12]

Despite some signs of inchoate legislation in this period, even one of the latest and most extensive collections of Anglo-Saxon law, that of Cnut the Dane, is thought to have largely codified existing law.[13] In certain other cases, the text of Anglo-Saxon laws appears to have been a written record of previous oral pronouncements or decrees made by the king. Risto Hiltunen's linguistic analysis of the Anglo-Saxon codes also suggests that many of them are oral in origin. He notes, for instance, that they sometimes contain the introductory phrase "we have pronounced" before the statement of certain rules.[14]

Although there was a slowly developing consciousness that laws ought to be written down, the validity of legislation at the time did not depend on whether it was, in fact, memorialized on paper or parchment. Kings may have been able to have innovative laws written down, but it was not the only way in which they could make law. And the fact that a rule of conduct was written did not necessarily create law where none had existed before. To quote Wormald once more, "*Legislation*, commitment of the law to writing, showed what the law was, whether in custom or as a result of royal adjudication or decree. It was not, at this stage, necessarily the same thing as *making law*."[15]

The notion that writing was not yet essential to the lawmaking process is supported by the observation that many Anglo-Saxon kings seem to have produced no written laws at all, even after Æthelberht and other Kentish kings established a precedent for doing so, and even if they had clerics at their disposal to do the drafting. Perhaps these kings simply did not legislate. They may have been content to govern entirely by custom, lacking either the will or the power to innovate. Other kings clearly did engage in legislative activity but made no effort—as far as we know—to have their product reduced to writing. Edward the Confessor, for instance, is said to have abrogated bad laws and, with the advice of his counsel, to have established good ones. But there is no evidence that he ever made written law.[16]

The Anglo-Saxon codes were therefore mainly records of the law or evidence of what the law was. Unlike modern legislation, the written codes did not constitute the law. Wormald points out that there is not a single lawsuit from this period in which one of the participants referred to written legislation.[17] Part of the reason, no doubt, was that the supremacy of written law had not yet been established. In addition, there were often severe practical problems in obtaining copies of the royal codes, so judges may not have had easy access to them.[18] Whatever the reason, resolving disputes by referring to the language of a statute was still a thing of the future.

## The Normans and Beyond

In the century or so following the Norman Conquest in 1066, there was relatively little legislative activity. William the Conqueror legislated—if it can be called that—mainly by writs, which could be loosely defined at this stage as letters from the sovereign to officials or subjects, containing commands, prohibitions, declarations, and similar legal speech acts. The famous example is William's writ to the citizens of London, soon after he assumed power, in which he declared that they were to enjoy the same laws that were in effect in King Edward's time and that the existing rules of inheritance would be respected.[19] No doubt William could instead have issued an oral proclamation, which would probably have been no less effective during his lifetime. But the fact that he made his declaration in writing did have significance, if not for its validity, then certainly for its durability. The original document has been kept ever since by the City of London, and one may assume that—at least initially—it was not merely a historical curiosity.[20]

More akin to modern legislation are various *assizes* from a slightly later period. This word, which refers in the first instance to a council or court session (*assize* means something like "sitting"), later came to refer to the enactments that were made at such sessions. Thus, the Assize of Clarendon (1166) contained various rules relating to criminal procedure. The introductory language makes clear that the king and his council are acting as lawmakers: "King Henry established by the counsel of all his barons. . . ." Moreover, the contents were not always restatements of established custom but at times were innovative. The first chapter provided that the justices and sheriffs should place twelve men under oath from every *hundred* (an administrative unit), and four men from every *vill* (a village or subdivision of a hundred), and inquire whether any crimes had been committed in their hundred or vill. This is commonly thought to have given birth to the grand jury.[21]

Although these assizes were written documents, generally issued in the name of the king and his counsel, there is no indication that writing was deemed essential. The introductory formula in the Assize of Clarendon refers in the past tense to what the king established. Moreover, these assizes seem more like directions to various government officials. For the most part, they do not contain broad legal principles applicable to the population as a whole. It is thus debatable whether they should be considered lawmaking at all.[22]

In the early nineteenth century, the British government made an effort to print all English laws enacted since the Conquest in a series of books the *Statutes of the Realm*. The first statute in this series is the Provisions of Merton (1235–36) from the reign of Henry III.[23] Yet once again, the operative words of the Provisions are in the past tense (*provisum est*, or "it has been provided"), indicating that this is more a record of decisions that have already been made rather than text that has formally been enacted. While some of the provisions sound very much like legislation meant to govern future conduct and cases, there are also clauses that resemble the minutes of a meeting. The ninth clause reports on a disagreement between the bishops and the lords, and the final clause states that the king denied a proposal by the lords concerning trespass in parks and ponds.[24]

The Provisions of Westminster (1259), which forced Henry III to give up some of his power to the barons, reveal a growing literate mentality. A French draft text was prepared for Parliament in 1259. According to historian Paul Brand, the text of the document was originally drafted in French (the language of the aristocracy at the time). It was discussed at a parliament in 1259, and the text was then translated into Latin. After being approved, it was read out in public in Westminster Hall, and copies were made for sheriffs and justices.[25]

Thus, a gradually increasing corpus of written documents that were in some sense legislative was being produced during the first half of the thirteenth century. But writing was hardly essential. Henry III is reported to have made law orally. For instance, in 1248 he "ordered it to be proclaimed as law by the voice of the crier" that from that time forward, a man could no longer castrate someone else for engaging in fornication, an exception being made for a husband who caught another man in flagrante delicto with his wife.[26]

More inclined to rule by means of written documents was Edward I (1272–1307), who instituted a number of bureaucratic and legal innovations during his reign. An example is the first Statute of Westminster, a voluminous series of laws dating from 1275. This appears to be the English legislation recorded in French, which became the dominant legislative language during the fourteenth and much of the fifteenth centuries. It refers to itself as containing the *establisementz* of the King. The operative language remains in the past tense, however: *le Rey ordine & establiles choses desuz escrites* ... [the King hath ordained and established these acts underwritten ...].[27] A year later, a statute on bigamy recited that it was "heard and published before the King and his Council" and that they agreed "that they should be put in Writing for a perpetual Memory, and that they should be steadfastly observed."[28] There was clearly a growing appreciation that laws, particularly those that related to important matters, should be perpetuated as written text.

Nonetheless, there remained a great deal of uncertainty surrounding this relatively novel form of governing. As Theodore Plucknett has observed,

Who could then say what a statute was, or be certain that any particular document was a statute? Who could say, even, what the actual words of any acknowledged statute really were? And what was the precise significance of *carta, assisa, constitutio, provisio, ordinatio, statutum, isetnysse,* all of which come before the courts for interpretation? If they were all equally statutes, why so many different titles? And if not, where do they differ?[29]

Plucknett later answered his own question by noting that at this time, the exact form of legislation seems not to have mattered much: "The great concern of the government was to govern, and if in the course of its duties legislation became necessary, then it was effected simply and quickly without any complications or formalities."[30]

## Legislating via Written Statutes

Not long afterward, legislation starts to assume greater regularity. The word *statute* appears more frequently. During this same period—starting in the latter part of the thirteenth century—we also begin to see clear signs of written laws being deliberately used to establish and change legal norms, akin to modern legislation. Statutes begin to stipulate when they go into effect, for instance, suggesting that their makers view themselves as making rules that are meant to govern future behavior and to be enforced.[31]

Moreover, the proclamation of statutes seems to have become customary, though perhaps not essential.[32] The chancery sent copies of the statutes to the sheriffs with a proclamation writ attached. The writ, in the form of a letter from the king to the sheriff, commanded the sheriff to proclaim and publish the statute.[33] The Statute of Winchester, enacted in 1285, specifically required that one of its more important provisions be cried out "in all Counties, Hundreds, Markets, Fairs, and all other Places where great Resort of People is, so that none shall excuse himself by Ignorance ..."[34]

Although the decisions of Parliament were now generally called *statutes* and were often proclaimed in public places, the word *statute* would not inevitably have suggested written law to people of this time. It derives from the Latin verb *statuo*, which literally means 'to cause to stand, put, place.' Even in classical Latin, however, it had developed a more abstract signification that referred to establishing something, settling a principle or point, giving a ruling, or deciding something.[35] A statute, therefore, was something that was established, settled, or decided. Its original meaning did not necessarily demand that it be written.[36]

Still, the rapid expansion of literacy and writing beginning in the thirteenth century would have encouraged the belief that legislation ought to be written. M. T. Clanchy observes that before this time, to record something meant to bear oral witness to it, not to produce a document.[37] "The spoken word was the legally valid record and was superior to any document."[38] Yet by the middle of the thirteenth century, the noun *record* had come to refer to a document.[39] If ordinary legal matters were increasingly memorialized in writing, one assumes that this principle would apply with even greater force to statutes. In addition, although it would have been possible for the king to send messengers with oral instructions to the sheriffs, the proclamation of new legislation would almost inevitably have required the production of written versions for them to promulgate.[40] At least on one occasion in 1306, there is a notation at the end of a statute that it is to be sent "word for word" into all the counties of England, there to be openly read and recited.[41]

## Consequences of Writing Law

Initially, the main function of writing laws must have differed little from the primary function of literacy in general: to preserve words for later use. But very quickly it would have become evident that there were some ancillary effects to setting down law in writing. Some of these effects are not direct results of literacy. For instance, in the process of writing down laws (or customs), kings could leave out those they did not like and make changes to others. Wormald points out that Kentish kings after Æthelberht apparently realized that they could benefit themselves by modifying rules for personal injury to require the payment of a fine to the royal treasury, which modified the customary rule of compensating only the victim.[42] In a kingdom largely governed by custom, the power to have existing law written down could potentially be converted into a power to subtly change custom or make new law.

Yet if the process of writing or codifying law allows for subtle modification, it is equally true that once written, law becomes increasingly static and resistant to change. Writing has a permanence that spoken language lacks. An unwritten law or custom can almost imperceptibly evolve or eventually disappear through disuse or fading memory. Clanchy has observed that

> [r]emembered truth was ... flexible and up to date, because no ancient custom could be proved to be older than the memory of the oldest living wise man. ... Customary law "quietly passes over obsolete laws, which sink into oblivion, and die peacefully, but the law itself remains young, always in the belief that it is old.[43]

Anthropologist Jack Goody has made the same observation on the basis of work done on traditional oral African legal systems.[44]

In contrast, once law is written down, the words remain fixed as long as the writing is legible. An example is that parts of the Statute of Marlborough, dating from 1267, are still in force today[45] Certain clauses of the first Statute of Westminster, enacted in 1275, also remain in effect.[46] The same is true for an act known as *Quia* Emptores, portions of which have been effective since 1289 or 1290.[47] It is virtually inconceivable that oral rules could have such longevity, and if they did, the exact words would long since have dissipated in the mists of time.

Related to permanence is the greater ability of writing—before modern inventions like the telephone or television—to accurately transmit a message over long distances. Of course, in a preliterate society, it is possible to summon a messenger and have him deliver an oral message to someone a substantial distance away. Yet having the messenger deliver a written document is far more likely to guarantee accurate transmission. The writ system in medieval England, under which the king was able to promulgate laws and administer a centralized system of justice by sending writs to sheriffs throughout the country, is a prime example.

Despite growing awareness of the advantages of writing during the thirteenth century, people did not yet equate law with written text. Law was less a matter of what was written on parchment and more a matter of what the king and his council desired or decreed. The king's word was still regarded as law. The first Statute of Westminster, for instance, often speaks of what the king "wills" or "commands" or "prohibits."

Relatedly, statutes were not nearly as autonomous as they are today. It appears to have been somewhat uncertain whether or to what extent statutes survived their makers. Soon after his coronation, Edward II saw fit to send a writ to his sheriffs noting that it would be useful to have the first Statute of Westminster, enacted by his father, "observed in all its Articles." The writ then proceeded to quote part of that statute and commanded the sheriffs to cause it to be proclaimed and published.[48] Just as a spoken order or command is eventually forgotten or dies with its maker, early laws—even if written down—were apparently considered effective only while their maker remained alive to enforce them.

Consider also that judges of this time were often members of the king's council and may have been present when a law was adopted. The written record of the legislation, assuming there was one and that it was readily accessible, might have mattered less to such a judge than his own recollection of what had been decided. At best, the text would have been a reminder of what had taken place, like minutes of a meeting. This is reflected by a well-known statement made by a judge to a lawyer in 1305. The lawyer was arguing why, in his view, a statute had been enacted. The judge replied, "Do not gloss the statute, for we understand it better than you; we made it."[49]

Even after the judiciary ceased to be involved in legislating, judges continued to view the law as consisting of the will or the intentions of the lawmaker, not as the text that resulted from the lawmaking process. Sometimes the judges appealed to their common knowledge or traditions regarding a statute's meaning or purpose.[50] Or they might ask the lawmakers what they intended. This is reflected in an incident from 1366, when there is a report of judges going to Parliament to ask what it meant by a recently enacted law.[51] If your job depends on pleasing your boss, then if there is any question about a statute's application, it is obviously more politic to try to find out what the king and his council actually intended to accomplish by the legislation than to focus on the text of the legislation itself.[52] It is a very oral mode of interpretation that fit the largely oral society in which it arose.

It is not surprising that during this era English courts did not have a consistent theory of how statutes should be interpreted. Sometimes they were strictly construed, sometimes loosely. Sometimes judges carved out exceptions to a statute, sometimes they extended its reach. And on occasion they ignored a relevant statute altogether.[53]

This looseness of interpretation is quite natural if we consider that statutes of the time were records made after the fact and that, in any event, judges did not have easy access to accurate copies of the text. Carlton Kemp Allen has pointed out that statutes in the twelfth and thirteenth centuries "were not so much exact formulas emanating from a supreme Parliamentary authority, as broad rules of government and administration, intended for guidance rather than as meticulous instruction, and meant to be applied on elastic principles of expediency."[54] Or, as Plucknett aptly observed, "Interpretation in this early period could not be precise. There was no sacrosanct text."[55]

## Notes

1. See Peter Salway, *Roman Britain 87* (1981); Peter Salway, *The Oxford Illustrated History of Roman Britain*, 358–59 (1993).

2. The Anglo-Saxons were familiar with runes. Additionally, they had probably already had some contact with the Roman alphabet. See H. G. Richardson and G. O. Sayles, *Law and Legislation from Æthelberht to Magna Carta*, 157–59 (1966). But the arrival of Christian clerics was clearly the critical impetus to the development of written culture in Anglo-Saxon England.

3. For more on the history of Æthelberht's laws, as well as a text of the laws in Anglo-Saxon and modern English, see Lisi Oliver, *The Beginnings of English Law* (2002).

4. Oliver, *Beginnings of English Law*, 66–67.

5. Patrick Wormald, *The Making of English Law: King Alfred to the Twelfth Century: Volume 1: Legislation and Its Limits*, 95 (1999). Wormald points out that the language is archaic in places and the syntax quite simple. *Id.*

6. *Id.*, 101–2.

7. *Id.*, 103 (emphasis added).

8. *Id.*, 272.

9. *Id.*, 106.

10. *Id.*, 104. The same is true of Edward the Elder, who commanded his reeves to follow the rules in his *domboc* or code. *Id.*, 286.

11. *Id.*, 317.

12. *Id.*

13. *Id.*, 349.

14. Risto Hiltunen, *Chapters on Legal English: Aspects Past and Present of the Language of the Law 36* (1990).

15. Wormald, *Making of English Law*, 284.

16. *Id.*, 128.

17. *Id.*, 143.

18. *Id.*, 300.

19. *Regesta Regum Anglo-Normannorum: The Acta of William I (1066–1087)* 593 (David Bates ed., 1998).

20. Wormald, *Making of English Law*, 398.

21. Theodore F. T. Plucknett, *A Concise History of the Common Law* 112–13 (1956).

22. See Desmond Manderson, *Statuta v. Acts: Interpretation, Music, and Early English Legislation*, 7 Yale J. L. & Hum. 317, 328–31 (1995).

23. I *Statutes of the Realm* xiv, 1 (1810). Modern scholars are of the view that legislation had begun earlier. See Plucknett, *Concise History*, 318.

24. I *Statutes of the Realm*, 4.

25. Paul Brand, *Kings, Barons and Justices: The Making and Enforcement of Legislation in Thirteenth-Century England* 33–38 (2003). It is unclear if ordinary statutes were drafted in this way. *Id.*, 394.

26. M. T. Clanchy, *From Memory to Written Record: England 1066–1307 264* (2d ed. 1993).

27. I *Statutes of the Realm*, Statutes, 26.

28. *Id.*, 42.

29. Theodore F. T. Plucknett, *Statutes and Their Interpretation in the First Half of the Fourteenth Century 1* (1922/1980).

30. Plucknett, *Concise History*, 322.

31. Manderson, *Statuta vs. Acts*, 342, citing the second Statute of Westminster, 13 Edw. I, c. 50 (1285).

32. Plucknett, *Concise History*, 328.

33. I *Statutes of the Realm*, xlv.

34. Statute of Winchester, 13 Edw. I, c.l, reprinted in I *Statutes of the Realm*, 96. At the same time, the requirement of publication was to some extent undermined by the competing notion that every man was deemed to know what happens in Parliament, even if it had not been publicly proclaimed. Plucknett, *Statutes and Their Interpretation*, 103.

35. D. P. Simpson, *Cassell's New Latin Dictionary 569* (1959).

36. Plucknett comments that the word statute in the fourteenth century means "the provision made rather than the instrument embodying it." Plucknett, *Statutes and Their Interpretation*, 12.

37. This is reflected in the Spanish word *recordar*, which in the reflexive form means "to remember." The root *cord* comes from the Latin word for "heart."

38. Clanchy, *From Memory to Written Record*, 77.

39. *Id.*

40. It might not always have been the case. At least on some occasions, the "Knights, Citizens, and Burgesses" were simply charged "upon their Return into the Country to shew and publish to the People the Matters agreed on in Parliament." *Statutes of the Realm*, xlv, fn.1.

41. The Statute of Carlisle, 35 Edw. I (I *Statutes of the Realm*, Statutes, 152).

42. Wormald, *Making of English Law*, 96, 103.

43. Clanchy, *From Memory to Written Record*, 296, citing F. Kern, *Kingship and Law in the Middle Ages 179* (S. B. Chrimes trans., 1939).

44. Jack Goody, *The Logic of Writing and the Organization of Society 136* (1986).

45. 52 Hen. Ill, c. 23 (1267). The relevant provision, which relates to waste, is set forth in 23 *Halsbury's Statutes of England and Wales* 35 (4th ed. 1997 reissue). In addition, chapters 1, 4, and 15, dealing with distress, are also still in force in England and Wales. 13 *Halsbury's Statutes*, 628–30.

There are several things that complicate identifying the oldest statute still in force. One is the very basic issue of what is a statute. I follow the table in *Halsbury's Statutes Citator 2003* and therefore accept Halsbury's judgment on this issue. Another problem is that there are some statutes of uncertain date that might well be older. An example is another statute on distress, the Statutes of the Exchequer (temp, incert.), set forth in 13 *Halsbury's Statutes* at 632–32. According to *Halsbury's* (631), this statute is also still in force and is often thought to have been enacted in the fifty-first year of Henry III, which makes it a year older than the Statutes of Marlborough. Yet *Halsbury's* also suggests that it may date from the reign of Edward I, which would make it several decades younger.

46. 3 Edw. I (1275). Chapter 5 on elections is still in force (5 *Halsbury's Statutes*, 1326), as is chapter 50 (10 *Halsbury's Statutes*, 13). The statute was cited a mere fifty years ago in Attorney-General v. Colchester Corporation, [1952] Ch. 586, 595 (Chancery Division).

47. 18 Edw. 1, c.1; see 37 *Halsbury's Statutes of England and Wales* 25 (4th ed. 1998 reissue). A case in 1901 referred not only to *Quia Emptores* but to a statute dating from 1315 that had never been printed but was contained in a Parliament roll. Carlton Kemp Allen, *Law in the Making* 440 (7th ed. 1964).

48. Of the Not Taking Undue Prises from Ecclesiastical Persons or Others, 2 Edw. II (I *Statutes* of the Realm, 153–54). Similar is the Statute of Stamford, 3 Edw. II.

49. J. H. Baker, *An Introduction to English Legal History* 239–40 (1990), citing Aumeye's Case (1305), YB 33–35 Edw. I, p. 82.

50. See Plucknett, *Statutes and Their Interpretation*, 50–53.

51. R. E. Megarry, *Miscellany-at-Law: A Diversion for Lawyers and Others 358* (1958).

52. Consider the comment of one reporter that judges made a decision "more for the king's profit than for the vindication of law, and they did it through fear." Plucknett, *Statutes and Their Interpretation*, 139. And as noted previously, some kings of this time explicitly claimed the right to interpret their own laws, and it was only gradually that the power to construe statutes came to be viewed as an exclusively judicial prerogative. Plucknett, *Statutes and Their Interpretation*, 21.

53. *Id.*, 57–90.

54. Allen, *Law in the Making*, 454.

55. Plucknett, *Concise History*, 340.

4

# Some Myths about Legal Language*
Peter M. Tiersma

The final myth I'd like to discuss is that legal language is itself a myth. Obviously, I couldn't resist a catchy heading. But there are indeed those who suggest that the language of the law is in reality nothing but ordinary language, with a lot of technical terminology appended to it.[1] Likewise, there are those who suggest that legal language can be interpreted just like ordinary language, which presupposes that legal language is not fundamentally different from ordinary speech and writing.[2] Other scholars have posited that many of the distinct conventions of legal interpretation are derivable from principles regulating ordinary conversation, and thus are not at all unique to law.[3]

Given how peculiar and incomprehensible legal language can often seem to the average speaker of English, the notion that lawyers speak and write ordinary English may seem highly counterintuitive. But it seems to me that this notion must be taken seriously, although perhaps not for the reasons previously advanced for it. Although most rules governing ordinary conversation also apply to legal language, the language of law is in many important respects quite different from ordinary *speech*. On the other hand, it is much harder to distinguish legal language from ordinary but highly formal *written* language.

The most commonly cited linguistic features of legal language are the following:[4]

1. *Technical vocabulary.* This includes words such as "asportation," "demurrer," "interpleader," "estop," "quitclaim," "reverter," or to "expunge a lis pendens," along with many other examples. We might also include jargon like "black-letter law," "boilerplate," "case on point," "chilling effect," "conclusory," and "judge-shopping."

* Excerpt from Peter M. Tiersma, Some Myths about Legal Language, *Journal of Law, Culture and Humanities* 2: 9, 44–50 (2006).

2. *Archaic, formal, and unusual or difficult terminology.* We have already discussed archaic language. Examples of formal or unusual terminology include the lawyerly proclivity to speak of "commence" and "terminate" in place of "begin" and "end," or the use of "indicate" and "advise" to mean "say" or "tell" ("my client has advised me . . .").

3. *Impersonal constructions.* Illustrating this feature is avoidance of first and second person pronouns ("I" and "you"), and preference for the third person in referring to oneself (as in "this court finds").

4. *Passive constructions.* Much legal writing prefers verbs in the passive voice, especially favoring what are called *agentless* passives, as in "mistakes were made," which hides or deflects attention from the person who was responsible for the action.

5. *Nominalizations.* Another characteristic of legal language is preference for nouns and nominalizations (nouns derived from verbs, such as "consideration" or "injury") over verbs ("consider" or "injure"). This feature can also reduce emphasis on the actor.

6. *Negation.* It has also been suggested that legal language contains high levels of negation. In fact, the problem seems to be multiple negation rather than negation per se.[5]

7. *Long and complex sentences.* Legal English tends to have long sentences, in some extreme cases going on for hundreds of words before reaching a period. Blackstone's Commentaries contains an appendix that reproduces an indenture from the year 1747; one sentence goes on for 1,463 words before coming to a complete stop.[6] Often the sentences have high levels of embedding, which leads to syntactic complexity. Consider a sentence from the California jury instructions: "Do not assume to be true any insinuation suggested by a question asked a witness."[7]

8. *Wordiness and redundancy..*

We have seen that some of these features are characteristic of only certain types of legal language, or are no longer as true as they once were. Nonetheless, the list certainly contains the linguistic features most commonly attributed to legal language. What is interesting about this list is that it shows a remarkable overlap with features that linguists have associated with written language in general, and especially more formal types of prose.

A study by Wallace Chafe and Jane Danielewicz found, not surprisingly, that writing generally contains a more literate (i.e., formal) vocabulary than speech. They found that academic papers in particular packed a lot of material into "information units" (roughly comparable to a sentence). They also discovered that writers use more nominalizations and passives than speakers do. And as opposed to casual speakers, who tend to produce simple sequences of coordinated clauses, writers generally use more elaborate syntax that requires more processing power to interpret. Chafe and Danielewicz also noted that there were few first-person pronouns in academic writing, and that generally writing is more detached (i.e., impersonal) than speech.[8]

An overview of linguistic research into the difference between speech and writing by F. Niyi Akinnaso confirms most of Chafe and Danielewicz's conclusions. Although the research is sometimes inconclusive or contradictory, most studies have found that writing (compared to speech) generally has higher levels of abstraction and verbal density, more difficult and more Latinate vocabulary, fewer personal pronouns, and more elaborate syntax (including more subordination, as well as greater use of passive and nominal constructions).[9]

It turns out that just about all the features attributed to legal language are also characteristic of formal written prose. One exception is that there are no studies finding more negation in writing, as far as I know, and at least one study suggests that speech in fact has more negatives.[10] This is not a serious problem, since the overuse of negation in legal writing has never been clearly established.

The other exception is that the research on writing with which I am familiar does not establish that use of technical terminology is particularly characteristic of writing, especially when comparing similar genres (such as a spoken lecture and a written article on the same topic). It's quite possible to use a lot of technical vocabulary in speech. Thus, leaving aside negation, our comparison might lead us to conclude that the only major difference between legal language and ordinary formal writing is that the former uses more technical vocabulary. This conclusion offers small comfort to those who claim that the language of the law is special and distinct from ordinary communication. After all, there are large numbers of trades and professions—carpentry, plumbing, accountancy, medicine, software development, and many others—that have extensive technical terminology.

Should we therefore conclude that legal language is nothing more than ordinary English with a lot of specialized vocabulary? Is there no essential distinction between the language of lawyers and that of plumbers?

I think that this would be the wrong lesson to draw. For one thing, legal language has some minor deviations from ordinary language in terms of pronunciation, spelling, and punctuation.[11] It also has drafting and interpretive conventions that differ from ordinary writing, such as the one-meaning-one-form principle (avoid elegant variation), the repetition of nouns where in ordinary writing the second and later occurrences of the noun would be replaced by a pronoun ("Buyer promises that Buyer will pay . . ."), and similar linguistic quirks that may or may not be justifiable but are nonetheless distinct from ordinary writing. Normally, the use of two or three terms to refer to a single person or object ("car," "automobile," "wheels") is considered unremarkable, but in legal texts it is generally assumed that use of a separate word is intended to refer to a distinct referent. Similarly, repeating a noun is usually taken, especially within a single sentence, to indicate that the second occurrence of the noun refers to something or someone different. If I say, "John kissed John's girlfriend," we normally assume that there are two distinct people named John, because otherwise I would have said that John kissed *his* girlfriend. But this convention is not followed in legal usage: "Buyer promises that Buyer will pay" is normally assumed to refer to one person, not two.

More importantly, what we might broadly call the textual or literary conventions of the profession are sometimes very distinct from ordinary conventions relating to writing. To mention just two examples from the law of wills, a person who handwrites her will on a bedroom wall and signs it has made a valid will in many American jurisdictions. But if she types the will on paper, and signs it, it is *not* effective. Or suppose that a woman goes to a lawyer and executes a valid witnessed will giving $10,000 to her niece, Sarah. She later crosses out that bequest and puts her signature in the margin. In many states the gift remains effective.[12] These results seem completely antithetical to ordinary conventions of literacy.

There are also many genres of text in the legal realm that do not exist in ordinary language, such as various types of contracts, deeds, wills, rules, and statutes. Each has its own relatively rigid format and sometimes requires specific forms of language.

Moreover, the legal mode of interpreting text is very different from how we interpret ordinary writing. Suppose that you are reading a book of some sort and come across an ambiguity. You might reread the text several times, examine the context, and then use whatever intuitions and information you have at hand to resolve it as best you can. You do not consciously apply rules of interpretation that someone taught you.

Judges tend to have very explicit rules about interpreting legal texts, especially statutes. An intentionalist judge may research a statute's history, previous drafts, statements by sponsors on the floor of the legislature, committee reports, etc., each of which will carry greater or lesser weight. A textualist judge, on the other hand, will look only at the text itself, and perhaps some related texts, as well as dictionaries. He may also invoke certain canons of construction.[13] In other words, an intentionalist judge does not simply rely on whatever information she has before her, but digs through often obscure archives for additional clues to a text's meaning. A textualist judge, in contrast, refuses to consider certain types of information even if it is known to him. Both of these approaches are different from how we normally interpret text.

In sum, it would be a gross mischaracterization to suggest that lawyers have a language of their own. But it would also be inaccurate to say that legal language is nothing more than formal written language with some additional technical vocabulary. Elsewhere I have suggested that it is a *sublanguage* of English. Whatever the label, it is somewhere between a separate language and ordinary English, and it is much closer to ordinary English than many people seem to think.

There is an interesting variation on the myth that legal language is a myth. Some people agree that legal language differs in some important ways from ordinary speech and writing, but argue that these differences are indefensible and should be eliminated. Essentially, their point is that law *can* and *should be* expressed in ordinary English.

During the Commonwealth period in England, the Levellers advocated abolishing the common law and replacing it with a pocket-book of law in "plain man's English."[14] Many supporters of the codification movement also espoused the making of codes of law that ordinary people could understand. In Europe, where it was widely implemented, codification may have helped rationalize and clarify the law, but it does not seem to have enhanced knowledge of the law among the citizenry.[15] In the United States, David Dudley Field argued that codification would make the law so simple that it could be understood by any person of ordinary intellect,[16] but once again this goal was not achieved.

Can the law be expressed in ordinary English, or is this also a myth? The short answer is that in theory it can be, but probably not in practice. The law can certainly be expressed more plainly, but it is unlikely that ordinary citizens will ever understand it completely.

We have seen that one thing that makes the language of lawyers distinct is its large technical vocabulary. Such terms would obviously have to be converted into plain English. I have no doubt that this can be done, but is it a good idea? Even if we convert the Latin *malum prohibitum* into the plainer English phrase "prohibited wrong," its technical meaning in criminal law will be just as obscure to the uninitiated. Many technical terms are useful, and it is senseless to try to eliminate them entirely.

Of course, it should be possible to define technical terminology in plain language. A very interesting approach to explaining complex technical terms is that of Natural Semantic Metalanguage (NSM), developed by linguist Anna Wierzbicka and her colleagues. NSM endeavors to reduce any word to a few semantic primes, which it claims to be universal.

Wierzbicka has applied her approach to the concept of "reasonable man." Thus, "I think that X is a reasonable man" is reduced to:

a. I think about X like this:
b. X can think well about many things
c. when something happens to X, X can think well about it
d. because of this, X can think about it like this:
　'I know what is a good thing to do now'
　'I know what is a good thing not to do now'

    e. if other people think about it for some time they can think the same
    f. when I think about X like this, I think: this is good
    g. I don't want to say more
    h. I don't want to say that X is not like many other people.[17]

Clearly, NSM is an interesting approach, although I might quibble about some of the details. But notice that a two-word phrase requires around 100 words of explication. One of Wierzbicka's students, Ian Langford, applied her approach to criminal law, claiming that "highly complex and obscure legal definitions can be replaced by simple explications which are clear, accurate and noncircular."[18] His explications of the various crimes are indeed clear, but at times seem to have glossed over legal complexities that would require many more words to explain. Part of his explication for "murder" is that "people say: it is very bad if someone does something like this." This seems to be aimed at the requirement that a killing be "unlawful." But this requirement actually relates to excuse and justification, each of which is itself quite complicated. Despite his prodigious efforts, Langford on occasion finds himself admitting defeat, observing that explicating a particular term would be "a complex exercise outside the scope of this thesis."[19] These problems would be less severe if we used ordinary English, of course, but the need to define legal concepts would remain, and would almost certainly result in statutes being much more verbose than they are now. It's not so clear that this would be an improvement over the current state of affairs.

    Efforts to write law in plain English would also have to deal with the textual conventions of the legal profession, which allow the meaning of a word or phrase to be explained or sometimes modified by judicial decision. Either we would have to abolish the ability of courts to do so, which would radically change our legal system, or we would have to require judges construing legislation to literally rewrite the language, or insert definitions, in ordinary English, so that the language of the statute remains transparent. Obviously, drafting the law in plain language would be pointless if readers have to consult judicial opinions in order to know what a statute really means.

    Thus, the main obstacle to writing the law in plain English is that, unless the law itself is vastly simplified, it will require the use of so many words that there will be nothing plain about it.

    Most advocates of plain English recognize this problem. Although they continue to agitate for plainer language in legal documents, including statutes, they realize that many parts of the law are too complex to allow them to be fully and comprehensibly explained to ordinary citizens. They therefore advocate that those legal areas in which citizens have particular interest, like criminal law, be officially summarized and explained.[20] Not only would such summaries help people understand the law, but they could place a limit on how much of the law citizens are presumed to know, so that ignorance of a statute's text would indeed be an excuse, but ignorance of the summary would not be.

## Notes

1. See Mary Jane Morrison, "Excursions into the Nature of Legal Language," *Cleveland State L. Rev.* 37 (1989), p. 271.

2. See Jan Engberg, "Statutory Texts as Instances of Language(s): Consequences and Limitations on Interpretation, " *Brooklyn J. Int'l L.* 29 (2004), p. 1135. See also "Symposium: What Is Meaning in a Legal Text?," *Wash. U. L.Q.* 73 (1995), pp. 771–970.

3. Geoffrey P. Miller, "Pragmatics and the Maxims of Interpretation," *Wis. L. Rev.* (1990), p. 1179; M. B. W. Sinclair, "Law and Language: The Role of Pragmatics in Statutory Interpretation, *U. Pitts. L. Rev.* 46 (1985), p. 373.

4. The list is based on David Mellinkoff, *The Language of the Law* (Boston: Little, Brown and Company, 1963), p.13; and Peter M. Tiersma, *Legal Language* (Chicago: University of Chicago Press, 1999), pp. 203–210.

5. Robert R. Charrow and Veda R. Charrow, "Making Legal Language Underst andable: A Psycholinguistic Study of Jury Instructions," *Colum. L. Rev.* 79 (1979), pp. 1325–1326.

6. William Blackstone, *Commentaries on the Laws of England, Book the Second, Appendix* (Oxford: Clarendon Press, 1765–1769), pp. iii–v (the sentence in question is from the document entitled "Deed of Release" and begins with the words, "Whereas the marriage is intended . . .").

7. California Jury Instructions, Criminal, No. 1.02 (St. Paul, Minn.: West, 1996).

8. Wallace Chafe and Jane Danielewicz, "Properties of Spoken and Written Language," in R. Horowitz and S. J. Samuels, eds., *Comprehending Oral and Written Language* (San Diego, Calif.: Academic Press, 1987), pp. 83–113.

9. F. Niyi Akinnaso, "On the Difference Between Spoken and Written Language," *Language and Speech* 25 (1982), pp. 97–125.

10. Douglas Biber, *Variation Across Speech and Writing* (Cambridge: University Press, 1988), p. 245.

11. Tiersma, *Legal Language*, pp. 51–55.

12. See Peter M. Tiersma, "From Speech to Writing: Textualization and Its Consequences," in Marilyn Robinson, ed., *Language and the Law: Proceedings of a Conference* (Buffalo, NY: William S. Hein & Co., 2003).

13. See generally William N. Eskridge, Jr., "The New Textualism," *UCLA L. Rev.* 37 (1990), p. 621.

14. J. H. Baker, *An Introduction to English Legal History* (London: Butterworths, 1990), p. 244.

15. Helmut Going, "An Intellectual History of European Codification in the Eighteenth and Nineteenth Centuries," in S. J. Stoljar, ed., *Problems of Codification* (Dept. of Law, Research School of Social Sciences, Australian National University, 1977), pp. 16–25.

16. Maurice Eugen Lang, *Codification in the British Empire and America* (Amsterdam: HJ Paris, 1927), pp. 160–162.

17. Anna Wierzbicka, "'Reasonable Man' and 'Reasonable Doubt': The English Language, Anglo Culture and Anglo-American Law," *International Journal of Speech, Language, and the Law* 10 (2003), pp. 1–22.

18. Ian Langford, "The Semantics of Crime: A Linguistic Analysis," unpublished PhD thesis, Australian National University, 2002, p. 293.

19. Op. Cit., p. 302. See also pp. 313 and 320.

20. See Paul H. Robinson, Peter D. Greene, and Natasha B. Goldstein, "Making Criminal Codes Functional: A Code of Conduct and a Code of Adjudication," *J.. Crim. L. & Criminology* 86 (1996), p. 304.

# 5

# On the Relationship Between Legal and Ordinary Language

Frederick Schauer

In *Parchment, Paper, Pixels*, Peter Tiersma (2010: 120) raises the important question of what he calls "Conflicting Conventions of Literacy." His immediate target is the parol evidence rule, the substantive rule of contract law (and not really a rule of evidence at all) according to which a final contract "supersedes" and "integrates" all prior writings and discussions, such that evidence about such writings and discussions cannot be used to add to, subtract from, or otherwise modify the terms of the contract. And for Tiersma, what is most interesting and jarring about the parol evidence rule is that it "runs counter to ordinary conventions of literacy."

Tiersma's observations about the parol evidence rule are important and valuable, but they are based on his identification of an issue that is more important and valuable still. That is, legal language generally is in important ways different from ordinary language. In some respects this is obvious. Ordinary people simply do not talk about "assumpsit," "res judicata," "interpleader," or "covenants running with the land." And so we can start by observing that law not only contains some of its own technical language, but that the definitions of such words and terms are created by the law itself. If you want to know what "interpleader" means, you need to know about the law of interpleader, just as the definition of "covenants running with the land" comes from centuries of common law legal history and legal doctrine and not from either the diction-ary or the ordinary language of the ordinary person.

Things get more complicated, however, once we realize that everything we can say about the law-dependent meanings of terms like "interpleader," "res judicata," and "covenants running with the land" can also be said about "contract," "trust," "complaint," and "assault." The student who on a law school examination relies on the dictionary to define and apply such terms will fail, and justifiably so. And this is so despite the fact that the terms in the latter group, unlike the terms in the former group, are ones that can be found in ordinary non-legal dictionaries, and are terms that ordinary people use in their ordinary non-technical and non-legal conversations. But once we understand that such terms have ordinary non-legal as well as legal technical meanings, we find ourselves faced with the important and under-analyzed problem of legal technical language, and of the relationship between legal technical language and the law's own frequent use of ordinary language.

The nature of the problem was hinted at by Oliver Wendell Holmes, Jr. (1897: 464), who observed that it is a common "fallacy" to take words with moral content and import, such as "rights," "duties," "malice," "intent," and "negligence," and assume that they have the same moral content and import when they are used in law, or used to describe the law. Somewhat more specifically, and about half a century later, the contracts, insurance, and jurisprudence scholar Edwin Patterson suggested that it might be preferable to use entirely made-up words in place of much of legal language—like the word "contract," for example, that simultaneously and confusingly looked outward to the larger linguistic world and inward to the linguistic world of the law and its inhabitants.[1] And perhaps most prominently, Lon Fuller (1967: 20–23), in writing about legal fictions, saw legal fictions as the remedy for the impossibility of a legal regime in which all language used in law was understood as technical language. Indeed, in his famous debate with H. L. A. Hart, Fuller (1958: 662–64) appeared to flirt with the idea of going somewhat further, approaching, but not quite embracing, the idea that the word "vehicle," as part of the sign prohibiting vehicles from the park, might be understood not as ordinary language, but as legal technical language, as such incorporating all of the goals, values, and doctrines of the legal system in which the particular rule existed.[2]

As Fuller and others who have discussed the issue have recognized (see Patterson 1953: 252–258), of course, legal language cannot plausibly be understood as a language unto itself. Legal English is related to ordinary English in ways that Estonian is not.[3] And that is as it should be, because an important dimension of law is captured in the way in which it speaks to its subjects and not just to the legal professionals who manage the system from the inside.[4] Legal rules and legal decisions that could not be understood by the "man on the Clapham omnibus," as the English so quaintly put it, would fail to provide the guidance function so essential to law, and would fail in such a way that, at least for some, and again Lon Fuller is the major figure here (see Fuller 1969: 49–50, 63–65), secret law is essentially no law at all.

Thus the problem of technical language in law is the problem, as yet unsolved and barely addressed, of the relationship between ordinary language and technical legal language. The word "speech" in the First

Amendment plainly has a definition that is not coextensive with the ordinary language meaning of that word,[5] but it would be a mistake to infer from this that the word "speech" in that context is totally unrelated to the idea of speech as discussed by non-lawyers in non-legal settings. So too with a "contract" or "combination" or "conspiracy" in the context of the Sherman Antitrust Act's prohibitions, "or a "device" or "artifice" to "defraud" in the context of the prohibitions of the American securities laws. In these and countless other legal contexts, it is an error to interpret the legal language as simply being ordinary English, but it is also a mistake to take such terms as entirely terms of art with no connection at all to the ways in which they are used in ordinary talk. Tiersma is entirely correct, and importantly so, in observing that the conventions of language, of literacy, and of interpretation of the law are hardly congruent with the conventions of language, literacy, and interpretation of ordinary non-technical life. And of course these conventions in law also differ from the conventions that exist in the other specialized disciplines, each with their own technical language. The work that remains to be done, however, is that of analyzing the relationship between the conventions of the technical and the conventions of the ordinary, and to do so in a way that recognizes law's parallel needs to speak to itself and at the same time to speak to those outside it. It is common for legal insiders and commentators to refer to "terms of art," but all too often such references are largely question-begging. When the terms of legal terms of art are ones that are found elsewhere in the language, we need a way to distinguish, conceptually even if not with perfect precision, the terms that are legal terms of art from those that are not. And even when we have identified what is a legal term of art, we need a way to interpret it that is faithful to the way that even legal terms of art are commonly written in English and not in Latin or Law French. If we can grasp these tasks, and if we can make some headway in performing, we will have made progress in understanding the language of the law. Consequently, and as Tiersma has long insisted, and properly so, when we understand more about the language of the law, we understand more about law itself.

## Notes

1. Preliminary manuscript for a treatise on the law of contracts, available at the Columbia Law School Library.

2. In a more sophisticated version, somewhat of the same flavor appears in Moore (1985: 381–396).

3. On the relationship between technical language and ordinary language more generally, see Charles E. Caton's "Introduction," in Caton (1963: v–xi).

4. Moreover, and as Peter Tiersma has usefully explored, even decisionmakers inside the legal system—jurors, most obviously—may not be legally trained or sophisticated, and the language of the law must be able to speak to them as well. See Tiersma (1993a).

5. See Schauer (1979, 1981, 2004); Tiersma (1993b).

## References

Caton, Charles E. (1963) *Philosophy and Ordinary Language.* Urbana, Ill.: University of Illinois Press.

Fuller, Lon L. (1958) Positivism and Fidelity to Law—A Reply to Professor Hart, *Harvard Law Review* 71: 630–672.

Fuller, Lon L. (1967) *Legal Fictions.* Stanford, Calif.: Stanford University Press.

Fuller, Lon L. (1969) *The Morality of Law* (Rev. ed.). New Haven, Conn.: Yale University Press.

Holmes, Oliver Wendell, Jr. (1897) The Path of the Law, *Harvard Law Review* 10: 457–478.

Moore, Michael S. (1985) A Natural Law Theory of Interpretation, *Southern California Law Review* 58: 277–398.

Patterson, Edwin W. (1953) *Jurisprudence: Men and Ideas of the Law.* Brooklyn, NY: The Foundation Press.

Schauer, Frederick (1979) Speech and "Speech"—Obscenity and "Obscenity": An Exercise in the Interpretation of Constitutional Language, *Georgetown Law Journal* 67: 899–933.

Schauer, Frederick (1981) Categories and the First Amendment: A Play in Three Acts, *Vanderbilt Law Review* 34: 265–307.

Schauer, Frederick (2004) The Boundaries of the First Amendment: A Preliminary Exploration of Constitutional Salience, *Harvard Law Review* 117: 1765–1809.

Tiersma, Peter Meijes (1993a) Refining the Language of Jury Instructions, *Hofstra Law Review* 22: 37–78.

Tiersma, Peter Meijes (1993b) Nonverbal Communication and the Freedom of "Speech," *Wisconsin Law Review* 1993: 1525–1589.

Tiersma, Peter Meijes (2010) *Parchment, Paper, Pixels: Law and the Technologies of Communication.* Chicago: University of Chicago Press.

# 6

# Legal Language and Its History

*QUO IMUS? QUA IMUS?*

## Ronald R. Butters

Peter Tiersma's writings on the history of legal language, excerpted in this volume, together offer a succinct, comprehensive survey of significant aspects of the development of the Western traditions of legal speech and writing from the earliest code of Hammurabi to present-day online publication of laws and judicial opinions. Tiersma embeds his understanding of his subject—as an anthropologist rightly would—in a consideration of the history and culture of the law-producing peoples that are his focus, deducing as best anyone could the oral legal traditions in preliterate societies (e.g., Germanic law before the influence of Rome, delineated in medieval Icelandic literature), and in Western societies that had not yet set their laws into written form or, like ancient Sparta, seem to have deliberately eschewed written codes. Legal language has evolved into a number of quite different, only-sometimes-intersecting categories, but it surely began as (1) communally understood practical and ethical precepts, often of a religious nature, and (2) ritualized ways of their enforcement.

Today in the United States, for example, these two precepts are still at the heart of legal language. However, both written and spoken language break down into a number of legal categories, and the rules governing legal utterances are so extremely complex that learning these rules must surely be one of the important functions of legal education.

Spoken legal language includes the language of courtroom proceedings, where matters of spoken decorum and ritual vary with the type of court. Traffic court and small claims courts are marked by less formal language than are civil and criminal courts; appellate courts often restrict speech only to judges and pleading attorneys. Depositions involve a quite different kind of linguistic behavior. Trademark Board trials seem to have no spoken form at all, though they originate in deposition-like proceedings and the judges read the transcripts. Jurors can say only prescribed kinds of things at certain times. Judges are only allowed to say certain kinds of things to jurors. In all but the least serious of cases, a written record is made of the court proceedings, raising inevitable questions of whether the transcript adequately captures the meaning of the spoken words.

The spoken words in legal forums are themselves also subject to complex rules: Which languages are allowed? What is the role of translators? Of interpreters for the deaf? How far should court reporters go toward explaining gestures? When can questioners ask leading questions? What kinds of questions, if any, can one ask of children? Of prospective jurors in voir dire? Of witnesses in a grand jury investigation? What cannot be said in court about the sexual history of alleged rapists and their victims? What constitutes a perjurious statement? When language itself is the evidence, as, for example, in trademark disputes, libel cases, and criminal cases involving extortion or solicitation, who has the authority to decide that language's relevance and meaning? Written transcripts of undercover investigations, arrests, and police interrogations present just such thorny issues.

Similarly, written legal language comes in a wide variety of forms, with complex restraints that apply to virtually all of them. Tiersma necessarily restricts his historical consideration largely to statutes, constitutions, and written judicial opinions, but written law today takes many other forms, in addition to the transcripts of spoken proceedings. Written language with legal force today includes pardons, executive orders, regulations of innumerable state and federal regulatory boards, patents, trademark applications, and military orders to inferiors, as well as statutes and court opinions.

Thus, when Tiersma asks about the truth of various "myths" about legal language (in what is a most thought-provoking passage in his writings on the history of legal language), he is particularly right to wonder if the very concept of legal language itself is a "myth." Confining himself to written legal language, he notes that there are certainly characteristics of wills, contracts, and statutes that are conventionally different from any other kind of writing, sometimes justified as existing for the sake of clarity, itself a special goal of the law. Of course, Tiersma is right in asserting that the hoped-for "precision" of legal language is something of a myth in itself. It makes sense to say that numerous features of various kinds of legal language are indeed unique. At the same time, however, it would be mistaken to infer that, just because legal language is peculiar in a variety of ways, we should ignore the amazing heterogeneity within the domain of legal language, oral as well as written.

Tiersma's consideration of the many "myths" about legal language provide much continuing food for thought. As he convincingly points out, the myth that Latin is somehow the basis of legal language should be the first myth to go (hence my sardonic pseudo-legal-Latin subtitle, *Quo Imus? Qua Imus?*, which in ordinary, if less succinct, English would be, "Where are we going? How are we getting there?"). And anyone who believes the myth that legal language is invariably dull and pompous has never spent much time in a courtroom. On the other hand, the difficulties surrounding jury instructions are indeed no myth; of particular concern to Tiersma with respect to the future of legal language is the issue of the need to reform jury instructions, particularly in cases that may lead to death penalty verdicts (Tiersma 1999: 235ff.). Judges refrain from offering their own interpretations for fear of laying grounds for appeal, but the instructions that they are required to read to juries without explanation are sometimes incomprehensible to the jurors. For example, juries are asked to weigh a homicide's AGGRAVATING circumstances against MITIGATING circumstances—two words that are either not in the vocabularies of ordinary speakers of English or mean something different in legal language. The future, Tiersma hopes, will lead to greater clarity of jury instructions, recognizing however, that such reforms come slowly and are not always effective. In the interim, this non-lawyer wonders why defense lawyers do not simply ask prospective jurors about the meanings of such terms during the voir dire, laying grounds for their disqualification if the jurors seem unable to define them satisfactorily. But perhaps judges would not allow questions about legal terms—or disqualification on such grounds alone.

Tiersma's provocative suggestions for putting technology to use in drafting legislation are occasionally lighthearted and deliberately utopian, as where he speculates that future legislative and executive branches will be willing to cede power to judges to directly edit statutes online, making it unnecessary to write lengthy opinions (Tiersma 2010: 172). Similarly, Tiersma wonders if future legislators, each linked to a central computer, might draft statutes together, agreeing on the wording clause by clause (172). In reality today, Congress seems to find it difficult to agree even on fundamental principles, let alone on the wording of individual clauses, and members of Congress complain that the bills they vote on are so massive that they literally can't read them, let alone parse them line by line.

Yet Tiersma's *gedanken* experiments forcefully remind us that technology will inevitably change the future of the law in exciting and unpredictable ways. Just as the new technology of the printing press revolutionized both the process and substance of legislation centuries ago, so, too, is today's new technology replete with many possibilities for improving both the cooperative nature of the legislative process (a sort of official crowd-sourcing) and the quality of the product produced. Will the future see these more collaborative approaches to the legislative process and judicial interpretation of the law? Only time will tell. While today's reality is that bills are written by committees, and in turn the committees' work is done by staff members, one can imagine two or three congressional staffers, with linked MacBook Pros, following out Tiersma's scheme.

Certainly at the very least, Tiersma suggests, while wills will probably still have the greatest force of law in written form, they will increasingly have video and electronically stored adjuncts (Tiersma 2010: 76–77), and greater informality in their documentation (79–82). Tiersma also suggests (175) that electronic filing of committee reports, legislative preambles, and other statements of intent may be employed to clarify the issue of legislative intent. Of course, that may merely complicate the issue of legislative intent further, since they, too, will need to be interpreted.

Tiersma reminds us that legal language, spoken and written, has a rich and varied history, and there is no reason to think that the future will be one bit simpler—and every reason to hope that we will respond to technological and social change by making the most of our resources in novel and unpredictable ways.

## References

Tiersma, Peter M. (1999) *Legal Language*. Chicago: University of Chicago Press.
Tiersma, Peter M. (2010) *Parchment, Paper, Pixels: Law and the Technologies of Communication*. Chicago: University of Chicago Press.

# 7

# Philosophical Hermeneutics in the Age of Pixels

HANS-GEORG GADAMER, PETER TIERSMA, AND *DASEIN* IN THE AGE OF THE INTERNET

## Frank S. Ravitch

## Introduction

I am honored to contribute to this volume exploring the scholarship of Peter Tiersma, whose work has been immensely helpful to many of us who write in the area of legal interpretation. I will focus specifically on the implications of Tiersma's work on legal interpretation in the age of the Internet. Tiersma is one of the first scholars to address the impact that modern technology has on legal interpretation. He suggests some fascinating possibilities such as using wiki technology in drafting and interpreting legislation and inter-branch statutory editing. Here I will utilize his insights about legal interpretation and interpretive traditions in the age of the Internet to briefly explore the interrelationship among technology, *dasein*, and tradition in the understanding of law from the vantage of Philosophical Hermeneutics.

## A (Very) Basic Introduction to Gadamerian Hermeneutics and the Law

Hermeneutics are an inescapable part of everyday life. We are always interpreting, whether we know it or not (Ravitch 2007: 9–10). Interpretation is especially challenging when one attempts to apply a text written in a different time and culture to situations arising today (Ravitch 2010: 2–6, 9–12, 81–82). There are many approaches to interpretation, many of them overlapping on salient points. Philosophical hermeneutics seems especially useful in legal interpretation because of the time lag and cultural shifts that sometimes occur between the passage of legislation or ratification of constitutions and the present.

The philosopher Hans-Georg Gadamer explained that there is no absolute method of interpretation (Gadamer 1999; Gadamer 1981: 98–107). Each interpreter brings his or her own preconceptions into the act of interpreting a text—and Gadamer meant "text" in a broad sense not limited to written texts (Gadamer 1999: 265–271). These preconceptions are influenced by the tradition, including social context, in which the interpreter exists. The interpreter's tradition(s) provides her with a horizon that includes her interpretive predispositions. This horizon is the range of what the interpreter can see when engaging with a text. The concept of *dasein*, or being in the world, captures this dynamic (Gadamer 1999: 257, 264). We exist in the world around us and that world influences how we view things. Thus, our traditions and context are a part of our being. As Tiersma (2010) explains, the Internet has vastly expanded our access to the traditions to which we may be exposed.

Still, the text has its own horizon of meaning. That horizon is influenced by the context (or tradition) in which it was written, by those who influenced or interpreted it over time, by the words used, and by the context of the original author or authors (Gadamer 1999: 370, 374–375; 1981: 98). Here, too, technology could have an influence, as discussed later. Philosophical hermeneutics suggests that in order to understand a text, a give and take must occur between text and interpreter—a dialogue between one's being and the object that one seeks to understand. This conversation transforms both the text and interpreter as they engage in that give and take (Gadamer 1999).

The interpreter necessarily projects his or her horizon into the interpretive process, but should also reflect upon it and the horizon of the text. The horizon of the text has a binding quality in that if the interpreter openly enters into dialogue with the text, the horizon of the text will limit the range of preconceptions that the interpreter can project consistently with the horizon of the text (Gadamer 1999: 266–269; Eskridge 1990: 627). Since the text and interpreter are engaged in a kind of dialogue to reach a common meaning, neither text nor interpreter is the sole source of meaning.

Gadamer saw the quest for interpretive methodologies as interfering with the process of interpretation by obfuscating what is really going on. It is not that interpretive methodology is useless, but rather that it does not do what it purports to do—reach an objective and unquestionable meaning (Gadamer 1999: 266–277). Tiersma's work on legal interpretation helps frame this dynamic beautifully, because he recognizes the potential binding quality of words in the interpretive process while simultaneously understanding the limits of what the words of a text can do by themselves in situations where they must be applied to new contexts (Tiersma 2006; Tiersma 2007).

Gadamer would say that the process of reaching meaning requires a constant dialogue between text and interpreter. This dialogue is mediated, however, by tradition (Gadamer 1999: 257–264, 358–362). Significantly, Gadamer does not believe that the lack of a clear interpretive method prevents one from reaching truth, by which he means understanding. He simply shows us that truth can be variable when different texts and interpreters engage in the hermeneutic dialogue, or when that dialogue is engaged in over time by the same interpreter. Thus, while there is no methodological approach to interpretation in Gadamerian hermeneutics, there is a way for text and interpreter to interact to reach a meaning that is both consistent with the text and cognizant of the role the interpreter plays in reaching that meaning (Ravitch 2010: 9–12).

Tiersma's work adds two fascinating possibilities to this dynamic. First, in the modern world of the Internet, traditions may be framed in ways far more complex than would exist in a specific cultural or societal context (Tiersma 2010). Second, by using technology, the process of interpretation could more directly link judges who interpret the text of laws and legislators who write those laws (Tiersma 2010: 169–175), making fusion of horizons a potentially easier, or more open, task.

## Philosophical Hermeneutics in the Age of Pixels

Tiersma's work poignantly demonstrates the impact that technology can have both on the drafting and interpretation of law. Today, lawyers and the potential judges of tomorrow grow up in a legal culture that teaches and outwardly values many of the same interpretive presumptions used by earlier generations, including the need to ground or justify legal decisions through some form of accepted legal interpretation (Solan 1993: 2–3). Yet today's lawyers and future judges also grow up in a culture that is in some ways borderless. Blogs, Internet sources, wikis, Twitter, and so forth provide both a means to escape one's local traditions on a daily basis and at the same time a way for some to remain immersed only in those traditions that suit their preconceptions—we might call this informational forum shopping.

On the other hand, modern technology opens up potentially huge sources of information for judges attempting to understand and interpret legislation and legislative history. As Tiersma's discussion of wiki technology illustrates, this technology also opens the possibility of a literal dialogue between text and interpreter, a world where the text drafters in the executive or legislative branches may be able to edit as a group, and judges may be able to edit legislation after deciding a case where portions of the legislation are found unclear or unconstitutional (Tiersma 2010: 171–176). As Tiersma also suggests, it opens up the possibility that legislators editing as a group can leave a direct track record of authorial intent and editing, which judges can then rely on (Tiersma 2010: 172–174).

All of this raises serious questions for Gadamerian hermeneutics. The idea of a dasein—being in the world—was conceived at a time when cultural traditions were often homogeneous and based on a given society or subset within a society, such as judges and lawyers. One using hermeneutic theory to try to understand specific interpretive decisions may have had an easier time grappling with the horizon of the interpreter considering factors such as geography, profession, age, and so on. Today, however, many other factors and traditions may affect the horizon of the interpreter who is situated in even a relatively homogeneous community. Perhaps, in the end, even potentially limitless and boundary-less information would not create enough cognitive dissonance to overcome the preconceptions of specific culturally inculcated traditions. But, perhaps, as Tiersma's work suggests, the age of pixels and the Internet will create new interpretive and social traditions to affect old ones in a way that will challenge our use of philosophical hermeneutics to aid our understanding of the nature of interpretation and to challenge our own preconceptions regarding the very nature of traditions and dasein.

### References

Eskridge, William N. Jr. (1990) Gadamer/Statutory Interpretation, *Columbia Law Review* 90:609–681.

Gadamer, Hans Georg (1999) *Truth and Method* (2nd rev. ed.) (Joel Weinsheimer and Donald G. Marshall Trans.). New York: Continuum.

Gadamer, Hans Georg (1981) *Reason in the Age of Science* (Frederick G. Lawrence, Trans.). Cambridge: MIT Press.

Ravitch, Frank S. (2007) *Masters of Illusion: the Supreme Court and the Religion Clauses.* New York: New York University Press.

Solan, Lawrence M. (1993) *The Languages of Judges.* Chicago: University of Chicago Press.

Tiersma, Peter M. (2006) Some Myths about Legal Language, *Law, Culture and Humanities* 2:29–50.

Tiersma Peter M. (2007) The Textualization of Precedent, *Notre Dame Law Review* 82:1187–1278.

Tiersma, Peter M. (2010) *Parchment, Paper, Pixels: Law and the Technologies of Communication.* Chicago: The University of Chicago Press.

# 8

# The Language of Lawyers and
# the Language of Plumbers

Edward Finegan

The terms "legal language" and "the language of the law" have served as titles for books by Peter Tiersma and David Mellinkoff, respectively. In scholarly arenas they are the terms favored over "legalese," a term with a disparaging connotation that is more familiar to people outside communities of legal scholarship. Other referential terms serve as book titles for aspects of the language of the law, such as *The Language of Judges* (Solan 1993), intended for a scholarly audience, and *Lawtalk* (Clapp et al. 2011), illustrating a more popular discussion of legal expressions. In addition, titles and subtitles of monographs refer variously to "the language of criminal justice," "the language of statutes," "the language of bribery," "the language of perjury cases," while scores of books discuss "legal style" and "legal usage." Considerable published writing opts for the broad characterization enabled by the simple conjunction of "language and law." Inside handbooks and journals, one finds analyses of "the grammar and structure of legal texts," "discourses in the language of the law," "the rhetoric of constitutional law," and so on. When it comes to vocabulary, *Black's Law Dictionary* (Garner 2009), the legal dictionary favored in the American law community, runs to more than 1,900 pages, a magnitude that suggests heavy-duty specialization of legal vocabulary. Recently published is Heikki Mattila's (2013) *Comparative Legal Linguistics*, a substantial book that highlights an increasingly broad analytical focus on the language of the law across several languages.

But what exactly is the language of the law and what are its characteristics? In "Some Myths About Legal Language" Peter Tiersma (2006) undercuts several oft-repeated claims about its characteristics—that it is precise; that it uses archaic vocabulary; that it relies heavily on Latin and French terms; that it tends toward wordiness, redundancy, pomposity, and dullness.

Beyond those stock motifs, he tackles the knotty myth that the very concept of legal language is itself a myth. In his view, "it would be a gross mischaracterization to suggest that lawyers have a language of their own. But it would also be inaccurate to say that legal language is nothing more than formal written language with some additional technical vocabulary" (p. 48). He asks, "Is there no essential distinction between the language of lawyers and that of plumbers?" (p. 46), and in the end he concludes that, "Whatever the label, it is somewhere between a separate language and ordinary English, and it is much closer to ordinary English than many people seem to think" (p. 48).

He is right, of course. Whatever falls within the scope of the terms "legal language" and "the language of the law" does not constitute a separate language, certainly not in the sense that English is distinct from French or Japanese. Neither is it merely "formal written language" peppered with specialist or technical vocabulary. Tiersma is doubtless correct as well in saying that many people seem to think the language of the law more different from ordinary English than it is. Still, it is worthwhile to unpack some of the elements entailed in his conclusion that "it is much closer to ordinary English than many people seem to think."

Written texts have been the chief focus of analysis and criticism in discussions of legal language among those within and without the perimeter of legal professionals. Law school classes focus largely on published appellate decisions and, to a lesser degree, the texts of statutory law. Law students are required to take courses in legal writing, and numerous textbooks address legal writing in its many genres—office memos, motions, trial briefs, letters to clients, and more. Men and women outside the legal profession also confront the language of the law chiefly in writing, particularly in quotidian forms of contract—insurance policies, rental agreements, documents for automobile or home loans, credit card applications, skiing or snowboarding waiver release forms, and so on. While the Plain English movement has to a limited degree reduced the linguistic opaqueness of some forms of contract, ordinary readers frequently sign contracts with little more than a glance at them, partly because they anticipate that reading them will shed little or no light on the obligations incurred or the privileges forgone and partly because what they are chiefly interested in is the end product—rental car, credit card, access to a chairlift. To that extent, then, it is, as Tiersma says, impossible to regard such contract language—with its exceedingly long sentences and cumbersome syntax—as nothing more than formal language, akin, say, to a letter offering employment or a letter of resignation such as a layperson might have occasion to read or write.

There are still other arenas of legal language—spoken genres in particular—where laypersons are vulnerable to the exigencies and idiosyncrasies of the law. Gregory Matoesian (1993) has documented the not surprising power imbalance inherent in courtroom cross-examination. Taken utterance by utterance, questions asked by counsel and replies by witnesses may sometimes appear like ordinary English, as in examples 1 and 2 below:

1. Q: D'you know what- (.) road you turned right off to?
   A: No.
2. Q: Did you have any marijuana?
   A: No.

As Matoesian's meticulous analysis shows, however, the cross-examination of a rape victim, displaying talk exchanges whose effect he likens to reproducing the rape, is as alien to laypersons' ordinary interaction even in highly formal spoken settings, as it is familiar to defense attorneys. The variety of everyday speech events shows characteristic interactional norms, but they fall within broad bounds of ordinariness. Not so for cross-examination.

Consider this exchange from Matoesian's rape trial transcripts, illustrating how very different from ordinary conversation such interaction may be:

3. Q: You have used marijuana,have you not?
   A: Yes I have.
      (1.8 seconds elapse)
   Q: You enjoy its use do you not?

Matoesian deconstructs how the form of the defense attorney's questions first makes a statement and then by its tag question constrains the victim's answer. He further shows how the unusually long pauses a defense attorney can leave after a victim's answers serve to underscore her answers and ultimately undermine her claims, credibility, and personhood. A comparison of such transcripts with those of, say, a job interview (never mind a spontaneous conversation among young adults) would illustrate extreme differences between the interactional rules for questions under cross-examination on the one hand and ordinary discourse on the other, thus highlighting in ways more subtle—and more important—than those generally addressed in describing legal language just how far from ordinary English certain genres of legal language really are.

As another example of how legal language operates radically outside the rules of ordinary linguistic interaction, Janet Ainsworth (2008) has documented the alien interpretation of conversational implicatures that courts have imposed on the speech of criminal suspects who, by any standard of language use outside the legal arena, would likely be understood to have invoked their rights to consult with an attorney during a police interrogation but were not so understood under standards imposed by appellate courts. According to Ainsworth, each of these questions was judged by an appellate court to be a mere theoretical inquiry and not an invocation of the speaker's Miranda rights: "Could I call my lawyer?" (*Dormire v. Wilkinson* 2001); "Can I get my lawyer?" (*State v. Nixon* 1996); "May I call a lawyer? Can I call a lawyer?" (*State v. Payne* 2001); "Can I speak to an attorney before I answer the question to find out what he would have to tell me?" (*Taylor v. Carey* 2007). Going further, appellate courts likewise judged the following statements, softened only by the most pedestrian expressions such as "I think" and "it seems," as infelicitous invocations of the right to counsel—as unclear or ambiguous—and thus as allowing police investigators to continue their questioning: "I think I would like to talk to a lawyer" (*Clark v. Murphy* 2003); "I think I will talk to a lawyer" (*State v. Farrah* 2006); "It seems like what I need is a lawyer . . . I do want a lawyer" (*Oliver v. Runnels* 2006); "Actually, you know what, I'm gonna call my lawyer. I don't feel comfortable." (*People v. McMahon* 2005). It is taxing to see how these expressions could be regarded in ordinary English as not invoking the suspects' right to counsel, but in these and similar cases the judges can be seen as creating a genre of legal language by authoritatively interpreting everyday speech in a way that is remote from ordinary understanding and, more importantly, remote from the speakers' communicative intent.

When Tiersma concludes that legal language falls "somewhere between a separate language and ordinary English," he rightly captures the situation. As for his claim that legal language "is much closer to ordinary English than many people seem to think," that too is accurate, perhaps even for most genres of legal language. But in certain legal contexts, including many with serious consequences for ordinary speakers, legal language is only deceptively close to ordinary language, and those deceptively similar appearances warrant further scrutiny.

### References

Ainsworth, Janet (2008) "You Have the Right to Remain Silent . . ." but Only If You Ask for It Just So: The Role of Linguistic Ideology in American Police Interrogation Law." *International Journal of Speech, Language and the Law*: 15: 1–21.

Clapp, James E., Elizabeth G. Ghornburg, Marc Galanter, and Fred R. Shapiro (2011) *Lawtalk: The Unknown Stories Behind Familiar Legal Expressions*. New Haven, Conn.: Yale University Press.

Garner, Bryan A. (ed.) (2009) *Black's Law Dictionary*, 9th ed. Boston: West.

Matoesian, Gregory M. (1993) *Reproducing Rape: Domination through Talk in the Courtroom*. Chicago: University of Chicago Press.

Mattila, Heikki E. S. (2013) *Comparative Legal Linguistics: Language of Law, Latin and Modern Lingua Francas*, 2nd ed. Farnham, Surrey, UK: Ashgate.

Solan, Lawrence M. (1993) *The Language of Judges*. Chicago: University of Chicago Press.

Tiersma, Peter M. (2006) "Some Myths About Legal Language." *Law, Culture and the Humanities*: 2: 29–50.

# 9

# "Words, Words, Words"—But What's in a Legal Text?

Dieter Stein

One of the many things the discipline of law and language owes to Peter Tiersma is the description of a process that seems central for our legal culture: the transfer of legal authority to written language, a process he calls textualization, elaborated in his book, *Parchment, Paper, Pixels* (2010). This concept is, however, embedded in a broader and pervasive discussion of the extent to which "ordinary" language and legal language are the same and where they differ. It is an issue that Tiersma touched on in "Some Myths About Legal Language" (Tiersma 2006), and that I want to take up and develop a bit. Later I will return to the textualization phenomenon and related issues.

The issue for Tiersma is whether and to what extent the "language of the law" is different from "normal" language. There are difficulties in defining both ends of this comparison. Both are actually misleading myths in themselves. On the one hand, we cannot specify exactly what a "normal" language variety is. On the other hand, the "language of the law" is, as Tiersma has repeatedly pointed out, structured minimally into "operative," "persuasive," and "expository" genres (Tiersma 1999: 139–143). Restricting our discussion to the language of written statutes (an "operative," norm-establishing written type of genre), traditional lore has it that the main differences and distinguishing features are on what linguists now call the "microlinguistic" level, which is the grammar of the language, including syntax, morphology, the lexicon, and phonology. The lexicon includes legal vocabulary—concepts special to law that appear to lawyers to be the defining characteristic of legal language. While the existence of domain-specific concepts is beyond doubt, specialized vocabulary does not exhaust a linguistic characterization of this genre. Tiersma discusses what may be termed a "positive" list of grammatical features that are observed in operative legal texts, concluding that such a list does not offer conclusive evidence that the legal genre is radically different from other written formal language. He notes: "It turns out that just about all the features attributed to legal language are also 'characteristic of formal written prose' and that this conclusion offers small comfort to those who claim that the language of the law is special and distinct from ordinary communication" (Tiersma 2006: 46).

There are two main points that can be added to this argument. The first takes off from the work of Biber (1995), who characterized text types (clusters of linguistic co-occurring features, which are then, in a second step, interpreted as notional genres) in terms of what occurs and what does *not* occur. Obviously, what is absent reflects choices among grammatical options for selecting, presenting, and focusing content. Certain structures highlighting affected entities tend not to be chosen in legal texts, such as prepositional passives or middle voice structures. It appears that such a list of "negative" features has not been given enough weight in a linguistically oriented characterization of legal language. It is an interesting theoretical issue for the theory of varieties whether the absence of such features would be used to define either linguistic markers (exclusively characterizing a genre) or features (restricted to a class of genres) as set out by Biber (1995: 28). Generally, these terms are applied to actually "occurring forms." It is understandable that, in the age of computerized corpus linguistics, the focus is on positive features, whereas the absence of features is well-nigh impossible to handle computationally.

Tiersma himself pointed the way to an even more important repository of "negative" features that can serve as "markers" or "features" of legal discourse. He discusses a number of local interpretive conventions of a type represented by contrasting the following two examples:

> John kissed John's girlfriend
> vs
> Buyer promises that Buyer will pay

Only in the second, legal example will the referent of the second-mention of "Buyer" be construed as the same person, whereas in the first example, from "ordinary" language, the second mention of "John" will ordinarily be construed as another John. Such rules of interpretation and inference are not in the "words." Rather, they appear to be pragmatic rules that apply to legal language only, and, pending further systematic investigation, remain amongst the prime candidates for a further type of "negative" marker of legal language, in the sense of not being represented on the linguistic surface. These rules of pragma-linguistic interpretation are not just negative in the sense of the absence of grammatical structures, but they are part of genre competence.

There is massive evidence of the existence and the effect of this type of rules of inference and interpretation. Apart from the examples of such rules supplied by Tiersma himself, work by Drew and Heritage (1992) has turned up genre (activity type) specific rules. And despite the fact that even the so-called "canons" offer a rich repository of such rules (the "codified canons" (Scott 2010), such as "ejusdem generis," "expressio unius est exclusio alterius"), there has up to now not been a systematic study of the type and scope of these rules, and how they differ from other genres and domains. Such a systematic study would certainly go some way to remedy the definitional deficit observed by Tiersma.

My second point is that these observations, emanating from Tiersma's work, have significant theoretical ramifications. If legal genres are defined—and communication in them functions not only through words but also through non-verbal rules of interpretation, local and global, which text-producers rely on in drafting texts—then we can no longer take seriously a notion that what is interpreted is "the text." What does this imply for the concept of "textualization" and for any notion of "literal interpretation"?

In a modern view of the ontology of social objects, Ferraris (2013) has pointed out that for social objects, such as the system of law, the linguistic text is nothing but a trace, or a symptom, of the original "inscription" (origination in an act of social contractual constitution) of law. Increasingly, the act of inscription, though still logically and ontologically separate, is also performed and coincides by its packaging into the text itself. This phenomenon, as described by Ferraris (2013) from a philosophical point of view, corresponds to Tiersma's concept of "textualization": the increasing transfer of performative authority from the social-contractual inscription to the written text, especially in the common law system.

A related and equally significant concept repeatedly discussed by Tiersma (e.g., 2001) is the issue of the autonomy of the legal text. Tiersma pointed out that autonomy of a text, its ability to be interpreted without pragmatic, specifically deictic, context, is a defining characteristic for a legal text, and certainly for a statute. However, in the light of the previous discussion, interpretive rules of cooperation for any genre, including statutes, would mean an increase in non-autonomy of a statute. Non-autonomy implies less reliance on information extracted from words. If textualization implies packaging a social legal contract (an "inscription" in Ferraris's words) into not just words, but also genre-rules of interpretation and cooperation, then this would imply a stronger oral element in written discourse: the assumption of mutual knowledge includes more non-verbalized, non-autonomous communication—an idea arguably not very palatable to some legal theorists.

How, then, can literal interpretation be based on what is a mere symptom, or a trace, of an act of communication or socialization? While the purportedly rock-solid legal concepts in the shape of words have their own social and philosophical underpinnings, histories, and fluidities, what about the rules of inference and interpretation that define the identity of a genre and any given text—are they not "in the text"? Are they included in Tiersma's concept of "textualization"? Or are only some content elements explicitated in words, the rest left as redundancies in the shape of tacit genre-interpretation rules?

So the law is not in the words, and the words are really indexical of the existence of the law. "Interpreting" really applies to the socialized inscription of which the linguistic inscription is a trace. How, then, can we assume the "plain meaning" to be in the words, or in the words only? In a lucid analysis of the notion of what is in a "text," Tiersma (2001: 5f) has pointed out a fact that should have sounded the death knell for any hope from the side of jurists to see linguists supply any sort of a watertight explication of a notion of "literal" meaning. Any reading implies an interpretation, unless we refer to the physical inscription. Tiersma refers to the words of Paul Campos: "Words do not mean; people do" (Tiersma 2001: 6). Whoever uses words at all intends us to imagine some mental or cognitive scenario: always a constructed, already interpreted one. Some Platonic idea like an uninterpreted system-sentence potentiality, without the rules of interpretation adumbrated in Tiersma (2006), is not a realistic possible construct of language use. So the exact ontology of "plain meaning" must remain an unexplicated, if not inexplicable, mystery from the linguistic point of view.

Finally, Tiersma (2006: 50) critically points out that spelling legal concepts out in a plain language version would make statutes "much more verbose than they are now" (Tiersma 2006: 50). But, in the context of my present discussion, would the "spelling out" also have to include making explicit or giving explicit instructions how to pragmatically interpret the words? Telling non-linguistically knowledgeable readers how to interpret and how to differently interpret? Adding legal rules of interpretation would certainly add to the verbosity of the "plain" language—or should the "plain language" rules apply? How would we know? How would we decide? Or, even worse, add, the "judicial opinions in order to know what a statute really means" (Tiersma 2006: 50). This is another wave generated by a modernist stone, amongst many others with even greater impact, thrown in the water by Peter Tiersma.

### References

Biber, Douglas (1995). *Dimensions of Register Variation: A Cross-Linguistic Comparison.* Cambridge: Cambridge University Press.

Drew, Paul and Peter Heritage, eds. (1992). *Talk at Work. Interaction in Institutional Settings.* Cambridge: Cambridge University Press.

Ferraris, Maurizio (2013). *Documentality. Why It Is Necessary to Leave Traces.* Translated by Richard Davies. New York: Fordham University Press.

Scott, Jacob J. (2010). Codified Canons and the Common Law of Interpretation. *The Georgetown Law Journal* 98: 341–431.

Tiersma Peter M. (1999). *Legal Language.* Chicago: The University of Chicago Press.

Tiersma, Peter M. (2010). *Parchment, Paper, Pixels. Law and the Technologies of Communication.* Chicago, London: The University of Chicago Press.

Tiersma, Peter M. (2006). Some Myths about Legal Language. *Law, Culture and the Humanities* 2: 9–50.

Tiersma, Peter M. (2001). A Message in a Bottle: Text, Autonomy, and Statutory Interpretation. *Tulane Law Review* 76: 431–483.

PART II

# The Language of Contracts and Wills

10

# Text, Tape and Pixels in the Making of Wills*

Peter M. Tiersma

As people become increasingly accustomed to new technologies for communicating and storing information, the pressure to allow wills to be made in novel ways is likely to intensify. Even if the profession defends its textual practices and the primacy of the written word, it may have to give way if torrents of video wills or e-wills start to appear in court. If they have not yet done so, people will almost certainly try to create wills in the form of a multimedia presentation, with graphic images of the items they wish to bequeath, links to their bank accounts or to property descriptions in the county recorder's office, and video clips of the testator explaining who should get what. Can the law continue to insist that a valid will must be a written text of some sort, preferably made by placing ink on paper?

## Audio and Video Wills

People have already started to experiment with audio and video wills. A lawsuit from Wyoming involved a tape-recorded (audio) will that was contained in a sealed envelope on which was handwritten "Robert Reed To be played in the event of my death only! [signed] Robert G, Reed." The proponent argued that it could be viewed as a valid "holophonic" will, akin to a holographic will. In Wyoming, a holographic will must not just be signed, but it must also be entirely in the handwriting of the testator. The will's proponent suggested "that in this age of advanced electronics and circuitry the tape recorder should be a method of 'writing' which conforms with the holographic will statute."[1]

---

* Excerpt from Peter M. Tiersma, *Parchment, Paper Pixels* 75–82 (2010).

The court acknowledged that in evidence law, a tape recording might well be considered a "writing." Yet the rules of evidence did not change the substantive requirement of a writing in wills law. Hence, the tape recording was not a legally effective will.[2] To date, no American case has held that an audio recording can be a valid will.[3]

Recently, it is not uncommon to make a video that shows the testator executing the will. A video recording can constitute valuable evidence of whether there was undue influence or whether the testator had capacity. But can a person's oral statements, if recorded on videotape, take the place of a will written on paper? Despite predictions about how videotape and other "paratextual" communication technologies will revolutionize the law,[4] virtually no jurisdiction, if any, considers a video recording to be a writing that satisfies the requirements of wills law.[5]

It seems likely that there have been or will be additional cases on the validity of audio and video wills. Nonetheless, they have clearly been a rare species, and in my opinion audio and video are likely to remain adjuncts to will making, mostly as a means of presenting evidence regarding whether the testator still had his wits about him.

## E-Wills

What about wills stored on a computer? A computer can easily deal with sound and graphics these days, making it possible for a testator to orally state her will and have it captured in a digitized form that is preserved on a hard drive or other storage medium. Despite the more modern technology, it remains an audio recording that is not all that different from an old-fashioned recording on tape. The same is true of video, which can also be either recorded on tape or captured by a computer in digital form. None of these recording technologies produces a writing, so they are likely to remain marginal in the culture of will making.

Electronic wills, on the other hand, can consist entirely of written text. Although letters of the alphabet are presented on a computer display as tiny dots, or pixels, and are printed in a similar fashion, the overall impression they create is one very similar to traditional writing with ink on a sheet of paper.

Given that in many American jurisdictions a handwritten and signed letter, or a scribbled note with a signature, can constitute a valid holographic will, it may seem strange that the status of an e-mailed will or one contained in a file on a computer's hard disk is currently very uncertain. If you print it and properly execute it (with two witnesses, etc.), there is no problem, of course. On the other hand, if you print it and sign it, without witnesses and the other formal requirements, it will almost certainly be invalid under the current law of most states.

What if the will is not printed out but resides solely on a computer or in cyberspace somewhere? To date, the only state to allow true e-wills is Nevada, which has enacted legislation on the issue. Such a will must be created and stored in such a manner that

1. Only one authoritative copy exists;
2. The authoritative copy is maintained and controlled by the testator or a custodian designated by the testator in the electronic will;
3. Any attempted alteration of the authoritative copy is readily identifiable; and
4. Each copy of the authoritative copy is readily identifiable as a copy that is not the authoritative copy.

Moreover, it must contain the date and the electronic signature of the testator and include at least one authentication characteristic (such as a retinal scan or fingerprint) of the testator.[6] It's hard to imagine that many Nevada residents have taken advantage of this innovative statute. I would think that if your computer is attached to a printer, it is less risky and more efficient to press the print button and to sign the will in the presence of two witnesses. Admittedly, the law might be useful for technologically savvy hermits or astronauts in space, especially if they do not have access to a printer or cannot locate two witnesses.

As far as I can tell, there has not yet been a case testing the validity of an e-will (one that has not been printed) in American states.[7] There is, however, a case from Quebec, *Rioux v. Coulombe*, involving a will on a computer diskette. After being printed on paper, it was admitted to probate.[8] Quebec is a civil law jurisdiction, however, whose law is more similar to that of France than to the common law of England or the United States.

There is a case from Tennessee in which a man composed a will on his computer and, in the presence of two witnesses, attached a digital signature (apparently a scanned version of his normal signature). The witnesses then signed the will. The facts are not entirely clear, but it seems that it was printed before the witnesses signed it. The court held it valid, in large part because Tennessee defines a signature as including any mark intended to authenticate a writing.[9] The fact is that courts tend to be fairly relaxed regarding the signature requirement; a mark or very informal signature often suffices. But they have been quite strict in enforcing the rule that a will must be written, and because in this case the will seems to have been printed and then signed by witnesses, it does not deviate much from current practice.

Whether e-wills are ever going to supersede wills on paper is impossible to say, but it seems probable that Nevada will not be the only state to legitimize them. Of course, there are still technical issues to overcome. Because computers and software become obsolete so quickly, a will composed on a computer twenty years ago might not be decipherable today. And digital storage media still do not last as long as paper.[10]

Yet unlike audio and video recordings, which immortalize sound waves and graphic images, computers can store and transmit information, that can be made to look like traditional text or writing. Moreover, it is technically feasible to create digital signatures that are at least as secure as those that are written by hand. In addition, the process of writing (or typing) on a computer allows for careful planning of the text, just like traditional writing. Such planning is more difficult with audio and video recordings. Finally, the problem of obsolescence of computers and software will almost certainly be solved at some point. If a computer can produce a written text that is accompanied by a secure digital signature of the testator and two witnesses or some other reliable method of authentication, there seems to be little reason to deny validity to the will. Of course, the judge would probably insist on a printed copy!

## The Future of the Testamentary Text

### WRITTEN TEXT WILL ENDURE

Even in a world that in decades to come will offer communication technology that we cannot imagine, I believe that the significance of written text, as well as many of the textual conventions of the legal profession, will persist. One of the reasons is that language is a defining characteristic of human beings. Various nonverbal means of communication, such as gesturing, touching, or making graphic images, can also transmit a person's intentions, but usually only in limited contexts that do not require a precise message to be conveyed. Typically, gestures and pictures help us understand language; they do not replace it. It is hard to imagine that the supremacy of language as the primary means of human communication will be seriously challenged by technical innovations, certainly not during the lifetime of anyone alive today.

Second, writing is an extremely efficient way of representing human language in a durable form. It is true that new technologies have made it possible to preserve speech as speech and to transmit it over long distances, leading to a revival of orality in modern times. But when it comes to important legal transactions, writing has the advantage that it can be carefully planned and edited in a way that is much more difficult to accomplish orally. If you wish to specify exactly what should happen to your possessions when you die and hope to have your wishes carried out, creating a written document is surely your best option. Moreover, executing a written text is very useful in signifying to testators that they are engaging in an important legal transaction, something that sending an e-mail to your lawyer, or posting your intentions on a website or blog, does not do.

Writing on paper or some other durable medium will continue to be practiced for a long time to come, especially to memorialize solemn or important events. A hundred years from now, I imagine, colleges and universities will still be issuing paper diplomas to graduates in live ceremonies rather than just e-mailing them electronic degrees. The president will still be signing legislation printed on paper rather than clicking on a link ("I approve" or "I veto") in an e-mail sent to her by Congress. The perceived solemnity and significance of these acts will only increase as the use of paper becomes increasingly rare in ordinary life. That will enhance the value of writing wills on paper, since the testamentary act is one of the more solemn and significant transactions that a person can undertake.

Not only is the continued vitality of written wills likely, but so is the process of textualization. It may not endure in its present form, but it can be very helpful to have a formal procedure for authoritatively fixing the text of a will, guaranteeing that it represents the intentions of the testator and authenticating his identity as its author. This is especially valuable when fraud, undue influence, or declining mental capacity are realistic possibilities.

Of course, not all testators want or need such a high level of security. Some may wish to create or modify wills more informally, without having to go to the trouble and expense of hiring a lawyer. If someone is not particularly concerned about the possibility of a will contest after her death, why not allow her to express her testamentary desires in any way she wishes, as long as we have adequate evidence of those intentions?

To some extent, holographic wills are already an informal means of creating a will that functions more like a record of the testator's intentions, rather than formally textualizing them. In stark contrast to attested wills, holographs do not need to be witnessed and can usually be changed by the testator after the will is signed, with or without formalities.[11]

The law of holographic wills is useful as far as it goes. But the technology of writing and the textual conventions of society are certain to change. It will become increasingly archaic to maintain that the only alternative to a formal textualized will is one fixed on paper in the handwriting of the testator.

The reason for allowing holographic wills (which are a clear exception to the textual conventions of the law) is generally held to be that handwriting analysis can provide strong evidence that it really was written by the person in question. Many such wills, incidentally, consist of letters sent to family members. But if an ordinary letter can be a will, why should the same principle not apply to electronic mail, as long as its authenticity can be established with equal certainty? Handwriting will probably never completely disappear, but many younger people today are more comfortable with writing on some kind of keyboard. It may well be that handwriting will largely be supplanted by typing or keying in text. As new forms of writing develop, it will be increasingly unrealistic to insist on handwritten wills as the only alternative to the formal and highly textualized variety.

## A MODEST PROPOSAL

I propose that we need to rationalize the law of wills. Currently, we have detailed and to some extent archaic rules relating to the execution of wills, with a slew of exceptions that rather haphazardly recognize ordinary literary conventions but which in the process sometimes create unjustifiable inconsistencies. Instead, we should recognize two basic categories of wills, one formal and the other informal.

My proposal differs in important respects from reforms suggested by other scholars. Some, including John Langbein and Lawrence Waggoner, support retaining at least some of the formalities while giving courts the power to dispense with them on an ad hoc basis in appropriate cases.[12] Others would dispense with most formalities in all cases. James Lindgren has argued that the only requirements for will making should be writing and a signature.[13] Adam Hirsch has made a similar proposal.[14] While I am sympathetic to this idea, it implies that all wills would be relatively informal and more consistent with ordinary textual conventions.

Yet I hope to have made the point—a point borne out by long practice—that the literary practices of the legal profession, and especially textualization, can sometimes be useful. My proposal is therefore that we reduce the formalities of execution when they are not necessary, but allow people the option of expressing their intentions in a more formal manner if they prefer to do so.

People who wish to make their estate plan as fixed and secure as possible would thus be able to go to a lawyer to make a formal will. Currently this requires the attestation of two witnesses and the other formalities of execution that we previously discussed, but the nature of those formalities might very well change as new means to fulfill their functions become available. What is critical is that such wills provide a high level of protection against fraud or undue influence, strong evidence of the testator's desires, and a certain amount of ritual to emphasize the importance of the transaction. In addition, the resulting text should be regarded as the definitive expression of the testator's intentions. Informal changes would undermine the integrity of the text and should therefore be discouraged. Because these textual practices are foreign to the average person, they should be clearly explained before the will is executed. In fact, it might not be a bad idea to include in a formal will a notice, in plain English, explaining that it can only be revoked or changed by following a prescribed procedure (such as going to a lawyer and executing a new will).

Informal wills would follow a much more relaxed set of rules. As mentioned, the only such option these days is holographic wills. One problem is that they are not valid in many jurisdictions. Also, the requirement that they be entirely handwritten or that the material provisions be in the testator's handwriting is a continual source of litigation when part of the text is typed or printed.[15] Finally, it seems likely that handwriting will soon be to some extent supplanted by new technologies of writing or recording speech.

A broader category of informal wills could address many of these issues. Borrowing a phrase from copyright law, we should probably insist that such a will be "fixed" in a "tangible medium of expression," a flexible phrase that should accommodate future technological developments. And the person who makes it should intend it to be her will. People should be able to make changes, even after the will is made, using normal textual conventions. And it should be interpreted as ordinary language with the aim of carrying out the testator's actual intentions.

While practitioners of estate planning may find this a fairly radical proposal, it is worth pointing out that living trusts, which are increasingly being used to transfer assets at death, can already be created and amended with far fewer formalities than wills. Ironically, lawyers draft almost all trusts. In contrast, a person who does not have a large enough estate to justify going to a lawyer is much more likely to try to write a will on his own. The textual practices of the legal profession are therefore most likely to stymie the intentions of those who are least familiar with them and who are least able to hire the services of a lawyer.

My proposal differs from alternative suggestions by leaving it up to the testator to decide the degree to which he would like to textualize his testamentary intentions. If the proposal is adopted, the textual practices relating to wills would become more similar to those governing contracts. Parties who enter into a contract generally have the option of making a purely oral agreement, or making an oral agreement with a writing that records the more important terms, or textualizing their contract by creating a writing that is regarded as the definitive and complete repository of the terms of the agreement. In modern wills law, testators have only the third option. If parties to a contract can generally choose whether to textualize a contract, why should testators not be allowed to decide whether or not to textualize their wills?

In other words, the testator should be able to choose how much protection he would like to have against the possibility of fraud, undue influence, and so forth. If a family is riven by dissent or cursed by greed, or if a testator is wealthy and without apparent heirs, fully textualizing his intentions by means of a traditional will is an excellent idea. Yet if someone dies without having made such a formal will but has left behind other reliable indicators of his testamentary intentions, the textual conventions of the law should not get in the way of bringing those intentions to fruition.

## Notes

1. *Estate of Reed*, 672 P.2d 829, 831 (Wyo. 1983).

2. *Id.* at 834.

3. Gerry W. Beyer and Claire G. Hargrove, *Digital Wills: Has the Time Come for Wills to Join the Digital Revolution?*, 33 Ohio N.U.L. Rev. 865, 882 (2007).

4. Ronald K. L. Collins and David M. Skover, *Paratexts*, 44 Stan. L. Rev. 509 (1992).

5. Beyer and Hargrove, *Digital Wills*, 884. See also Lisa L. McGarry, Note, *Video-taped Wills: An Evidentiary Tool or a Written Will Substitute?*, 77 Iowa L. Rev. 1187 (1992) (concluding that virtually all courts continue to insist that wills be in writing, rejecting videotaped wills, as opposed to videotaped evidence of a written will's validity, which is generally admitted); Gerry W. Beyer and William R. Buckley, *Videotape and the Probate Process: The Nexus Grows*, 42 Okla. L. Rev. 43 (1989) (listing other articles on the subject in footnote 18 and concluding that while videotape is used as evidence, its use as testamentary instrument will require legislation).

6. *Nevada Rev. Stat. Ann.* §133.085.

7. This was the case in 2002, at least, according to Christopher J. Caldwell, *Should "E-Wills" Be Wills: Will Advances in Technology Be Recognized for Will Execution?* 63 U. Pitts. L. Rev. 467,476 (2002).

8. The case is critically discussed in Nicolas Kasirir, *From Written Record to Memory in the Law of Wills*, 29 Ottawa L. Rev. 39 (1997/1998).

9. Taylor v. Holt, 134 S.W.3d 830 (Tenn. Ct. App. 2003).

10. Beyer and Hargrove, *Digital Wills*, 890–97.

11. Stanley v. Henderson, 162 S.W.2d 95 (Tex. Comm. Appeals 1942); *Estate of Archer*, 239 Cal. Rptr. 137 (Cal. Ct. App. 1987).

12. John H. Langbein and Lawrence W. Waggoner, *Reformation of Wills on the Ground of Mistake: Change of Direction in American Law?* 130 U. Pa. L. Rev. 521 (1982); John H. Langbein, *Substantial Compliance with the Wills Act*, 88 Harv. L. Rev. 489 (1975).

13. James Lindgren, *Abolishing the Attestation Requirement for Wills*, 68 N.C. L. Rev. 541 (1990).

14. Adam Hirsch, *Inheritance and Inconsistency*, 57 Ohio St. L.J. 1057, 1075–76.

15. For examples, see Witkin, *Summary of California Law, Wills*, 12 at § 205.

11

# Reassessing Unilateral Contracts*
## Peter M. Tiersma

### Unilateral Contracts Are Not Formed by Offer and Acceptance

Several critical distinctions separate offer/acceptance from promise as vehicles for creating commitment. These differences can be summarized as follows:

1. An offer must be accepted; a promise need not.
2. An offer does not commit the speaker until it has been accepted and is thus revocable until then; a promise commits the speaker when it is made and is not freely revocable.
3. Two parties must perform the "ritual" of offer and acceptance to create commitment; a promise is made unilaterally.
4. With offer and acceptance, the offeror and acceptor are both bound, whereas with promise only the promisor is bound.

In this section, we will see that unilateral contracts fit the criteria for promise rather than those for offer and acceptance. As a consequence, an "offer" of a unilateral contract is in fact a promise or set of promises rather than a true offer.

The observation that unilateral contracts do not fit comfortably in the offer and acceptance mold is not novel. As Atiyah has put it, "unilateral contracts do not always fit happily into a legal framework devised largely for bilateral contracts."[1] Simpson has noted that "[t]he application of the offer and acceptance analysis to [unilateral] promises has never been [a] happy [one]."[2] And Stoljar, discussing the distinction between bilateral and unilateral contracts, observed "how much the language of offer and acceptance falsifies the picture."[3] This section takes these thoughts to their logical conclusion: that unilateral contracts do not belong in the offer and acceptance framework at all.

---

* Excerpt from Peter Meijes Tiersma, Reassessing Unilateral Contracts, *U.C. Davis Law Review* 26: 1, 24–34 (1992).

## Unilateral Contracts Do Not Require Acceptance

According to the generally accepted view, unilateral contracts, like bilateral contracts, require formation by offer and acceptance. The offeror, who can invite the offeree to accept in any way that pleases him, requires that the offeree accept the offer not by saying "I accept," but rather by completing a particular act. For example, if I run a restaurant, I might tell a waitress that I will give her a bonus if she sells ten special desserts. In the traditional theory of unilateral contracts, my promise does not become binding until all ten desserts have been sold because this is what I, the "master" of my offer, desire. Before that time I am at least theoretically free to revoke at my pleasure, even after the waitress has sold nine desserts and has said "I accept" a dozen times.[4]

Of course, saying "I accept" is the prototypical way of accepting. The *Restatement* defines acceptance as a "manifestation of assent" to the terms of the offer.[5] And it defines an "offer" as inviting "assent" to a proposed bargain; indeed, the offeror intends that "assent" by the offeree will conclude the bargain.[6] If acceptance is assent to the terms of a bargain, the offeree should be able to accept the offer in any way that is comprehensible to the offeror as assent. She might explicitly say that she accepts. Or she might begin to do the requested performance in such a way that the offeror can infer that she is symbolically communicating assent. All of these manners of acceptance are consistent with viewing an offer as a speech act that commits the speaker to a proposal once the other party—via the speech act of acceptance—also commits herself.[7]

Several commentators have observed that "acceptance" of a unilateral contract is very different from acceptance in the bilateral context. Llewellyn noted that "[a]cceptance ... as it shuttles and shifts between the unilateral and the bilateral situations, [is] a term with radically divergent *legal* connotations."[8] He continued that bilateral acceptance bars an offeror, on his own motion, from revoking before he has received "an iota" of the ultimate substance of his bargain.[9] Acceptance in the context of unilateral contracts, on the other hand, refers to obligating an offeror only after he has received the "uttermost jot" of everything he bargained for.[10] Likewise, Stoljar remarked that "acceptance" in the context of bilateral contracts relates to *formation* of a bargain, while with unilateral contracts it relates to its *fulfillment* by one party.[11]

Obviously, "acceptance" of a unilateral offer by completing the requested act is not a "manifestation of assent." If a unilateral contract must be accepted, saying "I accept" or symbolically assenting by *beginning* performance in such a way that the offeror will notice would be perfectly sufficient.

But a manifestation of assent by itself never suffices to constitute acceptance of a unilateral contract.

Although lawyers have become accustomed to the notion that an offeror "invites" the offeree to "accept" by performance,[12] consider how strange this must sound to the uninitiated: "I offer to pay you $100 to repair my bicycle. I invite you to accept this offer, but do not want your promise to repair my bicycle. You may accept only by completing the job, and I do not consider myself obligated in any way until then." More natural—and hence more likely to reflect how people actually structure their commercial relations—is the following: "I promise to pay you $100 to repair my bicycle. You don't need to accept or to promise anything. I just want you to do the work, if possible. I will pay you after you have finished the entire job."

Requiring the offeree to "accept" a unilateral contract suffers from another flaw. Perhaps the most important rationale for holding parties to an agreement is that they have committed themselves to it by means of a commissive speech act, such as an offer, acceptance, or promise. The other party relies on the commitment and may be injured if it is not enforced. But acceptance of a unilateral contract—in contrast to one that is bilateral—is not an act of commitment. As noted previously, the speech act of acceptance cannot make an offeror's proposal binding in the traditional theory—only full performance will achieve that goal. The offeree cannot and need not commit herself to a unilateral proposal. Because a unilateral offeree is *never* bound, an act of commitment by the offeree is superfluous. As a result, the offeree does not logically need to accept the so-called offer. The offeree simply performs the requested act and expects to be paid as promised.

The traditional view of unilateral contracts is quite correct in holding that the unilateral "offeror" does not want words of acceptance. Where it went astray was in presupposing that commitment can only arise by offer and acceptance. Because with unilateral contracts there is no real speech act of acceptance, it was necessary to label some other act or event an "acceptance" if the offer/acceptance model was to remain intact. The traditional theory chose to identify completed performance as "acceptance." Several commentators subsequently recognized that full performance does not resemble acceptance in any reasonable sense of that word. Unfortunately, rather than question the hegemony of the offer and acceptance model, they strove to find acceptance elsewhere, as in reliance or beginning performance. In reality, the fact that the offeror does not want words of acceptance simply means that no acceptance is necessary to make the promise binding.

We may conclude, therefore, that with respect to not needing acceptance, unilateral contracts resemble promises rather than offers.

## Unilateral Contracts Commit the Speaker from the Time the Promise Is Made

The second criterion that distinguishes offers from promises is that offerors commit themselves only after acceptance, and can therefore freely revoke until that time. With a promise, on the other hand, there is no need for acceptance. The promise is an unconditional act of commitment that goes into effect immediately and therefore cannot be freely revoked.[13]

Although the traditional view posits that the unilateral offeror does not wish to be bound until he has obtained full performance and can freely revoke until that time, the modern rule of *Restatement* section 45 is less clear. Practically speaking, when the offeree commences or tenders performance, revocation is no longer possible. Oddly, however, the *Restatement* seems to free the offeror from commitment until the offeree finishes performance.[14] Section 45 therefore assumes, like the traditional rule, that the offeror has not committed himself until completed performance, but by imposing an option contract it prevents him from revoking after the offeree begins to do the requested act.

Closer examination reveals how unlikely it is that someone would make an offer of the type envisioned by the traditional theory or the *Restatement*. Preliminarily, one should realize that an offeror can fully commit himself before the occurrence of completed performance. Even the common law recognizes this by enforcing certain promises without acceptance or consideration, as well as acts in exchange for a promise.[15] All the "offeror" has to do is use a promise to bind himself unilaterally, instead of invoking the mechanism of offer and acceptance.

Not only can people bind themselves unilaterally, but no reasonable person would intentionally create the sort of agreement that the traditional theory of unilateral contracts assumes. Suppose that a person, asserting his freedom to contract and his mastery over his offer, specifically intends to make a promise that will bind him not at the time he makes it, but only after the other party has completed a particular act in exchange. In other words, this promisor wishes to create the traditional unilateral contract. For example, he might tell the offeree that if she paints his house, he will—once she is finished—commit himself to paying her $1,000. He makes it clear that he does not wish to be bound until she is completely finished, explaining to her that before she is finished he may revoke with impunity. What rational person would even buy the paint if she believed the speaker had not committed himself? No one would realistically begin to perform such an agreement. Nor should the law give damages to an offeree injured by acting so rashly; expending money and effort on the basis of such a non-promise is hardly justifiable reliance, and the law is loath to protect fools.[16]

The primary purpose of unilateral contracts, such as reward offers or promises to pay a commission to a real estate broker, is to motivate the offeree to do the requested act. In other words, their goal is precisely to induce reliance. Obviously, an "offer" to pay someone to paint a fence or find a lost dog provides precious little inducement if it remains freely revocable until full performance. An offer to pay that becomes irrevocable after the offeree commences performance (the *Restatement* approach) is more apt to entice the offeree, but even beginning performance costs time and effort, and the offeree must take the risk that she will forfeit money she spends on *preparations* to perform if the offeror revokes before she can commence.[17] Clearly, the offeror is most likely to induce reliance if he commits himself at the time of the making of the unilateral contract. He can only do this by the speech act of promising, rather than offering.[18] The presence of commitment justifies the promisee's preparation or initial performance. If the law truly believes that the offeror is master of his offer, it should recognize that when he truly wants the promisee to perform a particular act, he will make a promise, thus binding himself from inception.

In fact, probably the best-known illustration of unilateral contracts in the second *Restatement* provides proof that they bind the speaker when made:

> A, a merchant, mails B, a carpenter in the same city, an offer to employ B to fit up A's office in accordance with A's specifications and B's estimate previously submitted, the work to be completed in two weeks. The offer says, "You may begin at once," and B immediately buys lumber and begins to work on it in his own shop. The next day, before B has sent a notice of acceptance or begun work at A's office or rendered the lumber unfit for other jobs, A revokes the offer. The revocation is timely, since B has not begun to perform.[19]

Preliminarily, note that this hypothetical reveals the "unsatisfactory distinction between 'beginning to perform' and 'preparing to perform' which haunts unilateral contract theory."[20] According to the illustration, the carpenter "begins to work" on the lumber that he bought for the project but "has not begun to perform"!

Even more telling is the merchant's comment to the carpenter, "You may begin at once." Recall that if unilateral contracts are promises, they do not require acceptance before it is reasonable to begin performing. In fact, "you may begin at once" is strong evidence that no return promise is expected or required. Amazingly, however, even though the merchant tells the carpenter he may begin immediately, the *Restatement* suggests that it is not necessarily reasonable for the carpenter to prepare to perform, because the merchant has not yet committed himself and may therefore yet revoke.[21]

In reality, "you may begin at once" confirms that the so-called "offer" of a unilateral contract is intended as a promise that commits the merchant *ab initio*. The merchant, who wants the job done in two weeks, is attempting to induce immediate reliance. To accomplish this, the merchant must have committed himself to paying the carpenter for his efforts, conditional, of course, on completion of the job.

Obviously, no reasonable person can expect another to carry out a requested act if he has not committed himself to rewarding her for her efforts. Why, therefore, has the law so long insisted that the offeror does not intend to be bound until completed performance, a position even maintained, albeit with little enthusiasm, by the second *Restatement*?[22] The answer lies, I believe, in the fact that with many unilateral contracts, in particular those like rewards and brokerage agreements, offerors do not want to contribute their part of the bargain until they have received all that they asked for in exchange. Partial performance of a proposal to pay a reward or broker's commission is useless to the offeror, who simply wants a lost pet found or a house sold. He does not want to pay for failed or incomplete efforts. But this is no reason to assume that the offeror does not wish to commit himself until full performance.

[Discussed earlier in this Article is] the legal distinction between *conditional commitment* and a *conditional duty*. Obviously, the offeror's *duty to perform* is contingent on the offeree performing her part of the contract. Therefore, he need not pay her until she has found his dog or produced a ready, willing, and able buyer for his house. At the same time, however, the offeror is unconditionally committed to pay if and when the condition is met. There is no reason to posit, as does the present rule, that the offeror intends to commit himself only after "acceptance" by full performance.

Another good indicator of the presence of commitment is reliance behavior. For example, in the bilateral context, it is generally always reasonable for the parties to rely on an offer that has been accepted and where the parties have thus committed themselves to a proposal. Compare this to the situation before the offer has been accepted, when there is usually no commitment. In that case, a bilateral offer may become binding as an option contract only if the offeror "should reasonably expect [the offer] to induce action or forbearance of a substantial character on the part of the offeree before acceptance and which does induce such action or forbearance."[23] Nevertheless, the offer is binding only "to the extent necessary to avoid injustice."[24] Courts have been reluctant to protect offerees who have relied before accepting.[25] The reason for this reluctance is obvious: until the offeror is committed, reliance on the offer is seldom reasonable. Under normal circumstances, what rational offeree would begin to spend substantial amounts of money in reliance on an offer before she has exercised her power to make the proposal binding by accepting it? What court would protect such rash behavior?

In the unilateral context, on the other hand, section 45 of the *Restatement* creates an option contract as soon as the offeree begins to perform *without inquiring* whether the reliance on the offer was reasonable.[26] In fact, a comment to section 45 states that the rule "is designed to protect the offeree in justifiable reliance on the offeror's promise."[27] The only way to explain why reliance is presumptively justified long before acceptance by completed performance is that the offeror has already committed himself. Only when the offeror attempts to reserve the power to revoke is reliance not justified, because an unlimited power to revoke is inconsistent with a true promise.[28]

The fact of the matter, as the *Restatement* implicitly recognizes, is that very reasonable people spend substantial time and money doing the sorts of things that unilateral contracts attempt to induce them to do. The only rational explanation for such behavior is that, as in the *Restatement* illustration of the merchant who requests the carpentry work, people believe the speaker is in fact committed *then and there* to paying the price if the conditions of the offer are met.

One possible objection to this explanation is that people rely on unilateral offers not because they believe that the offeror has committed himself to the proposal, but rather because they trust the courts to protect their reliance under *Restatement* section 45 or similar decisional law. There are several problems with this suggestion. First, under this objection the offeree reasonably relies on a unilateral offer because the law will impose an option contract as soon as performance begins. But as noted, the law imposes an option contract precisely because reliance is reasonable. The way out of this conundrum is to posit that when reliance begins, commitment already exists. In addition, the present law protects reliance only after beginning performance. It therefore cannot easily explain why people prepare to perform. In any event, it is highly unlikely that most people who make and act on unilateral contracts have any idea of the legal principles involved. They do know, however, that a promise creates commitment and that it is generally reasonable to rely on the promisor keeping his word. Additionally, the judgments of generations of law students and contracts scholars that the traditional Langdellian rule was unjust suggests that intuitively they also must have believed that the professor committed himself *before* the hapless student completed the journey across the Brooklyn Bridge, since otherwise the professor's abrupt revocation of the offer would not have stirred the indignation that it did. Finally, the fact that offerees commenced performance of unilateral contracts long before courts protected such reliance proves quite convincingly that reliance before completed performance cannot be explained by the availability of legal remedies.

Reliance is thus prima facie evidence of the existence of commitment. As Atiyah has observed, "For if promises were not binding, they might not be relied upon."[29] Of course, reliance is sometimes caused by a mistaken belief that a promise has been made. Yet reliance on unilateral offers is not the result of mistake. Rather, it is a commonplace and quite reasonable reaction. It is, in addition, precisely the reaction that the offeror wishes to induce. The only logical conclusion is that unilateral "offers" commit the speaker from the time the speech act is performed. In other words, unilateral "offers" are really promises.

## Notes

1. P. S. Atiyah, AN INTRODUCTION TO THE LAW OF CONTRACT 82 (4th ed. 1989).

2. A. W. B. Simpson, *Innovation in Nineteenth Century Contract Law*, 19 LAW Q. REV. 247, 262 (1975).

3. Samuel J. Stoljar, *The Ambiguity of Promise*, 47 Nw. U. L. REV.1, 19 (1952).

4. Of course, the law may protect the promisee with an option contract. But the general principle that I can revoke at any time before completed performance is the only logical view in the traditional framework, even according to the second *Restatement. See* RESTATEMENT (SECOND) OF CONTRACTS § 45 (1979).

5. *Id.* § 50(1).

6. *Id.* § 24.

7. Of course, the offeror may dictate that the proposal be accepted in a particular way, such as waving a flag, but with bilateral agreements, the acceptance, whatever its mode, must be an act of communication. Corbin cites an example of conduct communicating agreement that illustrates this. If A says to B that B can accept his offer by hanging out a flag so that A can see it as he goes by, this is communication and a bilateral contract has been formed. But if A simply wants a flag hung on a certain flagpole and offers B a certain amount of money to do so, the act of hanging it constitutes B's acceptance, just as above, but now the act is not sign language and B makes no promise. 1 ARTHUR L. CORBIN, CORBIN ON CONTRACTS, § 62, at 255–56 (1963).

8. K. N. Llewellyn, *On Our Case-Law of Contract: Offer and Acceptance, I*, 48 YALE L.J. 1, 33 (1938) (emphasis added).

9. *Id.*

10. *Id.*

11. Stoljar, *supra* note 3, at 520–21. Elsewhere, Stoljar remarked that acceptance of a unilateral contract is a myth; a unilateral contract simply involves one party making a promise upon which the other party may justifiably rely. Stoljar, *supra* note 3, at 19.

12. *See, e.g.,* RESTATEMENT (SECOND) OF CONTRACTS § 53(1) (1979) ("An offer can be accepted by the rendering of a performance only if the offer invites such an acceptance."); *id.* § 54(1) ("Where an offer invites an offeree to accept by rendering a performance. . . .").

13. Of course, a promisor can break a promise, or performance may be excused. This may be a general rule governing speech acts: until they go into effect, they can freely be revoked, but after that time revocation is wrongful, at least if it causes injury to another. Consider wills, for example. A will is conditional on death, and its dispositive power does not go into effect until that time. Thomas E. Atkinson, HANDBOOK OF THE LAW OF WILLS 1 (2d ed. 1953). As a result, the testator can revoke the will at any time before death. *Id.*

14. *See* RESTATEMENT (SECOND) OF CONTRACTS § 24 cmt. a (1979).

15. *See, e.g.,* 1 CORBIN, *supra* note 7, § 12, at 27–28. On acts for a promise, see *id.* § 71, at 298.

16. A similar point is made by Stoljar, *supra* note 3, at 522–23: Suppose X tells Y "I'll give you $50 if you go to Rome, but remember that I'm at liberty to revoke this promise at any time before you reach the Holy City." A promise of this type would be as unusual as it is absurd. Because it is merely a statement of intention that X *might* give Y the money, but X is free to change his mind, the promise is illusory.

17. Perhaps a more serious problem is that it is highly unlikely that most offerees know the rule of § 45. Unlike the mechanisms of offer and acceptance, which rest on social institutions of which most people are aware, § 45 is an ad hoc solution to the injustice of the traditional rule and does not necessarily pretend to mirror what the parties intend to accomplish.

18. One could argue that the offeror might prefer the traditional theory, or otherwise the *Restatement*, because under these approaches his liability for breach may be less. We must assume that the promisor intends to carry out his promise, however, so calculations based on possible breach should not be given much weight.

19. RESTATEMENT (SECOND) OF CONTRACTS § 62 cmt. d, illus. 1 (1979). The example is based on White v. Corlies, 46 N.Y. 467 (1871), although the offeror in *White* seems to have anticipated a bilateral contract.

20. Mark Pettit, Jr., *Modern Unilateral Contracts*, 63 B.U. L. REV. 551, 591 (1983).

21. RESTATEMENT (SECOND) OF CONTRACTS § 24 cmt. a (1979).

22. *See id.* § 1 reporter's note, cmt. f.

23. RESTATEMENT (SECOND) OF CONTRACTS § 87(2) (1979).

24. *Id.*

25. *See, e.g.*, Gruber v. S-M News Co., 126 F. Supp. 442 (S.D.N.Y. 1954) (disallowing recovery for costs incurred before contract); Hough v. Jay-Dee Realty &: Inv., 401 S.W.2d 545 (Mo. Ct. App. 1966) (stating that plaintiffs are not entitled to recover damages suffered prior to execution of contract); E. ALLAN FARNSWORTH, CONTRACTS § 3.25, at 197 (2d ed. 1990).

26. RESTATEMENT (SECOND) OF CONTRACTS § 45 cmt. b (1979).

27. *Id.*

28. *See id.*

29. P. S. Atiyah, ESSAYS ON CONTRACT 38 (1986). *See also* Charles Fried, CONTRACT AS PROMISE, 19 (1981) ("There is reliance because a promise is binding, not the other way around.").

# 12

# Philosophy of Language, Unilateral Contracts, and the Law

Brian H. Bix

Among the many important and incisive contributions Peter Tiersma has made to our understanding of law and language are two wonderful pieces on what speech act theory can teach us about offer and acceptance in contract law. (Tiersma 1986, 1992) These works and others by Tiersma raise questions that are central for theorists who wish to bring insights from philosophy of language into the study of law.

There has been growing interest among legal scholars in the way that speech act theory, and other ideas from modern philosophy of language, might assist legal practice. For example, Lawrence Solum's influential work on originalist approaches to constitutional interpretation relies on distinctions between semantic content and legal content, and on Paul Grice's distinction between speaker's meaning and sentence meaning. (e.g., Solum 2009, especially 944–955) Andrei Marmor uses a different aspect of Grice's work, on implicature, to show how and when non-textualist understandings of legal norms are appropriate, reflecting similar ways of understanding in ordinary speech.

In most cases of bringing philosophy of language to law, what the theorists are doing in their use of ideas from philosophy of language is *not* prescribing any radical change to legal practice, but primarily articulating a clearer understanding of what legal actors already do: that is, the work helps better to explain, rationalize, or justify our existing practices. What prescriptions there are in such works are usually on the margin, frequently the cleaning up of doctrinal uncertainties "in the corners," as it were. I have argued elsewhere (Bix 2005) that many attempts to use Ludwig Wittgenstein's views on rule-following as the basis for changing legal practices were based either on a misunderstanding of legal practice, a misunderstanding of Wittgenstein's theory, or both. A proper understanding of Wittgenstein's views, I have argued, leaves legal practice just as it was.

However, in Tiersma's writing on unilateral contracts (Tiersma 1992), we see a proposal for significant change, as well as a radically new understanding of unilateral contracts: that offers for unilateral contracts should be seen as promises, as commitments, but not really as offers. As Tiersma shows, this is just the exceptional sort of context where a focus on language and philosophy of language can help ground arguments for change in legal practice and doctrine.

With unilateral contracts, we have a situation where the doctrinal law has been awkwardly constructed over time. Parties' expectations do not well match the rules, and the legal outcomes of some even quite ordinary cases are uncertain under current rules and principles. This is just the sort of place where an approach based on linguistics or philosophy of language can converge with an understanding of contracting practices and doctrinal rules for a convincing prescription.

The history of unilateral contracting rules is well known. The transactions that fall under the rubric of "unilateral contracts" are generally ones where the performance sought is uncertain or unlikely—for example, rewards, dares, or employment bonuses. Historically, the effort to place these transactions within the structure of "offer and acceptance" and the once often-espoused principle of "mutuality of obligation" created an anomaly, where the person offering the transaction could lawfully withdraw the offer even after the party responding had nearly completed performance. The solution to this problem—or at least the Band-Aid over it—was Section 45 of the First and Second *Restatements of Contract*, under which once an offeree had begun performance in response to a unilateral contract "offer," the person making the offer lost the power to revoke the offer. A sort of option contract was created.

However, as Tiersma points out, awkwardness and anomalies remain. The parties' understanding of unilateral contracts often varies significantly from the doctrinal rules—not least in the arbitrary cut-off line in the offeror's ability to revoke the offer. A party's preparation for performance in response to the "offer" of a unilateral contract, even when significant, costly, and reasonable is not protected under Section 45, whereas a similar party who begins performance will get the protection of Section 45, even if his performance costs are slight. Additionally, it is far from clear what the proper remedy should be when an offeror of a unilateral contract improperly reneges after the recipient of the offer has begun performance.

Tiersma's analysis points out that looking at the proposal for a unilateral contract as a promise—a commitment—rather than as an offer, which becomes a commitment only if and when it is met by an acceptance—better matches both party expectations in relation to unilateral contracts and the existing legal doctrine. Finally and most importantly, it creates clearer and better answers to remedies questions when the proposal for a unilateral contract is reneged after the recipient has incurred significant expenses in reliance. It is important to note, however, that Tiersma shows in his work how his analysis is grounded both in actual practices and party expectations, as well as in existing doctrinal rules—as in the way that Sections 87(2) and 90 of the *Second Restatement* may apply to the problem of reneged promises of unilateral contracts. Section 90 is the general reliance section, allowing enforcement of promises where they have induced action or forbearance in reasonable reliance on the promise, and injustice can only be avoided by enforcement of the promise; Section 87(2) creates a similar option of legal enforcement based on pre-acceptance reliance on an offer. Tiersma persuasively shows that these sections may apply to this problem, either directly or by analogy. Additionally, he points out that there have been court decisions on the question of damages that were more consistent with his prescriptions than they were with existing black-letter law—another strong sign that his approach tracks moral and practical intuitions.

In general, I think we need to have modest expectations when applying philosophy of language to law, aspiring primarily to better re-characterizations of existing practices, but there are exceptional circumstances, as Tiersma has shown, where the insights of philosophy of language can ground arguments for significant doctrinal change.

## References

Bix, Brian H. (2005), Cautions and Caveats for the Application of Wittgenstein to Legal Theory, in Joseph Keim Campbell, Michael O'Rourke & David Shier (eds.), *Topics in Contemporary Philosophy* 217–229 (Cambridge, Mass.: MIT Press), 217–229.

Marmor, Andrei (2011), Can the Law Imply More Than It Says? On Some Pragmatic Aspects of Strategic Speech, in Andrei Marmor & Scott Soames (eds.), *Philosophical Foundations of Language in the Law* (Oxford: Oxford University Press), 83–104.

Solum, Lawrence B. (2009), *District of Columbia v. Heller* and Originalism, *Northwestern University Law Review* 103: 923–981.

Tiersma, Peter Meijes (1986), The Language of Offer and Acceptance: Speech Acts and the Question of Intent, *California Law Review* 74: 189–232.

Tiersma, Peter Meijes (1992), Reassessing Unilateral Contracts: The Role of Offer, Acceptance and Promise, *U.C. Davis Law Review* 26: 1–86.

# 13

# How to Do Legal Things with Words

THE CONTRACTS SCHOLARSHIP OF PETER TIERSMA

## Sidney W. DeLong

Law is a system of speech acts. Legally operative communications are not just bits of information. They are actions that have immediate legal effects. Because people use speech acts to create private legal relations, any comprehensive theory of private law requires an account of how legal speech acts succeed or fail. Speech act theory provides such an account of the conditions under which speech acts are performed in natural language (Austin 1962; Searle 1969, 1979; Grice 1999). Peter Tiersma's scholarship demonstrates both the theoretical and practical value of speech act theory to an understanding of the relationship between natural language and the law.

Speech act theory distinguishes among three dimensions of every utterance (Searle 1969, 23–26; Searle 1979). As a "locution," a speech act conveys a semantic meaning. As an "illocution," a speech act affects the world as an action in its own right, such as asserting or promising. Successful interpretation (or "uptake") of a speech act requires a correct interpretation by its recipient of both its semantic meaning and its illocutionary force. Finally, every speech act will have numerous personal and institutional effects—in speech act theory terminology, its perlocutionary effects—on its hearer and on third parties. Speech act theory describes the conditions that are necessary to the successful (or "felicitous") performance of each kind of illocution and the essential point or force of the act.

Tiersma's "The Language of Offer and Acceptance: Speech Acts and the Question of Intent" was the first sustained application of speech act theory in American legal scholarship. His work demonstrated the analytic value of speech act theory in dealing with a persistent problem of contracts jurisprudence—the interpretation of whether a sequence of communications should count as offers and acceptances. Classifying communications in this way requires courts to correctly interpret the illocutionary point as well as the semantic content of both express and indirect speech acts.

One of the first puzzles addressed by speech act theory was how to explain the phenomenon of indirect speech acts, in which we can say one thing and yet be correctly understood to be saying something else with a different illocutionary force (Searle 1979: 30–58). Paul Grice accounted for our ability to understand indirect speech acts by positing that in conversation we follow a Cooperative Principle (Grice 1999: 22–41). We understand apparently irrelevant things said by our conversational partners by making a very strong assumption that everything they say is helpful and relevant to our shared purpose in the conversation. Indirect speech acts succeed because that assumption is usually correct.

A court informed by this insight will correctly interpret the exchanges in a contract negotiation as being relevant responses to be understood in context rather than as self-contained units of meaning. The principle applies to the interpretation of both semantic meaning and illocutionary force. Thus, the course of a contract discussion might lead a court to construe a response to an offer as an acceptance even though it has the apparent surface form of a directive rather than a promise.

Judges who interpret oral statements need to be wary of the Cooperative Principle, however. If people in conversation are able to understand apparently non-responsive speech acts because they hear them as being what they expect to hear, then they will tend to misconstrue responses that are not intended to be what the hearer expects. If an employee demands that his employer renew his contract, the employer's response to get back to work will be heard by the employee as an acceptance instead of a perhaps-intended deflection. The hearer's assumption of cooperation may also override contrary evidence given by verbal nuances and pragmatic clues.

Mistrustful of such interpretations, modern courts often refuse to give legal effect to inferential commitments, insisting instead on explicit promissory expressions (for examples, see DeLong 2001). Courts construe reliance-inducing expressions of implied commitment as mere expressions of hope and optimism, with the illocutionary force of assertions or expressives rather than as promissory commissives. This "new formalism" represents an effort to channel people's speech act behavior into formal language that courts consider to be more reliable for their purposes.

In "Reassessing Unilateral Contracts: The Role of Offer, Acceptance and Promise," Tiersma tackled another contracts conundrum, reaching an original and surprising conclusion. In a unilateral contract, only one party makes a promise of performance, which he offers in return for a specified performance by the offeree. "I will gladly pay you Tuesday for a hamburger today," proposes a unilateral contract. Because the offeree's performance may take time to complete, a problem arises if the offeror attempts to revoke the offer after the offeree begins performance but before she has finished. Although scholars now all agree that the revocation is ineffective, they disagree about why.

The Restatement of Contracts takes the position that the offer is not yet binding on the offeror as a contract because it has not been accepted in the way required by the offeror and because the offeror has not yet received consideration. When the offeree begins performance, however, the offer becomes irrevocable until the offeree has a chance to finish, at which point the offer becomes binding because it has now been "accepted" and consideration has been given.

Tiersma argued that this analysis misidentifies the illocutionary force of the initial proposal: "A unilateral contract is not an offer that commits the speaker only after acceptance, but is rather a promise that, like all others, need not be accepted at all. Like other promises, a so-called 'offer' of a unilateral contract commits its maker immediately" (Tiersma 1992, 4). Although the promisor is bound at the moment of her promise, her duty of performance is conditional and does not "ripen" until the promisee fully performs. But the proposal, because it is a promise rather than an offer, is binding and irrevocable from the moment it is uttered.

This was a bold move. To reason from the illocutionary rules defining offers and promises to the (perlocutionary) consequences of promising is to step over the boundaries of speech act theory and natural language into the jurisdiction of ethics and law. The domain of speech act theory is to describe the constitutive rules of natural language, the necessary and sufficient conditions for the successful performance of illocutionary acts, such as promising (Searle 1979, 33–42). The constitutive rules for successful promising stipulate that it creates an obligation (Searle 1969, 63), but they do not determine what the nature of promissory obligation is, whether promises are ever revocable, or what the consequences of breach are. The answers to these questions lie in the perlocutionary rather than the illocutionary realm, where they are governed by conventional morality and the positive rules of contract law. Whether a unilateral contract offer is revocable is normatively determined by the law of contracts rather than the natural language conventions relevant to promising.

But Tiersma did not bottom his argument on the Restatement's mislabeling of unilateral offers and promises and did not seek to move the common law with the lever of prescriptive speech act theory. Instead, he supported his speech analysis with policy arguments that treating revocable unilateral contract offers as irrevocable unilateral promises would make contract law more consistent with the expectations and understandings of the businesspeople who make and receive such offers.

There is probably no universal expectation about revocability in the business world. The economic issue posed by Tiersma's proposal is whether making all unilateral contract "offers" irrevocable would increase or decrease the total transaction costs incurred by future contractors. How might businesspeople who prefer to make *revocable* offers for unilateral contracts react to the new rule? They could easily "contract around" it by making unilateral contract offers that expressly reserve a power to revoke before the offeree begins performance. Of course, that is not a promise under anyone's definition. In a system that promotes "freedom of contract," however, legally sophisticated people can be expected to create any new speech acts necessary to achieve the legal effects they desire. It is this creative potential for private law making through the use of speech acts that makes an understanding of speech act theory essential to an understanding of contract law.

### References

Austin, J. L. (1962) *How to Do Things With Words.* New York: Oxford University Press.

DeLong, Sidney W. (2001) Placid, Clear-Seeming Words: Some Realism about the New Formalism (With Particular Attention to Promissory Estoppel), *San Diego Law Review* 38: 13–51.

Grice, Paul (1999) *Studies in the Way of Words.* Cambridge, Mass.: Harvard University Press.

Searle, J. R. (1969) *Speech Acts: An Essay in the Philosophy of Language.* Cambridge: Cambridge University Press.

Searle, J. R. (1979). *Expression and Meaning: Studies in the Theory of Speech Acts.* Cambridge: Cambridge University Press.

Searle, J. R. (1964) How to Derive "Ought" from "Is." *Philosophical Review* 73: 43–58.

Tiersma, Peter Meijes (1986) The Language of Offer and Acceptance: Speech Acts and the Question of Intent, *California Law Review* 74: 189–232.

Tiersma, Peter Meijes (1992) Reassessing Unilateral Contracts: The Role of Offer, Acceptance and Promise, *University of California, Davis Law Review* 26: 1–86.

14

# Tiersma *Contra Mundum:* in Defence of Promises

Peter Goodrich

In the spirit of Dutch antidisestablishmentarianism, or perhaps in the last kick of youthful rebellion, in 1992, Peter Tiersma published a lengthy law review article on speech acts and contracts (Tiersma 1992). Flouting the received wisdom of Christopher Columbus Langdell, of Karl Llewellyn, the Second *Restatement of Contracts*, and of legal realism more generally, he argued that there is a significant conceptual difference, and distinction to be made, between bilateral contracts and unilateral promises. Tiersma's argument, *in nuce*, is that a promise is a unilateral commitment, in the language of the courts, a sacred pact, a solemn covenant, a binding avowal between the subject and their future, the divinity or nature as one wishes, that is independent of any other subject's act or promise. A contract, by distinction, is from the Latin *contraho*, to draw together, and is a transitive process in which negotiations, offer, and acceptance lead eventually to a bilateral exchange of commitments and hence to contract formation, an exchange of promises. A proper grasp of this elegantly formulated and crucial distinction between bare promises and contracts, unilateral and bilateral, would spare the courts many errors of reasoning and on occasion legally perverse if not manifestly unjust results.

Lawyers, according to Martin Luther and many more modern divines, are fated upon their demise to an exceedingly rapid passage to Hell. It is perhaps for this reason, because of their secularism, that they seem to have been symptomatically uncomfortable in developing the doctrine of promising. The cases on unilateral contracts, which is to say bare promises, go back to *Rogers v. Snow*, and the promise to pay a man who walks from London to York to deliver a bond, but the more modern and variant discussions concern promises relating to climbing greasy flagpoles, walking across Brooklyn Bridge, or sending a tramp around the corner. Such *de minimis* examples tend to betray an evasion of the promissory basis of the commitment. There is no contract, no drawing together, no bilateral exchange, but rather, in good Christian terms, a promise, a commitment to perform if the conditions of the promise are met. As the unilateral promise is a commitment, a covenant with the divine or whatever other concept of higher power suits the illocutionary actor, it binds the promisor. That is the nature, the ontology, of the promise—it is an act of conscience, which according to the early legal authorities, means to "know with," meaning here to know with God.[1] If a promise is made, then it is breach of promise—*laesio fidei* in the ecclesiastical law—to retract or fail to perform. This is quite independent of any promise in return, and indeed in Christian doctrine it is precisely when it becomes unprofitable, when adverse circumstances challenge the promisor, that it is most necessary to keep the promise, to turn the other cheek. Such commitment is singly and solely the consequence of promising, the ontological entailment of the avowal that Saint Germain elaborates in *Doctor and Student* in terms consistent with the Roman law of *causa*: "And if the promise be good and with a cause though no worldly profit shall grow thereby to him that makes the promise but only a spiritual profit ... it is most commonly held that an action ... lies in law canon" (St. Germain, 1530/1974, 230).[2] It is this action that the common law took over from the spiritual jurisdiction in the mode most recently of promissory estoppel or non-bargain promise, an equity that subsists not in bargain but precisely in the illocutionary force and commissive speech act, the unilateral commitment of the promisor.

The modern conflation of the unilateral and bilateral in the shadowy notion of bargain is, as Tiersma correctly points out, a source of error. The perambulator from London to York, the climber of the greasy flagpole, the tramp who hazards to cross the road, are neither making a promise nor performing a promissory act; rather, they are much more simply putting faith in the promise, and believing the promisor. Attempts to create a contract out of such faith are both misguided and confusing. There is no mutuality of obligation, there is no return promise, there is at most behavior that indicates belief in the veracity of the promisor. Thus, it is perfectly correct to allow an equitable remedy where one of our perambulators or climbers has believed the promisor and acted accordingly, only to be shunned by the latter. This is not because there is a contract but because there has been breach of promise. Occasionally, though with an exceptionally tortured logic, the courts come to such a conclusion, as in *Cohen v. Cowles Media*, where journalists promised anonymity to a source and then were overridden by their editors (1991).[3] In a case that journeyed twice to the Minnesota Supreme Court, it was held (i) that there was no contract and (ii) that the plaintiff could recover in estoppel. The decision was based on the observation that a journalist's promises to a source are ethical, a matter of honor, and not amenable to the rigid and ill-fitting concept of contract. After refusing to smother such a chimerical, evanescent, and, in essence, spiritual relation with the callous categories of law, the court provides an extra-contractual remedy in promissory estoppel—one cannot change one's position to the harm of another. In sum, the promise was enforced, but because of the confusions of the modern doctrine estoppel, which is generally now deemed to be a contract, this particular judgment must therefore either be an aberration or a logical tautology.

The entirely accurate and logically pertinent point that Tiersma's argument allows us to make is that where a party acts on the faith of a singular, which is to say unilateral, promise, rather than entering a bargain, it is not their reliance that founds an action but rather the breach of commitment, the breaking of the promise that grounds the action and justifies a remedy. The importance of the distinction can be brought home by considering another erroneously decided case, that of *Browning v. Johnson*.[4] The plaintiff sold his osteopathic practice to the defendant. Some months later, he came to regret his decision and before the time for performance was due, negotiated the termination of the contract. The defendant was reluctant but eventually agreed to cancel the contract in exchange for $40,000. Browning then "tired of the bargain" and brought an action for declaratory judgment and restitution. Here the plot thickens. The trial court determined that the original contract was void for indefiniteness and lack of mutuality. It is important to note that if a bargain is too indefinite to be a contract, then the agreement is void *ab initio*—there never was a contract. The question that next arises is whether return of this non-contract can constitute consideration for the payment for the release, the termination of this original non-contract. Here, the judgment becomes confused and in failing to observe the proper distinction between unilateral promises and bilateral agreements, arrives at a legally erroneous conclusion.

Faced with the problem that Johnson has been paid $40,000 for nothing, for releasing Browning from a void contract, for the equivalent of what another court termed purchase and sale of the green cheese rights to the moon, Judge Langenbach is hard pressed to justify his determination not to rescind the latter contract. Hard cases often result in poor reasoning and in this instance the judge resorts to the distinction between bilateral and unilateral agreements and endeavors to avoid the problem of absence of any *quid pro quo*, the non-bargain nature of this non-exchange, by determining that this was a unilateral contract. Browning bargained for the act of returning the original contract: "This is a unilateral contract ... in which a promise is given in exchange for an act or forbearance."[5] By stepping outside the contemporary doctrinal consensus that refuses to distinguish the two categories, the judge hoped to avoid the problem of the insufficiency of the consideration. What matters in a unilateral contract, the judge argues, is the promise, the request for an act, and it is the doing of something that one does not have to do that constitutes the sufficiency, if not the adequacy, of the consideration. This, however, is a confused statement of the law. The unilateral promise is enforced because of the commitment entailed in the promise, the vow, the solemn trust, and not because of any imagined exchange or consideration. Here the act would in any event be *de minimis*, in that it was the handing over of a piece of paper or bundle of papers with no greater value than that of waste paper. These had no value whatsoever if they did not contain a promise and it is in this instance precisely the promise that is being sought. Returning a copy of a contract is not of value unless it is accompanied by the promise to cancel the contract, in other words to destroy all other copies. If there was an act, a returning, it was symbolic and of no significance as an act unless accompanied by an exchange of promises, a bargain, a bilateral contract in which the money was paid for release.

The problem that the judge sought to avoid is that you cannot bargain for nothing—the exchange of a considerable sum for a promise not to do what it is impossible for you to do, namely to enforce an agreement that is void *ab initio*, is no bargain at all. Judge Langenbach resorts to old English common law, to *Haigh v. Brooks*, to justify his conclusion.[6] In that case, Brooks gave up a note of guarantee in return for a second promise of guarantee. Langenbach supposes that the note given up was worthless and so assumes that it was the simple unilateral act of handing over a piece of valueless paper that constitutes the consideration for the second promise, but such is not what *Haigh v. Brooks* decides at all. It is crucial to the decision in *Haigh* that the original note had some value, that even if it was unlikely to be enforced, there was a genuine possibility that it might have been enforceable. The judge pondered the grammar of the note, and decided that the expression "being in advance" was transitive and so allowed for the possibility that the first transaction was in process and not yet complete when Haigh signed the original guarantee. Had the note had no value, were it void *ab initio*, as in the case in hand, then it would have been no consideration, and if there were to be a cause of action it would be unilateral, in equity, upon a promise, and without either contract or consideration.

The problem that Langenbach thus faced was that if this were to be classified, as it should be, as a bilateral exchange, it was without consideration. No court has held that a promise to forbear to sue on a void claim is good consideration. There has always in fact been some possibility, as in *Haigh v. Brooks*, of enforcement, some right or equity that will potentially support the action.[7] Otherwise, the action is a non-contractual one, and in this case a suit based upon an equity: having given Johnson $40,000 for nothing, for mere paper, Browning was entitled to restitution. It was not the case that Browning had other reasons for wanting the paper, but rather, I suspect, that Judge Langenbach had other reasons for wanting to deny

Browning recovery. These, ironically, had nothing to do with any contract but rather likely had to do with the plaintiff's refusal to honor his promises, his *volte face*, his fickle and changeable mind, and the ensuing porous quality of his word. Hard cases, however, make bad law. Langenbach here arrived at what was arguably an understandable result but supported it by confused reasoning and mischaracterization of legal doctrine and precedent. Tiersma's article would be salutary and instructive reading for such a court. Errors would have been avoided and a different determination handed down. The distinction between bilateral contract and unilateral promise would certainly have produced a more coherent and more candid decision. *Viva* Tiersma.

## Notes

1. Conscience is from *con-scire*, to know with, and means when two know together, meaning to know together with God, according to the divine William Perkins. See, for a juristic example, the English Renaissance humanist lawyer (Fulbeck, 1599/1829, 86–87).
2. Spelling modernized.
3. *Cohen v. Cowles Media* (1991).
4. *Browning v. Johnson* (1967).
5. *Ibid.* at 316.
6. *Haigh v. Brooks* (1839).
7. Judge Langenbach cites Fleishbein v. Thorne, but on examination, this case, on its facts, involved release of a mortgage that had a value and potential enforceability in equity even if at law it was barred by the statute of limitations. The other case that is often used in support of Langenbach's argument is *Cook v. Wright* (1861), but here again there were special circumstances. The consideration in question—release of an apparently invalid claim—was supported by old law that enforced promises to repair the king's highway as promises for spiritual benefit without any need of consideration.

## References

Browning v. Arthur Johnson, 422 P.2d 314 (1967).
Cohen v. Cowles Media, 501 U.S. 663, 111 S. Ct. 2513, 115 L. Ed. 2d 586 (1991).
Cook v. Wright, 121 ER 822 (1861).
Fleishbein v. Thorne, 74 P.2d 880 (1937).
Fulbeck, William (1829) *Direction or Preparative to the Study of the Law* [1599]. London: Clarke.
Germain, Christopher St. (1974) *Doctor and Student* [1530]. London: Selden Society.
Haigh v. Brooks, 10 A. & E. 309 (1839).
Tiersma, Peter Meijes (1992) Reassessing Unilateral Contracts: The Role of Offer, Acceptance and Promise, *U.C. Davis Law Review*. 26:1–86.

# 15

# Formalism, Speech Acts, and the Realities of Contract Formation

Jeffrey M. Lipshaw

Peter Tiersma's work on wills (Tiersma 2010: 75–82) and contracts (Tiersma 1992) is an important advance on Langdellian formalism. Lawyers traffic in words, but what, if anything, is *real* about them? In the parlance of speech act theory, the issue is "how the utterances of a speaker are related to, and have an impact on, the surrounding world" (1992: 15). The common thread between contracts and wills is that their operative statements have *illocutionary* force, whether of declaration ("I dub thee Sir Geoffrey") or commitment ("I promise to walk the dog"). In the appropriate context, when a speaker says, "I bequeath" or "I promise," she is not describing an action, but performing the action of bequeathing or promising itself (1992: 17).[1]

As to the law of holographic wills, Tiersma's application of speech act theory makes perfect sense and offers a bold solution: the testator's performative utterances in pixels or bytes have the equivalent illocutionary force of a formal writing, and the law ought to recognize it (2010: 82–83). Tiersma's assessment of offer and acceptance in classical formalism, it seems to me, is more respectful of the past. Nevertheless, it is still an admirable opening to even more radical critiques of misguided empiricism within classical formalism. That is what I propose here.

Langdell's approach, as modified by Restatement (Second) of Contracts §45, insisted on there being equivalence of "offer and acceptance" as between bilateral and unilateral contracts. As Tiersma (1992: 10) paraphrases Llewellyn, the key question is "when is the deal on?" Under classical bilateral contract doctrine, it is when there are corresponding performative utterances of promissory commitment by offeror and offeree. In the case of unilateral contracts, the offeror's performative utterance is a promise with the expectation the deal is on when the offeree performs the requested act. Hence, the great doctrinal question has been what, in terms of the return performance, constitutes the "acceptance," and how fairly to treat the offeree's pre-acceptance reliance on the offer if acceptance does not occur until completion. Tiersma rejects the need for equivalence between the bilateral and unilateral models, focusing instead on the promise as speech act (i.e., a performative utterance) and the responsive physical act. He concludes that formation of a contract should turn on acts, whether of speech or otherwise, signifying commitment that a deal is on (1992: 41).

Tiersma captures the correct issue: "how well the present doctrine of contract formation fits the intent of those who make agreements" (1992: 14) . Within the framework of classical offer and acceptance doctrine, he is clearly onto something. I would like to take the critique of formalism a step further. I am skeptical that any such intent can ever be divined or that the never-never land of offer and acceptance doctrine has anything to do with the real mutual intention of the parties, whether or not manifested in performative utterances (see Lipshaw 2005). Even Tiersma's enlightened application of the philosophy of language has not tempered my skepticism.

As Thomas Grey (1983: 6–11) observed in his review of Langdell's orthodoxy, we can assess legal systems by criteria, among others, of *formality, conceptual order* (can the system's bottom-level rules be derived from relatively few abstract principles and concepts?), and *acceptability* (does the system fulfill the ideals and desires of those subject to it?).[2] Hence, classical Langdellian orthodoxy was an ideology "the heart of [which] was its aspiration that the legal system be made complete through universal formality, and universally formal through conceptual order" (p. 11) .Conceptual order trumped acceptability if the two were in conflict. Indeed, the doctrine of offer and acceptance in unilateral contract cases demonstrates that "[c]onsiderations of justice and convenience were relevant, but only insofar as they were embodied in principles—abstract yet precise norms that were consistent with the other fundamental principles of the system" (p. 15).

Langdell himself rejected appeals to acceptability over conceptual order in unilateral offer and acceptance as "ingenious attempts [that] have been made to show that the offer becomes irrevocable as soon as performance of the consideration begins" (Langdell 1880: 4)[3] Tiersma's application of speech act theory allows the doctrine to maintain conceptual order while at the same time addressing the perceived unfairness that undercuts its acceptability.

As a matter of doctrine, Tiersma's arguments are almost irrefutable, but I am not satisfied simply to address the acceptability of the doctrine on its own terms. The reason is that I see the conceptual framework of the doctrine not as a descriptive characterization of subjective (or, worse, inter-subjective) intention, but as an after-the-fact normative model. Hence, we need to reassess odd empirical assertions such as contained in Restatement (First) of Contracts §22: "The manifestation of mutual assent *almost invariably* takes the form of an offer or proposal by one party accepted by the other party or parties." That was revisionist history at best. As Tiersma (1992: 5) himself notes, "Although contracts have a venerable history in the common law, the notion that they arise by means of offer and acceptance is comparatively recent."A. W. B. Simpson's account (which Tiersma cites) is more fulsome (Simpson 1975: 258). The doctrinal issues of offer and acceptance arose not in cases of breach of an oral commitment, but in written contracts by correspondence. In the nineteenth century, English legal scholars came to see the formation of these particular contracts as a question followed by an answer; indeed a leading treatise writer stated categorically, "Every expression of a common intention arrived at by two parties is ultimately reducible to question and answer."[4] Perhaps the boldness of this empirical conclusion troubled the drafters of the Restatement (Second), because the revised §22(1) asserts only that the manifestation of mutual assent *ordinarily* takes the form of offer followed by acceptance, and §22(2) concedes the possibility that parties might have manifest mutual assent by their conduct rather than by offer and acceptance.

I am not persuaded that this doctrine, even when informed by speech act theory, advances our understanding of the reality of before-the-fact contract formation (as opposed to the legal models used to resolve after-the-fact disputes). Clearly Tiersma gets it: in the real world, the deal can be on by way of all sorts of commitments that do not necessarily track the offer and acceptance model. I would advance his project by rejecting ideologies of contract law that continue to tap into a mysterious shared consciousness called "mutual intention of the parties." I do not believe the resolution of contract formation disputes has much to do with "how the parties themselves understand and use concepts such as offer, acceptance and promise" (Tiersma 1992: 14). Nor do I believe that the law is (nor must it necessarily be) "finely tuned to how people create obligations and how they expect those obligations to operate"(Ibid.). Indeed, cases of offer and acceptance never arise in precisely the kind of situation—large-scale deal making—that Tiersma's focus on commitment is intended to cure. It is true, as a matter of empirical description, that "[d]espite the clear presence of commitment [in complex transactions], it may be impossible to pinpoint offer and acceptance." As a matter of doctrine, that circumstance is trivial. Nobody in such a case is going to be litigating issues of offer and acceptance.

Contrast the making of a will, whether formal or holographic. The reality is that the testator has undertaken a performative utterance. The law merely supplies strictures to discourage fraud or frivolity in the process of inter-generational transfer. The only question is whether the bequeathing utterance counts. In contrast, the doctrine of contract formation has never been an empirical account of contract formation, much less an exploration of some shared mental state that is neither, on one hand, wholly observable by way of objective manifestations nor, on the other, the private and subjective inner experience of one of the parties. The doctrine consists instead of normative (and often conflicting) conceptual models of how contracts ought to have come into being and are used instrumentally after the fact of the event by litigants with a stake in showing that their manifestation did or did not create a contract.

The benefit of the Langdellian paradigm is that it works as a self-contained model to resolve disputes. Formality and conceptual order are efficient. But the notion that the doctrinal model necessarily reveals (or is capable of revealing) mutual intention is a fantasy. Tiersma's application of speech act theory was an admirable way to resolve the acceptability issue within the four walls of the doctrine itself. For real-world litigants (foolish enough to try rather than resolve disputes), acceptability of the doctrine more likely turns on whether they win or lose.

## Notes

1. In John Searle's (1989: 537) usage, "a *performative sentence* is a sentence whose literal utterance in appropriate circumstances constitutes the performance of an illocutionary act named by an expression in that very sentence in virtue of the occurrence of that expression. A *performative utterance* is an utterance of a performance sentence token, such that the utterance constitutes the act named by the performance expression in the sentence."

2. The other two criteria are comprehensiveness and completeness.

3. Quoted by Grey (1983: 15).

4. Simpson (1975: 258), quoting Anson (1882: 15).

## References

American Law Institute (1932) *Restatement of the Law of Contracts*. Philadelphia: ALI.

American Law Institute (1981) *Restatement (Second) of the Law of Contracts*. Philadelphia: ALI.

Anson, Sir William (1882) *Principles of the English Law of Contract 2d*. London: MacMillan & Co.

Grey, Thomas C. (1983) Langdell's Orthodoxy, 45 U. Pitt. L. Rev. 45: 1–53.

Langdell, C. C. (1880) *Summary of the Law of Contracts*. Boston: Little, Brown & Co.

Lipshaw, Jeffrey M. (2005) The Bewitchment of Intelligence: Language and Ex Post Illusions of Intention, *Temple Law Review* 78: 99–150.

Searle, John R. (1989) "How Performatives Work," 12 Linguistics and Philosophy, 12: 535–558 (1989), 537.

Simpson, A. W. B. (1975) Innovation in Nineteenth Century Contract Law, 91 *L.aw Quarterly. Review* 91: 247–278.

Tiersma, Peter Meijes (1992) Reassessing Unilateral Contracts: The Role of Offer, Acceptance and Promise, University of California, Davis Law Review 26: 1–86.

Tiersma, Peter Meijes (2010) *Parchment Paper Pixels: Law and the Technologies of Communication*. Chicago: University of Chicago Press.

# PART III

# Speech and Action

# The Meaning of Silence in Law

16

# The Language of Silence

IMPLICATION AND THE ROLE OF CONVERSATION*

## Peter M. Tiersma

Assuming that people can communicate by their silence, the next question is, how do they accomplish this feat? Normally, silence is an absence of speech, and communicates nothing, or at most allows for the drawing of certain inferences.[1] What, then, are the mechanisms by which saying nothing can become a means of communicating something?

*\*\*\**

Finally, an act or silence may obtain meaning by *implication*. In examples of convention, agreement and declaration, the meaning of silence is fixed in advance. Any political science student knows that inaction by the president for the specified period means that a bill will just become law. Similarly, certain colonists knew what the lamps in the church tower meant prior to Revere's historic ride.

Implication, on the other hand, gives meaning to an act on the spot and on a much more ad hoc basis. For example, if you ask me what I would like to do this evening, I could respond verbally by saying that I would like to play a game of chess. In the alternative, I could respond by conspicuously picking up the chess board and holding it up, while making eye contact to indicate my intent to communicate.[2]

Now suppose that I say nothing in response to your question. Rather, I silently leave to set up the chess board in another room. Here I have not intentionally communicated anything. It is rude as well, since while I obliquely suggest that I want to play chess, I have failed to answer your question directly; I have left you to deduce or infer my intent.[3]

---

* Excerpt from Peter Tiersma, The Language of Silence, *Rutgers Law Review* 48:1, 11–12, 74–80 (1995).

Another example of implication is if, in response to your question about what we should do this evening, I mimic the driving of an automobile, pretending to turn an imaginary steering wheel and changing gears while imitating the sounds of a roaring motor and screeching tires. Pretending to drive a car has no conventional meaning. Still, I have answered your question.[4] The reason is perhaps a more general interpretive convention that conspicuously mimicking a physical action can refer to, or symbolize, that action. Thus, ritualistically mimicking the driving of a car is not just the act of pretending to drive a car, but may *stand for* or *represent* the act of driving itself, especially when there are other indications, like eye contact, which show that the actor intends to engage in intentional communication.

In comparison to actions, silence provides fewer clues of intent to communicate. With people being silent the vast majority of their lives, how can we isolate the relatively rare occasions when their silence is meaningful by implication? Or to phrase it differently, when—if ever—can silence be meaningful if we can identify no convention, declaration, or agreement that gives meaning to the silence?

One fairly obvious requirement is that to be meaningful by implication, the silence must be part of a *conversation* or *discourse*.[5] The silence that most of us engage in during our daily existence, therefore, does not communicate if we are asleep or alone.

In light of the relevance of these phenomena, it is useful to outline in broad strokes some of the work that has been done recently on conversation or discourse. Traditional linguistic theory, which even today is heavily influenced by the work of Noam Chomsky, has almost exclusively concentrated on analyzing linguistic units no larger than the sentence.[6] Only more recently have linguists and other social scientists begun to systematically analyze larger units of speech, such as conversations.[7]

Modern research on discourse analysis has shown that conversations have a number of identifiable characteristics.[8] One focus of discourse analysis is what is called the *turn*.[9] A turn lasts as long as one speaker holds the floor.[10] A turn may be a complete sentence, of course, but it may also be more than one sentence, or an elliptical (partial or incomplete) sentence consisting of just one or two words.[11] Ideally, speakers' turns do not overlap, but rather follow each other sequentially, for obvious reasons.[12]

Turns, which are in many ways the building blocks of a conversation, are almost always organized into larger units.[13] The next larger unit is generally called an *exchange*.[14] It consists of at least two turns, one directly following the other. Consider the following short exchange:

Thea: "Did you go to the festival in Oak Park last weekend?"
Anne: "No."

Note that Thea's turn begins the exchange, and is therefore called the *initiation*.[15] Schoolmarms and legal writing teachers will be happy to observe that it is a complete sentence. Although this is not an essential trait of an initiation, it is quite common. Of course, there is a great deal of background information or shared knowledge (e.g., which festival the conversants are discussing; where Oak Park is located) that need not be explicitly mentioned. But someone who initiates an exchange must give enough information so other participants understand what is being said. Consequently, the initiation usually cannot be too elliptical or cryptic.

The second turn is Anne's *response*.[16] By definition, a response must follow an initiation.[17] Note further that because the initiation provides most of the essential information, the response can be very elliptical (i.e., it can omit most material that was already provided in the initiation). If Anne spoke in full sentences, she would have to say, "No, I did not go to the festival in Oak Park last weekend." But because of the information given by Thea in the initiation, all Anne needs to say is "no." The missing material can be "recovered" or filled in from the initiation.

Another attribute of the structure of such an exchange is that the initiation frequently *predicts* or *expects* a response.[18] This necessarily entails that the initiation cannot end the exchange; something else must follow. In the above example, the initiation does not predict whether the response will be positive or negative. It predicts only that a response of some kind will be forthcoming.[19] For Anne to fail to respond would indicate that something went awry: that she had not heard Thea's comment, did not understand it, or maybe did not want to talk to her.

A final relevant characteristic of exchanges is that the initiation not only predicts that there will be a response, but it greatly limits the range of appropriate responses. The potential topics of any initiation are vast; someone can always change the subject and raise a new topic. But assuming that conversational partners are relatively cooperative, an initiation in the form of a greeting ("Hi") expects or predicts that the response will be another greeting. A yes/no question ("Did you eat breakfast?") anticipates either a "yes" or a "no" in reply.[20] In fact, the range of expected responses can be reduced to one particular response. As every trial lawyer knows, the leading question "You were at the scene of the crime, weren't you?" clearly anticipates only one response: "Yes."[21]

If we posit that ordinarily silence is meaningful through implication only if it is part of a structured conversation, we come a long way in explaining when and how silence can communicate.[22] Most notably, it greatly narrows the occurrences of silence that can be considered meaningful. As one commentator has noted, participants in a conversation "can, by remaining silent, answer a question or agree to a request."[23] On the other hand, silence that is not part of a conversation is far less likely to involve intentional communication, although it may obviously support various inferences.[24]

It also appears that for silence to communicate, it must not only be part of a conversational exchange, but it must virtually always be a *response.*[25] In other words, silence or inaction cannot initiate an exchange. This is consistent with the observation that silence has no conventional meaning in isolation. Something that is meaningless in isolation cannot sufficiently convey the specific information required to initiate a conversational exchange.

Thus, absent convention, agreement, or declaration, silence normally is meaningful only as a response in an exchange.[26] This observation produces at least two significant benefits. One is that, as noted, it serves to define the context in which silence can be meaningful by implication. Not only must silence be part of a conversation, but it must occur as a response to a relatively complete initiation. The second benefit is that it shows how silence can communicate a relatively specific message absent convention, declaration, or agreement to give it meaning. In isolation, it is hard to say that silence has any articulable meaning. Yet recall that responses are often elliptical and derive much of their meaning from the initiation. Because a silent response secures meaning from the turn that it follows, the fact that no convention, declaration, or agreement exists to give meaning to the silence is not fatal.

Of course, these principles assume that the parties are indeed engaged in conversation. More specifically, the person initiating the exchange must have good reason to expect a response in the first place. Between strangers, for example, one person might be free to simply ignore a question, thereby refusing to engage in conversation. The fact that the person has remained silent in response to a question is meaningless in this situation, at least if the questioner has no right to expect or demand a response.

This principle is nicely illustrated by an example of Muslim marriage, [where the prospective bride's silence conventionally means consent only if she is asked by a close relative; it indicates rejection when asked by a stranger.] Presumably, where the family has arranged the marriage, the expectation is that she will consent. Thus, the family can expect a positive response. The woman does not need to say anything, unless she wishes to upset that expectation. But if a nonrelative asks, she is under no obligation to say anything. Her silence would therefore indicate a nonresponse, especially because it is probably impolite or unusual for a nonrelative to seek her consent. And practically speaking, a nonresponse is equivalent to a rejection.

A final issue is that although the conversational approach tremendously limits the range of possible meanings of silence, it does not always suffice. We have made a great deal of progress if we can interpret silence to mean either "yes" or "no." But the distinction between "yes" and "no" is fundamental. How can we select one of these two possibilities?

I propose that silence acquires meaning here on the basis of the participants' expectations. Sometimes these expectations can arise linguistically, often through the use of what are called tag questions.[27] For instance, the question "It's all right if I use your bathroom, isn't it?" anticipates a positive response. If you hear me and say nothing, I can safely conclude that you will let me use the bathroom, at least if I have the right to expect a response. In contrast, the question "You don't mind if I use your bathroom, do you?" expects a negative answer. These expectations can arise not only by linguistic structure, but also through real-world experience. For instance, someone may on many occasions have asked his friend Mary the neutral question, "May I use your bathroom?" and always have received a positive answer. Based on expectations of previous experience, he can construe Mary's silence as a positive answer.

Implicit in this discussion about the function of silence is that it is generally used to communicate when remaining silent is more convenient than speaking. The above examples work best if Mary is busily cooking a meal and does not want to be distracted. On the other hand, if I am engaged in a leisurely conversation with Mary and ask the same question, in response to which she simply says nothing, it seems somewhat more forced to interpret her silence as consent, because she could easily say yes. Observe that many other examples of communicative silence in this Article involve parties separated by distance, where it is more convenient to agree, for instance, that you need not contact me unless our planned fishing trip needs to be cancelled.

These basic concepts go only so far in explaining how silence can be legally significant. The remainder of this Article will apply these relatively abstract concepts, and elaborate on them, in the context of actual legal situations where silence has been deemed significant.

## Evidence

Another legal area where silence may be significant is evidence. A major part of evidence law is devoted to the hearsay rule, which excludes testimony regarding what other people said outside of court. Thus, if you hear John say that "the light was red when the car entered the intersection," your testimony regarding what John said is inadmissible under the hearsay rule.[28] The rule has numerous exceptions, however. One such exception relates to admissions.[29] If you hear John, who is now the defendant in a lawsuit, admit that the light was red when he entered the intersection and rammed into the plaintiff, John's statement is an admission. Thus, your testimony regarding John's statement is admissible.

What interests us here is what is called a *tacit* or *adoptive admission*. This is where a party, with knowledge of the contents of a statement, manifests his adoption of the statement by words or conduct.[30] As one might suppose, an adoptive admission may also be made by silence:

> You are on trial for holding up several businesses and killing three of their employees. The prosecution introduces evidence that after

your arrest, your sister visited you in prison and asked you, "Why did you have to shoot those three poor boys?" You did not respond. Your silence can be treated as an admission that your sister's accusation is true.[31]

One interesting aspect to the tacit admission rule is that technically it should only be the defendant's statement or silence that is admitted into evidence; the sister's question is obviously not an admission. Nonetheless, not only your silent response but also your sister's utterance is allowed into evidence.[32] This fits in well with viewing these utterances as part of a conversational exchange. Because a response is often elliptical, it must be given meaning by the initiation.

Traditionally, several factors must be met for the tacit admission rule to apply. Although the list can vary a bit, the following is McCormick's summary: (1) The party must have heard the speaker; (2) the party must understand the statement; (3) the subject matter must be within the party's knowledge; (4) the party must have no physical or emotional impediments that would prevent him from responding to the statement; (5) the personal makeup of the speaker must be considered; and (6) the statement itself must call for a denial if not true.[33]

Most of these factors are fairly self-evident. For instance—just as with the Roman law of manumission—the person whose silence is legally significant must be capable of speaking. What is more problematic is the sixth factor. In a sense, any untrue statement calls for a denial. Surely society has nothing to gain by dissemination of untruths. Some courts try to narrow this consideration by suggesting that the statement must "naturally" call for a denial, yet even this is inconclusive. As one court has observed, "Who determines whether a statement is one which 'naturally' calls for a denial? What is natural for one person may not be natural for another."[34] At one point, a "working rule" arose that anything said in a party's presence, and which he did not deny, was deemed an admission and was receivable in evidence against him.[35] For example, if Jane tells Betty that John shot someone, and John overhears the comment but says nothing, John may be deemed to have admitted that he shot the person.[36]

The tacit admission rule, for this and other reasons, has drawn its share of criticism. Academics have condemned it because sometimes people feel it best not to reply to an untrue or accusatory statement made in their presence, perhaps out of nervousness, fear, or pride.[37] At least one jurisdiction has rejected the rule entirely.[38] The United States Supreme Court has not gone as far, but it has written that "[i]n most circumstances silence is so ambiguous that it is of little probative force."[39] And, of course, limitations have been placed on the rule when applied to someone accused of a crime, who has a constitutional right to remain silent.[40] In light of these criticisms, is there any legitimate basis for this rule? Can silence mean anything in this context?

Recall that silence may receive meaning by convention, declaration, or agreement; none of these, however, are present here. Silence can also acquire meaning by implication, but usually only if it occurs as a response in a conversational exchange such as in the previous example. Nonetheless, people often prefer not to dignify false allegations of wrongdoing by responding. Numerous maxims suggest that this may be the wisest course of action. Abraham Lincoln observed that "If I should read much less answer, all the attacks made upon me this shop might as well be closed for any other business."[41] And as Ben Jonson wrote: "Calumnies are answered best with silence."[42]

Yet while silence—or nonresponse—may be the best policy in regard to many accusations, it is another matter when the person making the accusation can reasonably expect a response. In the previous example, the sister has the right, as a close relative, to an answer from her brother. Likewise, good friends can expect a response. If you are not going to reply, you at least ought to say so, perhaps by commenting that it is none of their business. Otherwise, the person who made the accusation can reasonably interpret your silence as meaningful.

Unfortunately, not all courts have recognized this point. Almost a century and a half ago, a Georgia court correctly commented that "what a stranger says to a party may, although uncontradicted, not always be evidence."[43] Yet other courts have allowed the statements of strangers to form the basis for a tacit admission,[44] including accusations made by police officers and hostile witnesses.[45] These people cannot compel a defendant to engage in a conversation; they are not entitled to expect an answer to a question or accusation.[46] As one court commented, the witness, "being a stranger to the accident, had no apparent right to require defendant to express himself."[47] Although a defendant's silence in this context may well lead to certain adverse inferences, it is not legitimately viewed as equivalent to a verbal admission.[48]

If a tacit admission can arise only as a response in a conversational exchange, it follows that a person's silence to a statement not directed at her is meaningless. Someone who simply overhears a conversation should not be expected to respond, because she is not a participant in the conversation. Of course, she might interject herself into the discussion, but the mere fact that she chooses not to interrupt a conversation by others is not an admission. At most, a person's silence in this situation supports a fairly vague inference based on the fact that she failed to deny her guilt when presented with an opportunity to do so. Here again, courts have been inconsistent. At times courts have refused to admit silence in the face of statements or accusations that were merely overheard.[49] Other courts, however, have admitted such statements.[50] In the approach of this Article, these latter cases are clearly wrong. Only silence that occurs as part of a conversation can, if other criteria are met, be deemed an admission. Even if silence is part of a conversational exchange, however, the silence must constitute an *admission*.

Traditionally, a person admits a statement made by someone else if that statement must naturally call for a denial if it is untrue.[51] Yet people do not always deny false statements.[52] Minor mistakes do not naturally call for a denial. For example, if a casual acquaintance mispronounces my name or incorrectly tells someone else, within my hearing, that I speak Friulian instead of Frisian, I might not correct the false statement to avoid embarrassing my acquaintance. In contrast, if I am accused of child molestation, I will almost certainly deny the allegations. Consequently, only in response to an allegation or accusation of wrongdoing is the silence of the accused person meaningful.[53]

A number of courts have recognized this principle, albeit often indirectly.[54] For instance, Justice Marshall once observed that:

> Silence is commonly thought to lack probative value on the question of whether a person has expressed tacit agreement or disagreement with contemporaneous statements of others. Silence gains more probative weight where it persists in the face of accusation, since it is assumed in such circumstances that the accused would be more likely than not to dispute an untrue accusation.[55]

The approach advocated in this Article thus suggests that silence will only rarely constitute an admission. First, the silence must come in response to an accusation of wrongdoing, because people often let minor errors stand uncorrected. In addition, the accusation must be made by someone entitled to expect a response. If a stranger accuses me of wrongdoing, I am free to refuse to answer his charges. Under the United States Constitution, the right to refuse to engage in conversation with strangers, when those strangers are governmental officials accusing a person of a crime, is protected by the Fifth Amendment. Finally, failure to respond to overheard comments is not an admission that those comments are true. When a person is not a participant in a conversation, he cannot be expected to respond to allegations contained in that conversation.[56]

## Notes

1. For a further discussion of the distinction between communication and the process of drawing inferences, see Peter M. Tiersma, *Nonverbal Communication and the Freedom of "Speech,"* 1993 WIS. L. REV. 1525, 1552–56.

As I note far more fully in that article, the distinction that I make between communication and inference owes much to the theory of meaning developed by the philosopher Paul Grice. *See* Paul Grice, *Meaning, in* STUDIES IN THE WAY OF WORDS 213 (1989). Note, however, that Grice uses different terminology. What I call "communication," he refers to as "nonnatural sense," and my "inference" is roughly equivalent to his "natural sense." *Id.* at 214; *see also* Dennis Kurzon, *The Right of Silence: A Sociopragmatic Model of Interpretation*, 23 J. Pragmatics 55, 60 (1955) (relating intended silence to the Gricean notion of nonnatural sense).

2. Note that the act of waving a chess board while looking you in the eyes has no conventional meaning, as far as I am aware. It is quite different from waving a white flag, a conventional nonverbal means of signifying truce or surrender. Nonetheless, conspicuously waving a chess board can communicate a fairly specific message in this narrow context.

3. Of course, even though the specific action of waving a chess board does not have a conventional meaning, there are more general interpretive strategies at work here. As I have demonstrated elsewhere, people can indicate that they are using a physical action to communicate by doing the act while maintaining eye contact with the "addressee." Tiersma, *supra* note 1, at 1554. Thus, maintaining eye contact, along with other factors, can be used to indicate that the actor is intentionally communicating, rather than just engaging in noncommunicative motor activity.

4. I would not have intentionally communicated an answer to your question if I had simply gone to the car and started it. In that case, I would have left you to try to figure out that I wanted to go for a drive, which seems rather rude precisely because I failed to answer your question.

5. Saville-Troike has also made this point. *See* Muriel Saville-Troike, *The Place of Silence in an Integrated Theory of Communication, in* Perspectives on Silence 3, 9 (Deborah Tannen & Muriel Saville-Troike eds., 1985) ("It is noteworthy that the silence here conveys a message precisely because it forms part of an interactional communicative structure.").

6. *See, e.g.,* Noam Chomsky, Syntactic Structures 13–14 (1972) (defining language as a set of sentences, and positing that the fundamental aim of linguistic analysis is to separate the set of grammatical sentences from ungrammatical sentences); Noam Chomsky, Aspects of the Theory of Syntax 8 (1965) (defining generative grammar as "a system of rules that in some explicit and well-defined way assigns structural descriptions to sentences").

7. For some legal applications of discourse analysis, *see* Linda F. Smith, *Interviewing Clients: A Linguistic Comparison of the "Traditional" Interview and the "Client-Centered" Interview*, 1 Clinical L. Rev. 541, 544 (1995) (presenting a linguistic analysis as a tool to achieve a more "client-centered" participatory client interviewing approach); Norman Williams, Jr., *Using Discourse Ethics to Promote Equality for African-American Children Forty Years After Brown v. Board of Education*, 5 B.U. Pub. INT. L.J. 99, 126 (1995) (noting that "[s]ilence ... has been to modern women's lives what Foucault has argued that knowledge and discourse have been to modern men's") (quoting Rubin West, *Critical Social* Theory and Law, 1989 U. Chi. Legal F. 59, 65); George H. Taylor, *Structural Textualism*, 75 B.U. L. Rev. 321, 353–54 (1995) (discussing a structural textual holistic approach to legal interpretation).

8. *See generally* Gillian Brown and George Yule, Discourse Analysis 226–31 (1983) (discussing sequencing utterances to create a coherent discourse); Georgia M. Green, Pragmatics and Natural Language Understanding, 141–53 (1989) (discussing conversational interaction); Michael Stubbs, Discourse Analysis: The Sociolinguistic Analysis of Natural Language 128–46 (1983) (same); Harvey Sacks et al., *A Simplest*

*Systematics for the Organization of Turn Taking for Conversation*, 50 LANGUAGE 696 (1974) (positing rules for determining who has the next turn in a conversation).

9. *See* GREEN, *supra* note 8, at 150–51.

10. There is no limit to the length of a turn in a conversation. Jan Renkema, DISCOURSE STUDIES 109 (1993).

11. *See id.*

12. Of course, this assumes only one conversation is taking place at a time.

13. *See* RENKEMA, *supra* note 10, at 112 (defining a conversational sequence as a "systematic succession of turns").

14. *See id.* at 131.

15. *See id.* at 104–05 (discussing the question-answer type of conversational exchange).

16. *Id.* at 104–05.

17. *See id.* at 135.

18. *Id.* at 136; RENKEMA, *supra* note 10, at 112–13.

19. Of course, because this is a yes/no question, the range of possible responses is limited to affirmative, negative, or evading or deferring a response.

20. *See, e.g., Kurzon, supra* note 1, at 59 (noting that polar interrogatives generally require a "yes" or "no" response).

The notion that a particular type of initiation constrains what will happen on the next turn is captured by the concept of adjacency pairs. *See generally* Emanuel A. Schegloff and Harvey Sacks, *Opening Up Closings*, 8 SEMIOTICA 289, 295–96 (1973).

21. *See also* Kurzon, *supra* note 1, at 66 (observing that when a question is a polar interrogative, the meaning of the silent answer is "yes" or "no" on the basis of the presupposition behind the propositional content of the polar question).

22. It seems possible to me that silence could be meaningful through convention, agreement, or declaration without being part of a conversation, although I believe it would be unusual. On the other hand, if silence is to be given meaning by implication, it seems to me that it must be part of a conversational exchange.

23. RENKEMA, *supra* note 10, at 112.

24. Inferences based on silence can vary greatly from person to person and across cultures. For some people, silence indicates that they are annoyed or angry; for others, that they are contented. Some cultures consider silence very polite, while others place less value on it. *See, e.g.,* Thomas J. Bruneau, *Communicative Silences: Forms and Functions*, 23 J. COMM. 17, 34, 36–42 (1973).

25. One potential exception is where, as illustrated in a rather stereotypical comic strip involving a Cockney-like character who seems to spend most of his time in the pub, the husband comes home far too late. His wife greets him in stony silence, perhaps also holding a rolling pin. He responds to the wife's silent accusation by muttering a feeble excuse. The wife promptly bops him on the head.

While the wife may indeed be communicating nonverbally that she is angry, it is not so clear that this happens purely by her silence. Other relevant factors to consider include her stance, the holding of the rolling pin, and her position by the door, where she can confront the husband when he enters. This is not a case where a conversation is initiated by silence alone, but rather by a combination of nonverbal cues.

26. So as not to overwhelm readers unfamiliar with this material, I do not consider the possibility that silence may constitute some other element in an exchange, such as feedback, which frequently follows a response. In any event, it seems to me that silent feedback does not conventionally communicate, but rather allows for certain inferences to be drawn. This is especially true because feedback is not generally predicted by a response.

27. *See* Janet E. Ainsworth, *In a Different Register: The Pragmatics of Powerlessness in Police Interrogation*, 103 YALE L.J. 259, 278 (1993) (noting that one use of tag questions is to solicit agreement or acquiescence).

28. FED. R. EVID. 801.

29. Under the Federal rules, an admission by a party-opponent is not considered an exception to the hearsay rule, but is rather defined as not hearsay. FED. R. CIV. 801(d) (2). On the other hand, California treats the admission of a party as an exception to the hearsay rule. CAL. EVID. CODE § 1220 (West 1966).

30. *See, e.g.,* CAL. EVID. CODE § 1230 (West 1966).

31. *See* People v. Medina, 799 P.2d 1282, 1294–96 (Cal. 1990).

32. As one court has noted:

[w]hen a matter is stated in the hearing of one, which injuriously affects his rights, and he understands it, and assents to it, wholly or in part, by a reply, both are admissible in evidence; the answer, because it is the act of the party, who is presumed to have acted under the force of truth, and the statement as giving point and meaning to the action.

State v. Kobylarz, 130 A.2d 80, 84 (N.J. Super. Ct. App. Div. 1957) (quoting Donnely v. State, 26 N.J.L. 601, 613 (1857)).

33. MCCORMICK ON EVIDENCE § 270, at 800–01 (Edward W. Cleary ed., 3d ed., 1984).

34. Commonwealth v. Dravecz, 227 A.2d 904, 906 (Pa. 1967).

35. JOHN H. WIGMORE, EVIDENCE IN TRIALS AT COMMON LAW § 1071, at 102 (James H. Chadbourn ed., 1972).

36. People v. Silva, 754 P.2d 1070, 1079–80, *vacated by* People v. Griffin, 761 P.2d 103 (Cal. 1988).

37. Charles W. Gamble, *The Tacit Admission Rule: Unreliable and Unconstitutional— A Doctrine Ripe for Abandonment*, 14 GA. L. REV. 27, 33-43 (1979) (arguing that the tacit admission rule is psychologically unreliable and unconstitutional). *See generally* Robert M. Hutchins and Donald Slesinger, *Some Observations on the Law of Evidence—Consciousness of Guilt*, 77 U. PA. L. REV. 725 (1929).

38. *Dravecz*, 227 A.2d at 909 (overruling earlier Pennsylvania case that allowed use of tacit admission rule).

39. United States v. Hale, 422 U.S. 171, 176 (1975).

40. Griffin v. California, 380 U.S. 609, 614 (1965) (holding that under the Fifth Amendment, the prosecution may not comment on the fact that the accused invoked his right to remain silent); Doyle v. Ohio, 426 U.S. 610, 619 (1976) (holding that the Due Process Clause of the Fourteenth Amendment prohibits impeachment on the basis of a defendant's silence following Miranda warnings).

41. *Dravecz*, 227 A.2d at 906 n.1.

42. BEN JONSON, VOLPONE, act II, sc. II.

43. Carter v. Buchannon, 3 Ga. 513, 522 (1847).

44. *See, e.g.,* Dill v. Widman, 109 N.E.2d 765, 769 (Ill. 1953) (holding a widow's silence upon reading of a will admissible as evidence of the truth of the asserted contract between her and the testator); Doherty v. Edwards, 290 N.W. 672, 676 (Iowa 1940) (holding admissible statement by fatally injured passenger that was not denied by the defendant); Dincare v. Tamayose, 182 Cal. Rptr. 855, 860–61 (Ct. App. 1986) (allowing into evidence plaintiffs failure to respond to accusations made by defendant's nurse).

45. *See, e.g.,* Kennedy v. State, 107 So. 2d 913, 919 (Ala. Ct. App. 1958) (holding defendant's silence in response to sheriff's statement admissible); People v. Smith, 184 N.E.2d 841, 844 (Ill. 1962) (holding admissible defendant's failure to deny accusation by rape prosecutrix in presence of police officer); People v. Homer, 133 N.E. 2d 284, 287 (Ill. 1956) (holding defendant's silence in response to statement by complaining witness admissible); Commonwealth v. Helfman, 155 N.E. 448, 449 (Mass. 1927) (admitting statement and subsequent silence in response to a letter read to defendant by police officer); Tillman v. Commonwealth, 37 S.E.2d 768, 773 (Va. 1946) (admitting silence of accused during conversation with investigator).

Of course, there are presently constitutional limitations on the use of statements by an accused in the presence of police officers or while in custody.

46. *See* Rhode Island v. Innis, 446 U.S. 291, 300–01 (1980) (holding Miranda safeguards applicable whenever a person in custody is subjected to express questioning or its equivalent), *on remand,* 433 A.2d 646 (R.I. 1981), *and cert. denied,* 456 U.S. 930 (1982).

47. Klever v. Elliott, 320 P.2d 263, 265 (Or. 1958) (refusing to admit statement of bystander to defendant in an accident).

48. *See* Secor v. Brown, 156 A.2d 225, 227 (Md. 1959), ("[M]ere silence in the face of an accusation does not always permit an inference of guilt, or that the statement is true.").

49. *See, e.g.,* People v. Lebell, 152 Cal. Rptr. 840, 845 (Cal. Ct. App. 1979) (holding that defendant's presence on a telephone extension during phone conversation between others was not sufficient to support a finding of an adoptive admission).

50. *See, e.g.,* People v. Silva, 754 P.2d 1070 (Cal. 1988), (classifying defendant's silence in response to accusation as an adoptive admission), *cert. denied,* 488 U.S. 1019 (1989).

51. McCormick's on Evidence § 270 at 799 (Edward W. Cleary ed., 3d ed., 1984).

52. Henry S. Hilles, Jr., Note, *Tacit Criminal Admissions,* 112 Geo. L.J. 210 (1964) (stating that failure to deny an accusation demonstrates agreement and adoption of the accusation).

53. A related rule in civil procedure provides that if a party does not respond (remains silent) to the accusations of a complaint, that party will have a default judgment entered against it. Fed. R. Civ. P. 55(a).

54. *See* People v. Medina, 799 P.2d 1282, 1295 (Cal. 1990) (discussing circumstances in which silence in response to an "accusatory" statement constitutes an adoptive admission), *aff'd.,* 505 U.S. 437 (1992); People v. Edelbacher, 766 P.2d 1, 17 (Cal. 1989) ("To warrant admissibility, it is sufficient that the evidence supports a reasonable inference that an accusatory statement was made under circumstances affording a fair opportunity to deny the accusation."); *see, e.g.,* State v. Kobylarz, 130 A.2d 80, 86–87 (N.J. Super. Ct. App. Div.) (discussing silence in the face of an "accusative statement"), *certif. denied,*

133 A.2d 395 (1957); State v. Howerton, 329 S.E.2d 874, 880 (W. Va. 1985) (noting that silent admission would require an accusation directed at the defendant which he should reasonably deny); *see also* Charles W. Gamble, *The Tacit Admission Rule: Unreliable and Unconstitutional—A Doctrine Ripe for Abandonment*, 14 GA. L. REV. 27, 28 (1979) (noting that courts generally require an "accusatory statement" for application of the tacit admission rule).

55. United States v. Hale, 422 U.S. 171, 176 (1975) (citations omitted).

56. For a somewhat different approach to this problem from a linguistic perspective, *see* Dennis Kurzon, *Silence in the Legal Process: A Sociopragmatic Model, in* LEGAL SEMIOTICS AND THE SOCIOLOGY OF LAW 297 (B. S. Jackson ed. 1994).

17

# Symbolic Destruction*

## Peter M. Tiersma

One of the more common ways in which people communicate by conduct is to destroy things, such as flags, draft cards, crosses, and other objects. The act of destruction is most often communicative if the object destroyed is symbolic (i.e., has conventional meaning). Consider, for example, the burning of a flag or an effigy of Uncle Sam, or toppling a statue of Lenin. Such displays can be dramatic and highly effective.

At the same time, the notion that destruction may be the equivalent of speech is troubling, because it suggests that some quite harmful activities may invoke the protection of the Free Speech Clause. After all, politically motivated rioting or a political assassination might also be described as symbolic destruction. As will be seen below, limiting "speech" to attempts to engage in deliberate communication greatly reduces the concern raised by Chief Justice Warren that "a limitless variety of conduct" can be labeled "speech."[1]

### Flag Burning

In determining whether flag burning is communicative, we begin by exploring the meaning of the act itself. As noted above, the principal way in which conduct can mean something is by means of convention. It is obvious that the United States flag has a very conventional and powerful meaning as a symbol for the nation.[2] Not only is the flag itself symbolic, but the act of burning likewise may convey meaning as a matter of convention. At least when intended to communicate, burning something is a symbolic act that signifies disapproval of the object that is burned, or what the object represents. For

\* Excerpt from Peter Meijes Tiersma, Nonverbal Communication and the Freedom of "Speech," *Wisconsin Law Review* Should be 1993: 1525, 1569–75 (1993).

instance, if government officials round up copies of a book that they believe is evil and burn them in the town square, they may aim to destroy copies of the book so that it cannot further corrupt impressionable minds. But this could just as well be done by disposing of the books in a less dramatic fashion. Clearly, the public nature of the burning conveys potent disapproval of the book's message. Likewise, a testator, by burning a will, may revoke it. Here again, the act of incineration signals disapproval of what the burned item represents.

Yet to establish that burning a flag has meaning is only the first half of the inquiry. In the vast majority of burnings, like disposing of trash, the actor does not intend to communicate at all. Nor does the fact that the burned item is a symbol with conventional meaning guarantee that incinerating it is intended to send a message: burning a flag while alone in one's backyard in order to dispose of it is not an instance of communication. To be the equivalent of speech, an act must not only convey meaning, but the speaker or actor must intend to communicate. Whether the indicia of communication are present requires reference to the circumstances. We will thus examine this issue on the basis of the facts of the well-known case of *Texas v. Johnson*, [in which the Supreme Court overturned the conviction of a demonstrator who burned an American flag during a political protest in Texas].[3]

First, Johnson's burning of the American flag was purely nonfunctional.[4] The natural function of burning a flag is to dispose of it, which would normally not be done in a public place. Furthermore, the facts intimate that the flag was in perfectly good condition. This suggests that Johnson was not merely ridding himself of a soiled banner; people do not normally discard useful objects.

Just as significantly, Johnson burned the flag before an audience, not in the privacy of his backyard. Not only was the burning meant to be viewed by many people, but it was done in front of City Hall, a forum conducive to publicizing a political message and likely to attract the attention of an even greater audience through media coverage.[5]

Finally, Johnson's action, as the Court recognized, took place in the communicative context of a demonstration against the Reagan administration. It also occurred against the more general backdrop of the Republican convention, which advocated many of the policies that the demonstrators opposed. The meaning of the act was further elaborated by the chant of the protestors while the flag was burning: "America, the red, white, and blue, we spit on you."[6]

Weighing all these factors, there is no doubt that Johnson's burning of the flag communicated a message. Indeed, even the dissenters recognized as much, arguing mainly that the importance of the flag as a national symbol justified a law against its desecration.[7]

## Draft Card Burning

The analysis of draft card burning in *United States v. O'Brien*[8] is quite similar to flag burning. As in *Johnson*, O'Brien performed his act before an audience in front of the South Boston Courthouse and the communicative context—opposition to the Vietnam war and the draft—was quite clear. For several reasons, however, burning a draft card might be a bit less communicative than burning a flag. In *Johnson* there was no natural purpose—such as disposal—for burning the flag. Of course, O'Brien likewise did not need to rid himself of the draft card because it was worn or tattered. But O'Brien might arguably have wished to dispose of it, at least in part, to frustrate the efficient operation of the draft. This functional reason for burning the card largely dissipates on closer examination, however. If he simply wished to impede the draft, O'Brien did not need to burn the card publicly and risk imprisonment by drawing attention to it. In addition, the impact on the selective service caused by one person not having a draft card was minuscule. What would impede the smooth functioning of the draft was not O'Brien's lack of a draft card, but his avowed refusal to be inducted into the military, and the fact that he urged others to follow in his footsteps.

Another possible difference between burning a flag and a draft card is that the American flag has a longstanding conventional meaning in a way that a draft card does not.[9] But bear in mind that for an object like a draft card to symbolize something, the convention need not have existed from time immemorial. It suffices that the object or act can at some time be identified with a particular meaning for a specific group.[10] Thus, for the vast majority of citizens of the People's Republic of China, small bottles most likely do not symbolize anything. Yet for students sympathetic to the protests at Tiananmen Square in 1989, small bottles ("xiaoping") represent Chinese leader Deng Xiaoping. Some students recently commemorated the anniversary of the protests by smashing small bottles.[11] Accordingly, the students could engage in communication by destruction even though small bottles, to my knowledge, have no generally recognized conventional meaning in China. What matters is that for the potential audience, these objects represent something.

Just as small bottles represent something to certain Chinese students, the draft card represented something to many draft-age American men: it stood for the Selective Service System and by extension, the possibility that they could be compelled to fight a war that many of them believed to be morally wrong. Because they had to keep the card in their possession at all times, it was for them the physical embodiment of that system. Burning the card quite clearly communicated opposition to all that the card embodied.

## Cross Burning

Burning crosses evokes a related analysis. Although the cross is a symbol of Christianity, burning the cross is apparently not meant to convey a message of opposition to the Christian religion. Yet although the symbolism of the cross in this context is not especially transparent, cross burning is conventionally linked to the Ku Klux Klan. It sends a message of opposition to certain ethnic groups or in favor of racial separation and the superiority of Caucasians.[12]

Burning a cross on the lawn of an African American family, as in the *R.A.V.* case,[13] is surely intended to communicate a message. Here, there was an audience: the other teenagers who were present viewed the action, and probably the residents of the house and neighbors also. As with burning flags and draft cards, there is no particular reason that someone would normally burn a cross in these circumstances, so burning cannot merely be fulfilling its natural function of disposing of an object or producing heat. The act's message of racial hatred, which is perhaps somewhat vague in the abstract, was crystallized by burning the cross on the lawn of an African American family. Finally, the act most likely had a certain ritualistic quality to it. Hence, even though cross burning hardly conveys the sort of message that furthers the democratic process, and in many ways is more like a threat than the equivalent of speech, it is sufficiently communicative that its regulation should invoke some type of First Amendment inquiry.[14]

## Destructive Protests

So far, the analysis of communication by destruction has dealt with cases where the destroyed object was largely symbolic and had little value. For example, the value of the flag that Johnson burned or of O'Brien's draft card was insignificant—they could be replaced at minimal cost. At least in theory, however, it is possible to claim that far more damaging types of political protest are capable of sending a message, including politically motivated bombings, rioting, arson, or looting.[15] The notion that such conduct "sends a message" evokes fears of opening a Pandora's box in which any manner of action can claim the protective mantle of speech. Virtually any crime can be interpreted as "communicating," in an expansive sense of the word, a message about poverty, hopelessness, hate, or greed. It is therefore worth analyzing these destructive actions more closely.

For destructive protests to constitute the equivalent of speech, they must be meaningful. Virtually the only way that destruction can convey meaning is if the destroyed object is a symbol, and the destruction is intended to express opposition to what the symbol represents. The Bastille may have had such symbolic meaning for the French, for instance. For this reason, more indiscriminate rioting or looting will generally fail to convey meaning. Of course, one might argue that destruction of businesses during social unrest has meaning because those businesses are symbolic of the "establishment" or the "system," or because the businesses are the location of injustices against customers forced to pay exorbitant prices for their goods. But for a place of business to be symbolic, it must *represent* or *stand* for injustice and not simply be the place where an injustice occurred.[16] A specific store can become a symbol of injustice, as might happen if it is the location of a racially tinged killing by the shopkeeper of a customer wrongly suspected of shoplifting. But unless destroyed targets are chosen for their symbolic value, acts of destruction will at best allow for fairly vague inferences that the actors are dissatisfied or that the political or economic system is unjust.

In addition, the actors must intend to communicate. It is important here to emphasize that an intent to protest is not equivalent to an intent to communicate. Someone can protest against an unjust war by secretly destroying the tracks of munitions trains or sabotaging other war efforts, but these acts do not normally communicate. As with all nonverbal communication, the acts must be done for an audience. Toppling the statue of a political leader in front of cheering masses meets this criterion, but surreptitious acts of protest normally do not.[17]

More problematic than the audience factor is that actors must somehow distinguish destructive protests from actions engaged in solely for functional reasons. The difficulty arises because actions like bombing, looting, and rioting are often noncommunicative, such as when disappointed soccer fans go on a rampage or when rioting follows a natural disaster. All of these destructive acts may be done for purely functional reasons—to destroy a building or obtain goods that the looters want. Thus, even if acts of destruction are intended to convey information, the fact that such actions are frequently indistinguishable from ordinary lawlessness weighs heavily against regarding them as communication. Without further clues, one cannot rationally expect viewers to realize that a specific act of looting was intended to send a message when identical instances of looting were motivated solely by a desire to obtain free merchandise.

Often the only factor that can show that destructive activities might be intended to communicate is the context. Destructive protests often occur in the communicative context of political debate, such as whether the government's military action in some foreign country is just. The protests themselves may include speeches and banners, or the purpose of the destruction may be explained in words later, as when a group takes responsibility for a bombing. By itself, however, context does not mean that ordinary destructive activity communicates. At best, the destructive activity may draw attention to a message that is independently being sent by other means. The mere fact that rioting accompanies a message being sent by a more traditional medium may add punch to the message, but it does not transform the rioting into communication.

The conclusion that not all protest activity communicates is quite consistent with the general rationales underlying the Free Speech Clause. The primary purpose of communication, at least in the context of the First Amendment, is to inform and/or persuade. In contrast, destructive protests aim to coerce. If a government accedes to the concerns of such protestors, it likely does so not because it has been persuaded by the rhetorical force of any communications, but because it wishes to avoid a recurrence of the violence.

## Notes

1. United States v. O'Brien, 391 U.S. 367, 376 (1968).

2. *See* Texas v. Johnson, 491 U.S., 397, 421 (1989) (Rehnquist, C. J., dissenting).

3. 491 U.S. 397, 404 (1989).

4. "Nonfunctional" here must be understood to mean that it does not carry out its normal *noncommunicative* function. Clearly, communication is also a function.

5. Interestingly, many statutes that forbid mutilation of the flag cover precisely those instances of mutilation that occur in public, i.e., before an audience or potential audience, and thus may be calculated to prevent speech of this sort. *See* Street v. New York, 394 U.S. 576, 577–78 (1969) (defendant was arrested and convicted for violating a statute that stated one could not *publicly* "mutilate, deface, defile, or defy, trample upon, or cast contempt upon, either by words or act," an American flag). *See also* Stromberg v. California, 283 U.S. 359 (1931) (invalidating statute that forbade the *public* display of a red flag).

6. *Johnson*, 491 U.S. at 399.

7. *Id.* at 421–29 (Rehnquist, C. J., dissenting).

8. 391 U.S. 367 (1968).

9. *See* Mary J. Morrison, *Excursions into the Nature of Legal Language*, 37 CLEV. St. L. REV. 271, 329 (1989) (arguing that O'Brien's burning his draft card is not speech in the ordinary sense of the word because we do not have a conventional meaning associated with burning a document, and the draft card also had no meaning).

10. In this sense, convention is similar to trade usage in contract law, which the Uniform Commercial Code defines as "any practice or method of dealing having such regularity of observance in a place, vocation or trade as to justify an expectation that it will be observed with respect to the transaction in question." U.C.C. § 1-205(2) (1987). Another analogy is that of a dialect. As long as a word or symbol is linked to a particular meaning for a recognizable community of speakers, even if this community is much smaller than the entire speech community of a specific language, the word or symbol has a conventional meaning.

11. David Holley, *China Tries Protester Imprisoned 11/2 Years*, L. A. TIMES, Dec. 7, 1991, at A4.

12. *See* Mar Matsuda, *Public Response to Racist Speech: Considering the Victim's Story*, 87 MICH. L. REV. 2320, 2365–66 (1989) (stating that in the context of history, the swastika, Klan robes, and burning crosses carry a clear message of racial supremacy, hatred, persecution, and degradation of certain groups).

13. R.A.V. v. City of St. Paul, 112 S. Ct. 2538 (1992).

14. Leaving aside the constitutionality of the disputed ordinance in the *R.A.V.* case, the act of cross burning is at best a threat of imminent harm akin to "fighting words," which are a type of speech which the First Amendment traditionally allows the state to regulate.

15. Scanlon, for example, defines acts of "expression" to include at least some bombings and assassinations. Thomas Scanlon, *A Theory of Freedom of Expression*, 1 PHIL. AND PUB. AFF. 204, 206 (1972). Such acts are not necessarily protected in his theory. *See id.*

16. In Franklyn Haiman's words, "symbols are not *it*, they are *about it*." Franklyn S. Haiman, SPEECH AND LAW IN A FREE SOCIETY 21, 31 (1981).

17. Of course, if destructive political acts are geared toward attracting media attention, this factor arguably may have been met.

# 18

# Law's Metalinguistics

SILENCE, SPEECH, AND ACTION

Elizabeth Mertz

In 1995 Peter Tiersma published a 99-page article in the *Rutgers Law Review* entitled "The Language of Silence," excerpted in this volume (Tiersma 1995). A creative blend of legal and linguistic scholarship, the article starts by asking under what circumstances silence can actually communicate meaning.[1] In the second part of the article, Tiersma goes on to examine a wide variety of areas of law in which silence is salient to legal communication. This impressive survey covers laws pertaining to contract, agency, perjury, defamation, fraud, consent, evidence (excerpted here), waiver, and legislative silence. He concludes that "[n]ot surprisingly, there seems to be no ironclad test for determining when a failure to speak can communicate" within legal settings (1995: 96). Nonetheless, as he notes, there are many situations in which silence can turn out to be legally meaningful. In this commentary, I will examine some of those situations in light of the recent attention in linguistic anthropology to what is called "linguistic ideology." Intriguingly, one of the many things Tiersma has done in his article is to demonstrate how law encodes tacit linguistic ideologies, projecting them as somehow given or natural and then using them as grounding for formal legal rules.

Let's begin (appropriately!) with Tiersma and his article on silence. There he argues that silence, which he defines as an "absence of speech" (1995: 11), can take on meaning in a number of different ways. In particular, he distinguishes between silence with "propositional content" and silence that is the basis of inferences, and he specifies how silence can become meaningful by convention, by agreement, by declaration, or by implication (1995: 12–23). Tacking between legal language and everyday speech, Tiersma charts the way ordinary linguistic patterns sometimes overlap with formal rules of law pertaining to silence. Here I will focus on his examples drawn from conversation and contract law, on the one hand, and his analysis of how the US law of agency infers acquiescence from silence, on the other hand.

Some background on the anthropological linguistic perspective that I'll be applying to these examples is in order. An important strand of thought in linguistic anthropology has been the exploration of the crucial role of contextual and metalinguistic levels in shaping how we understand each other (Silverstein 1976, 1993; Lucy 1993; Mertz 1985). Linguists speak of the contextual aspect of meaning as the "pragmatic" level; it is that aspect which relies upon the actual context of speech or writing. Thus, words like "here" and "there" or "you" and "I" generally require some information about the contexts in which they are being used in order for us to pinpoint their meaning. If we take the "meta-" level of language to be the way that language points to itself as it is used, then the "meta*pragmatic*" level is the way that language points to its own contextual character as it is used. An example of this is what anthropological linguists have called "linguistic ideologies"—that is, reflexive ideas about how language operates in social contexts (Silverstein 1979; Woolard and Schieffelin 1994; Schieffelin, Woolard, and Kroskrity 1998; Woolard 1998). If I think that a kind of speech is indicative of a kind of person, this is a linguistic ideology linking language with identity. If I don't consciously articulate this idea, but suddenly become condescending to someone who speaks in a certain way, this is simply an unconscious version of this ideology. At its most subtle levels, metapragmatic function and structure in language turn out to anchor much of linguistic interaction, according to this anthropological research (Lucy 1993; Silverstein 1993).

So, then, let's return to two of Tiersma's examples of legally meaningful silence. In the area of contract law, he offers a fascinating and insightful comparison between the laws governing whether a contract has been formed and tacit understandings regarding turn-taking in everyday conversations (1995: 24–31). Conversation analysts studying ordinary conversations in the United States have documented a set of "normal" understandings of how turn-taking works in those conversations. The first turn is not usually a silent one. The person who speaks first in a sense "takes the floor" and has control over subsequent turn-taking for a time.[2] In contract law, the first turn of contract formation is an "offer" (implying speech or writing, not silence); if the person to whom a question is addressed ("Want to go to dinner now?") fails to answer, in general, that silence cannot be taken to indicate acquiescence (absent some other specific signaling to the contrary). Without further contextual information to give other meaning to silence, silence in response to an offer does not indicate consent. Within the "economy" of turn-taking in conversations, the person who occupies the first part of something called a "pair-part" (i.e., question/answer, apology/acceptance, etc.) puts a kind of linguistic offer on the table; if the person to whom a question is addressed ("Want to go to dinner now?") fails to answer, that silence cannot be taken to indicate acquiescence. Underlying this tacit understanding is a complex set of metapragmatic structures, which interestingly have to be made explicit in legal settings.

In our second example, we focus on a situation in which law deems silence to be meaningful. In the law of agency, a principal (e.g., an employer) is ordinarily not bound to agreements made by his or her agent (e.g., employee) if the agent acted outside of the authority granted by the principal. However, if the principal fails to object when learning that an agent has exceeded that authority, this silence can legally serve as a kind of consent to, or ratification of, that out-of-bounds behavior. As Tiersma notes, the Second Restatement of Agency, an authoritative text summarizing the law in this area, explained this as follows: "[p]ersons ordinarily express dissent to acts done on their behalf which they have not authorized or of which they do not approve" (American Law Institute 1957: Section 43, comment a). Note that this statement is a metapragmatic description: it describes the way language does (or should?) function in particular social situations. There is no empirical evidence offered to support this proposition, nor is there any concern expressed about whether this approach to dissenting is widely shared across all sections of the population. In a fascinating way, it serves simultaneously as description and norm. Of course, as Tiersma points out—and as is amply borne out by research in sociolinguistics and anthropological linguistics—there is quite a bit of variation in why and whether persons might express dissent in such situations. But here law "naturalizes" what is in fact a normative decision about how to describe "what people ordinarily do" (or, more accurately, say). Something that is social, political, contextual, and contingent is represented as just natural—just "the way things are."

Thus Tiersma's article gives us a series of wonderful examples of how law copes with the tacit linguistic ideologies and norms that do so much of the regimenting of everyday speech through many layers of metapragmatic structuring (see Silverstein 1993). Formal law in the United States, then, renders the highly contextual metalinguistic norms and structures of human interaction at what we might call the "type" level; it has to freeze and typify very malleable aspects of linguistic meaning (see Parmentier 1994). In doing this, it erases meaningful differences among people as to those very norms and structures; there are systematic reasons why some people can speak up and others can't when they disagree with aspects of what is happening. The complexities of how and when a turn in conversation actually counts as the "first turn" (and how and whether having the first turn gives speakers control over subsequent turns) are myriad, but we struggle through those complexities in everyday speech against a rough backdrop of broad metalinguistic norms. How fascinating it is to find that taken-for-granted versions of these conversational norms in ordinary conversation have been translated into the formal rules of contract formation. And how important it is to consider the many contextual variables omitted in these formulations—from how ongoing relationships alter those norms (see, e.g., Macaulay 1985) to how differences in power matter to the meanings of silence.

## Notes

1. Tiersma cites the famous linguist Ferdinand de Saussure, who said: "So it is not even necessary to have a material sign in order to give expression to an idea: the language may be content simply to contrast something with nothing" (1986: 86) (the slightly different wording is due to the fact that I use a different edition than did Tiersma).

2. Conversation analysis itself has underlying tacit metapragmatic features, which have at times received attention in the literature; thus the idea that conversation involves a perpetual struggle for control of the "floor" does not always map well onto how participants themselves might view a conversation. However, the framework of conversation analysis does give us a grid from which to examine those instances.

## References

American Law Institute (1957) *Restatement (Second) of Agency*. Philadelphia: ALI.

Lucy, John (1993) Reflexive Language and the Human Disciplines. In *Reflexive Language*, ed. John Lucy, 9–32. New York: Cambridge University Press.

Macaulay, Stewart (1985) An Empirical View of Contract (1985) *Wisconsin Law Review* 1985: 465–482.

Mertz, Elizabeth (1985) Beyond Symbolic Anthropology: Introducing Semiotic Mediation. In *Semiotic Mediation: Sociocultural and Psychological Perspectives*, ed. Elizabeth Mertz and Richard Parmentier, 1–19. New York: Academic Press.

Parmentier, Richard (1994) *Signs in Society: Studies in Semiotic Anthropology*. Bloomington, Ind.: Indiana University Press.

Saussure, Ferdinand de (1986) *Course in General Linguistics*, ed. Charles Balley and Albert Sechehaye; trans. Roy Harris. Chicago: Open Court.

Schieffelin, Bambi, Kathryn Woolard, and Paul Kroskrity, eds. (1998) *Language Ideologies: Practice and Theory*. Oxford: Oxford University Press.

Silverstein, Michael (1976) Shifters, Verbal Categories, and Cultural Description. In *Meaning in Anthropology*, ed. Keith Basso and Henry Selby, Jr., 11–55. Albuquerque, NM: University of New Mexico Press.

Silverstein, Michael (1979) Language Structure and Linguistic Ideology. In *The Elements: A Parasession on Linguistic Units and Levels*, ed. Paul Clyne, William Hanks, and Carol Hofbauer, 193–247. Chicago: Chicago Linguistic Society.

Silverstein, Michael (1993) Metapragmatic Discourse and Metapragmatic Function. In *Reflexive Language: Reported Speech and Metapragmatics*, ed. John Lucy, 33–58. New York: Cambridge University Press.

Tiersma, Peter (1995) The Language of Silence, *Rutgers Law Review* 48: 1–99.

Woolard, Kathryn (1998) Language Ideology as a Field of Inquiry. In *Language Ideologies: Practice and Theory*, ed. Bambi Schieffelin, Kathryn Woolard, and Paul Kroskrity, 3–47. Oxford: Oxford University Press.

Woolard, Kathryn and Bambi Schieffelin (1994) Language Ideology. *Annual Review of Anthropology* 23: 55–82.

19

# The Sounds of Silence
Malcolm Coulthard

To be invited to contribute to a volume for Peter Tiersma is a daunting honour. He is the master of elegant argument and expression and a past master at choosing memorable examples—who can forget the Roman freeing his slave with a compulsory speech act realised by silence? Indeed, I was tempted to submit just an intriguing title and leave it to my readers to supply their own interesting content on the basis that "in some cases, silence . . . is used to communicate a relatively specific message" (Tiersma 1995: 6).

All of Tiersma's writings are excellent teaching texts—the bibliography for my current forensic linguistics course includes five of his publications, plus, of course, the magnificent book, *The Oxford Handbook on Language and Law* (Tiersma and Solan 2012). I have also long admired Tiersma's involvement in the re-drafting of the California Pattern Jury Instructions and always encourage my students to undertake research that will similarly have an impact outside the narrowly defined academic context. I am therefore delighted that three of my Brazilian doctoral students, introduced early to Tiersma, have chosen to research in topics related to silence, including the socially important areas of police interviewing, product warnings, and plagiarism.

## The Right to Silence

The Brazilian constitution asserts that an *"arrestee will be informed of his/her rights, among which is the right to remain silent,"* (translation quoted from Jorge 2014). However, unlike in the United States and the United Kingdom, in Brazil there is no fixed text for police officers to recite, nor detailed instructions about how the right is to be conveyed and when. But, as all know from the writings of Ainsworth (2010), Shuy (1997), and

Tiersma (op. cit.) on the Miranda warnings, the fact that suspects are told they have "the right to remain silent" doesn't mean they actually do so in practice, and confessions made before the reading of the Rights have been ruled admissible.

This is similar in Brazil. Although there is a law affirming that unlawful evidence, that is evidence obtained through violation of the constitutional norms, will not be accepted and should be disregarded in the criminal process (Jorge op. cit.), it is not difficult to find cases where appeals against conviction have been denied on the grounds that the confession was a "voluntary act." In our interactions with Brazilian police, we are urging them to adopt the English three-part model of: performing a fixed text; following this up, before any questioning begins, with a detailed explanation given by the police officer; and, essentially, rigorous enforcement by the judiciary, who must reject all evidence collected from suspects before they were cautioned.

Those who have never been arrested may wonder why anyone would ever say anything to a police officer after being told not only "You do not have to say anything" but also "Anything you do say may be given in evidence." Yet at the same time, as Tiersma points out,

> People commonly assume that someone who is wrongly accused of a crime would welcome the opportunity to explain why she is innocent; the defendant's silence thus supports an inference of guilt (op. cit. 10).

Indeed, this "commonsense" view is embodied in a sentence added to the English Police Caution some 20 years ago: "but it may harm your defence if you do not mention when questioned something which you later rely on in court" (English Police Caution, 1994 Revision).

As a result, English juries are now told they can make inferences from the accused's silence when being interviewed, even though at the same time they are not allowed to make any inferences from the other silence that Tiersma mentions—the option not to give evidence in one's own defence.

There is a more subtle point to be made about silence. The majority of jurisdictions in the world allow the police to summarise what was said; indeed, in Brazil any speech that is actually reported appears only in indirect form in the third person—in other words the suspect does not have a "voice." By contrast, for over a hundred years English judges have insisted on a verbatim record being made of the suspect's locutions and not simply of his illocutions and perlocutions as interpreted by the interviewing officer. This access to the suspect's voice is now embodied in the requirement in England that all significant interviews be audio-recorded.

There is one more point to be made about silence, which my colleagues in Aston University are currently working on with the local police. As noted above, the suspect in England is warned, "it may harm your defence if you do not mention when questioned something which you later rely on in court," yet it is the police officer who controls the interview and he typically sees his task as needing to find more evidence to support a prosecution. Thus, he often talks across attempts by the suspect to provide what seem at the time to be irrelevant details. As Haworth (2010) points out, the police should give the suspect a chance to contribute whatever evidence s/he may think relevant.

We now have contact with two lecturers at police academies in Brazil and Mozambique, both, highly unusually, trained to the doctoral level in linguistics, and we are working with them to try to introduce changes to the system.

### Silent Warnings

Tiersma observes that an adequate warning is one "whose content is understandable" and which conveys "a fair indication of the nature and extent of the danger" to the reader (2002: 55). The problem is that some product warnings are crucially silent, or, as Tiersma puts it, violate the "maxim of quantity," either by providing no information at all and/or allowing the reader to make incorrect inferences (see Coulthard 2014 and Coulthard and Hagemeyer 2013 for a detailed discussion of a set of misinterpretable warnings accompanying a portable BBQ).

Using observations on warnings by Dumas (2010), Shuy (2008), and Tiersma (op. cit.), we are analysing, with the aim of improving, some of the guidelines on warnings produced by ANVISA, the Brazilian government's Agency for the Control of Health Products, which is responsible for the guidelines on packages and package inserts. Shuy argues that warnings:

"should identify and describe the nature and danger of the risk. Then they should tell the reader how to avoid it" (2008: 72). Hagemeyer (2014) examines the ANVISA instructions for hair dye warnings and their realisation on three products. One of the required ANVISA warnings is *do not use on eyelashes and eyebrows*. Note that nothing is officially required by ANVISA in this warning about the nature of the risk involved. In fact, only one of the three products we examined spelled out the risk, which turns out to be severe—*not following these instructions can lead to blindness*. In her work on cigarette warnings in the 1990's, Dumas criticised the use of factual statements including technical terms, like "Cigarettes produce carbon monoxide" with no explanation of the significance to be attributed to this statement. This problem is still alive and kicking in ANVISA-approved warnings labels—labels are required to list the contents, but not to indicate the potential dangers. Thus:

"Contains phenilenodiamines, resorcinol and ammonia"[;]
"Contains ammonia. May contain: diaminotoluenes, resorcinol and phenilenodiamines."

Improving the underlying rationale for ANVISA guidelines will be a major linguistic challenge.

## Silent Witness

Plagiarism is a crime that is largely ignored in Brazilian universities (Abreu 2014)—very few use detection software, there are few systematic attempts to teach students how to avoid unintentional plagiarism, and little guidance exists on how to deal with cases of plagiarism when they arise.

Essentially, plagiarism is a crime of silence, a crime where one author passively denies credit for ideas or their textual encoding. I can imagine this might be a controversial assertion, but it was an idea that came to me as I was reading "The Language of Silence." On page 19 Tiersma refers to the analysis of spoken discourse using the terms *exchange* and *initiation/response*. I immediately recognised these as terms I had coined in the early 1970s and first published in Sinclair and Coulthard (1975). Out of interest I looked to the footnote to see what attribution there was, because anyone publishing in the field of linguistics would reference the 1975 Sinclair and Coulthard volume, but I saw only a reference to Jan Rankema's *Discourse Studies* (1993). Was this, I wondered, a case of an independent researcher devising the same categorisation system twenty years later, or was this plagiarism through silence?

What we do know is that we want our students to be able to reference correctly, so that silence can always be reliably interpreted as plagiarism. Currently, we are studying the English tertiary education system, where a combination of systematic use of detection software and explicit instruction about plagiarism and citation conventions has, over a ten-year period, halved the incidence of detected plagiarism (Abreu op. cit.). Our long-term aim is to produce a prevention/detection solution that consists of teaching materials for students and guidelines for staff on both how to reduce and deal with incidents of plagiarism and how to work with detection software.

"But now, for me, the rest is silence" (Coulthard 1985: 192).

## References

Abreu, B. (in preparation) ms chapter from *How to Become a Writer?: Investigating Plagiarism in the Academic Context*, draft doctoral thesis.

Ainsworth, Janet (2010) Curtailing Coercion in Police Interrogation: The Failed Promise of *Miranda v Arizona*. In Coulthard Johnson (eds.), 111–125.

Coulthard, Malcolm (1985) *An Introduction to Discourse Analysis* (2nd ed.). London: Longman.

Coulthard, Malcolm ( 2014) Have You Been Warned? In Casesnoves, R, M Forcadell, and N. Gavaldà (eds), *Ens Queda la Paraula. Estudis de Lingüística Aplicada en Honor a M. Teresa Turell*. Barcelona, IULA, Universitat Pompeu Fabra, 253–64

Coulthard, Malcolm and Alison Johnson, eds. (2010) *The Routledge Handbook of Forensic Linguistics*. New York: Routledge.

Coulthard, Malcolm and C. Hagemeyer (2013) PERIGO, CUIDADO, ATENÇÃO: a comunicação linguística de risco em advertências de produtos. *Cadernos de Linguagem e Sociedade* 14: 28–53.

Dumas, Bethany K. (2010) Consumer Product Warnings: Composition, Identification, and Assessment of Adequacy. In Coulthard and Johnson (eds.), 365–377.

Hagemeyer, C. (in preparation) ms chapter from *You Have Been Warned, or Have You? Product Warning Labels: Language, Components and Adequacy*, draft doctoral thesis.

Haworth, Kate (2010) Police Interviews as Evidence. In Coulthard and Johnson (eds.), 169–181.

Jorge, S. (in preparation) ms chapter from *A Study of Interviewing in Brazilian Police Stations Devoted Exclusively to Women*, draft doctoral thesis.

Renkema, Jan (1993) *Discourse Studies: An Introduction*. Amsterdam: John Benjamins.

Shuy, Roger (1990) Warning Labels: Language, Law and Comprehensibility, *American Speech* 65: 291–303.

Shuy, Roger (1997) Ten Unanswered Linguistic Questions about Miranda, *Forensic Linguistics* 4: 175–195.

Shuy, Roger (2008) *Fighting over Words*. New York: Oxford University Press.

Sinclair, John and Malcolm Coulthard (1975) *Towards an Analysis of Discourse*. London: Oxford University Press.

Tiersma, Peter M. (1995) The Language of Silence, *Rutgers Law Review* 48: 1–99.

Tiersma, Peter M. (1999) *Legal Language*. Chicago: University of Chicago Press

Tiersma, Peter M. (2002) The Language and Law of Product Warnings, in *Language in the Legal Process* (Janet Cotterill, ed.). New York: Palgrave Macmillan, 54–71.

Tiersma, Peter M. and Lawrence M. Solan (2012) *The Oxford Handbook of Language and Law*. Oxford: Oxford University Press.

# 20

# Speech or Silence

## WITHIN AND BEYOND LANGUAGE AND LAW

## Meizhen Liao

Reading Peter Tiersma's "The Language of Silence" (1995) and also his "Nonverbal Communication and the Freedom of 'Speech'" (1993) is a refreshing, intellectual, and enlightening journey. It is as if you revisit your hometown or your home village after having left it many years ago when you were young: you find the old, intimate, and time-honored willow trees still standing on the bank of the old familiar ponds and the old, mystic, and mossy Buddhist temple, but you are also enthralled by the new exotic villas you would never expect to see, the broad lighted avenues instead of those old narrow and shabby lanes, and the blue clear and straight river running by the village, which used to be muddy and rampant with wild plants. The things familiar to me in Tiersma's papers are the linguistic theories and models he adopted, which are tools I often use in my professional work. The unexpected changes are his creative and innovative application of the models and theories to the analysis and solution of real, important, even pressing controversial legal problems. Tiersma's paper strikes me as a masterful synthesis of linguistics and law, an excellent example of interdisciplinary study.

We can identify at least two main approaches to language and law research. The first approaches legal language from the perspective of the unique or exotic features of the language used in the legal context focusing on the language itself and the mechanisms by which law operates through language. Normally this approach is adopted by those scholars whose careers are in linguistics. The second approach also deals with legal issues from a linguistic perspective, as law is inseparable from the language with which it is constituted. This approach, however, is adopted largely by those trained as jurists and those with training in both jurisprudence and linguistics, and engages both the areas of linguistics and law in a significant way.

Tiersma's research is a perfect example of what can happen when the two approaches are combined. He makes full use of his linguistic knowledge in the service of understanding and critiquing law, providing new insights into legal problems that challenge judges, legislators, and legal scholars. In doing so, he extends the application of linguistic theories and models well beyond the ordinary boundaries of the discipline of linguistics. Hence, his work has implications for both the study of language and the study of law and are of interest to both fields and beyond.

For Tiersma is not only an expert in the grammar of sounds—his original field of study was phonetics—but also an artist of the grammar of silence. He has made an exhaustive study of the various ways in which people communicate through their silence, adding his own significant observations to those made in previous studies on silence or nonverbal communication.

Tiersma's work on silence is an excellent example of problem-oriented research, tackling a matter that is of importance to both theory and practice. Silence and its interpretation may not be routinely recognized as a problematic issue in ordinary life, but in a legal context, silence often has serious consequences. In the developing literature on nonverbal communication, the question of how people can communicate by their failure to speak—by their silence—has been under-studied. When people communicate, whether by means of language or through nonverbal behavior such as gesture, they actively convey information. How is it then possible for people to communicate by doing nothing—by the absence of language or gesture? In answering that question, Tiersma has identified the many ways in which silence can be legally significant. His exhaustive study of the meanings of silence promotes better understanding of when the law should require overt communication rather than merely drawing inferences from silence. His conclusion—that for silence to be considered legally relevant communication, meaning must be ascribed to it in fairly predictable ways—creates at least some assurance that the actor who remained silent is likely trying to communicate an identifiable message through that silence.

This understanding of the use of silence can have very important legal implications. Although Tiersma was considering the role of the interpretation of silence in the Anglo-American legal system, his arguments also have implications for the Chinese legal system. Beginning with his framework, I would like to take this opportunity to build upon it and make a related point, introducing the principle of goal direction for the study of communication.

## Encourage Speaking Rather than Silence

By definition, language is vocal. Hence, the language of silence is actually a metaphor. Human beings are designed to be speaking animals. Law should encourage people to speak rather than making inferences from silence, so that lawsuits marred by misunderstandings and misconceptions based on unreliable inferences from silence will be reduced, and even perhaps over time disappear. As Tiersma (1995: 97) observed, "many instances of legally significant silence have turned out to involve inference rather than communication." Drawing inferences from non-communicative behavior can be a dangerous endeavor. In China, I suggest an ideal of law not for the sake of law, or not even for the sake of rule of law, but instead an ideal of law for the sake of no law—a world where, as a result of enlightened law, human beings become so emancipated both physically and spiritually, so enlightened and so self-disciplined, that law or even the mere idea of law would seem shameful and unnecessary. This is a dream that can never be realized by silence, but using language or speaking definitely can move us toward achieving it.

## The Principle of Goal-Direction and Goal Analysis

When law encourages speaking, which is communication through action, action-oriented research paradigms may be used to illuminate the problematic nature of attempting to draw communicative inferences from silence. Communication presupposes a sender and a receiver of the information transmitted. Normally, the sender is responsible for communicating, and the receiver is responsible for the inference. What characterizes action—including communication through action—is its intentionality, the intention to represent and the intention to communicate(Searle 1969, 1983). Meaning, which is so important in communication, is derived from or *is* intentionality. So it is intentionality that distinguishes communication from non-communication. Based on this fact, I have posited the Principle of Goal Direction (Liao 2004, 2005, 2009, 2010). The Principle of Goal Direction is formulated as:

> Every act of rational human communication carries the guarantee that it is goal-oriented.

According to this principle, speaking or communication is an activity of expressing, pursuing, negotiating, and realizing one's goals. Thus, the most important aspect of communication study is goal analysis, including how those goals are expressed, pursued, negotiated, or realized. The corollaries of this principle are as follows: (1) the meaning of an utterance or action is related to or resides in the goals expressed and pursued; (2) any text or talk should be seen as a hierarchical system of goals; (3) coherence of a text or talk is assessed by whether the utterances are related with the super goals of the text or talk; (4) the interpersonal relationship in which the language occurs should be examined or evaluated in terms of whether the participants' goals are shared or convergent, conflicting or divergent, or neutral; and (5) the most important element of context is found in a consideration of the participants' goals. This model has been applied to analysis of Chinese courtroom discourse and has proven to be useful in addressing some of the challenges faced in attempting to apply the Principle of Cooperation in communicative interaction posited by Grice (1975) and the Universal Pragmatics Model of Habermas (1987) in the context of analyzing trial communication.

In my view, the articles under consideration would have benefited from a closer examination of the goals of the speaker's silence or attempt at nonverbal communication.

### References

Grice, H. P. (1975) Logic and Conversation. In P. Cole and J. Morgan (eds.), Syntax and Semantics 3: Speech Acts 41–58. New York: Academic Press.

Habermas, Jürgen (1979) *Communication and the Evolution of Society.* Toronto: Beacon Press.

Habermas, Jürgen (1987) *The Theory of Communicative Action, Vol. 2: Life World and System: A Critique of Functionalist Reason* (T. McCarthy, trans.). Boston: Beacon Press.

Liao, Meizhen (2004) The Principle of Goal Direction and Cooperation in Chinese Courtroom Trial Discourse. *Foreign Language Research* 5: 43–52.

Liao, Meizhen (2005) The Principle of Goal Direction and Goal Analysis: A New Way of Doing Pragmatics. *Rhetorical Learning* 3: 1–10, 4: 5–11.

Liao, Meizhen (2009) The Principle of Goal Direction and Communication. *Foreign Language Research* 4: 62–64, 6: 101–109.

Liao, Meizhen (2010) The Principle of Goal Direction and Dynamics of Context. *Journal of PLA University of Foreign Languages.* Volume 33: 4.

Searle, John (1969) *Speech Acts: An Essay in the Philosophy of Language.* Cambridge: Cambridge University Press.

Searle, John (1983) *Intentionality: An Essay in the Philosophy of Mind.* Cambridge: Cambridge University Press.

Tiersma, Peter Meijes (1993) Nonverbal Communication and the Freedom of "Speech," *Wisconsin Law Review* 1993: 1525–1569.

Tiersma, Peter Meijes (1995) The Language of Silence, *Rutgers Law Review* 48: 1–99.

# Consenting

21

# The Language of Consent in Rape Law*
Peter M. Tiersma

Perhaps the most important feature of the word *consent* is that it describes a state of mind. It is not primarily a performative verb. Of course, it is possible to consent by saying "I consent." So it might be more accurate to say that *consent* can be used in either a descriptive or performative sense. For our purposes, the critical point is that a person can consent without saying so, as reflected in the adage "silence is consent."

Compare consenting to promising. Promising is not a mental state. If I commit myself mentally to doing something for you, I have not promised, except perhaps in the derivative sense of promising myself to do something. Generally, for me to promise something, I have to communicate my commitment to the recipient of the promise. I do not, of course, have to use the word *promise*. But I do have to use words of some sort, or use actions that can communicate prepositional content. To consent, on the other hand, it usually suffices to have the right state of mind. *Consent* is like *believe* or *think*. I can say that I believe or think something, but I can also just believe or think it, without communicating my belief or thought to anyone.

Of course, there are many situations in which consent is expressed in words or actions. In fact, it may be legally required for consent to be expressed, sometimes orally, and sometimes also in writing. By way of illustration, the words "written consent" occur over 850 times in the statutes of California.[1] Rape law, in contrast, does not require written consent, or even express consent (that is, consent in words). It merely requires a certain state of mind.

It is instructive to compare the verb *consent* with *agree*. Consenting usually involves submitting to someone else's initiative or plan. It suggests that one person is proposing a course of action and that the other is going along

---

* Excerpt from The Language of Consent in Rape Law. In Janet Cotterill (ed.), *The Language of Sexual Crime* 91-97 (2007).

with it, or at least allowing it to happen. Although it need not invariably be the case, the person who consents often takes a relatively passive role. As Anna Wierzbicka (1987: 112) has pointed out, "consent implies a position of dependence on the part of the addressee." In contrast, she observes that agreeing generally involves a more symmetrical or reciprocal relationship. At the same time, she notes that *consent* does not just involve allowing an act to take place: "*consent* implies a more active kind of support than *permission*" (1987: 113). The latter distinction is important, because some courts seem to believe that it is enough for a woman to permit a man to carry out his sexual plans. Indeed, in many ways the resistance requirement is more consistent with permission, which is not the legal standard, than it is with consent.

In any event, the notion of consent remains problematic because, even if it is viewed as requiring support for the man's plan, the act of consenting is a mental state that may or may not be expressed verbally. Perhaps some of the difficulties with consent in rape law could be solved by requiring that consent must be made explicitly in words (see Remick, 1993). I t can be very challenging to determine a person's mental state by means of inferences from his or her conduct.

Yet there are some serious drawbacks to this proposal. One is that the language that people use to discuss sexual matters is typically vague and indirect. Although our society is no doubt changing in this regard, many people in Western society still consider it taboo to talk explicitly about sexual acts, even when they are engaging in them. In English we have a huge number of euphemisms for sexual acts. Moreover, some people seem to consider direct talk about sexual relations unromantic, especially in a dating situation.

Thus, many people in our society typically discuss sex—if they do so at all—by means of euphemism, double entendre, innuendo, or subtle suggestion. At least at the current stage of human development, it seems unlikely that the legal system could require men to obtain verbal consent, with the penalty for not doing so being a prosecution for rape.[2] There is, in addition, the consideration that if a man can force or intimidate a woman into having sex with him, he can certainly force or intimidate her into saying "I consent." In that case, the issue at trial would be whether she *really* consented, or whether she just *said* she consented because of pressure from the defendant. We would essentially be back where we started: debating whether the woman had a state of mind described by the word "consent."

We might also place the burden on women to verbally object if they do *not* consent. Under this approach, a woman could stop any unwanted sexual advances by saying "no" or "stop." If the man continues, he would be guilty of some kind of sexual crime, depending on what he did exactly. If he stops, he would be safe from prosecution. Like requiring express consent, this proposal would simplify matters by creating a bright-line rule. In that sense, it is similar to the former "physical resistance" rule. But it is unrealistic for the same reason that requiring verbal consent is unrealistic: it is not consistent with behaviour in our society; people do not always speak so clearly. It also places an unfair burden on women, who may be too intimidated by a man to verbally object.

If verbal standards are ultimately unworkable, we are left with a situation in which people often communicate consent indirectly, or where they signal their intentions by their actions, and perhaps even their silence. This may require that the man, and subsequently the jury, infer the woman's mental state from what she says or does. We have already mentioned some of the problems of using inferences to determine consent or lack thereof. There is also a substantial literature containing linguistic or sociolinguistic analyses of rape trials that highlight the problems associated with inferential reasoning in this situation. Susan Ehrlich, for instance, reports on alleged cases of date rape, involving the same man but two different women, that took place on or near a college campus in Canada. She points out that defence attorneys and, in this case, members of a university disciplinary tribunal, often interrogated the women about what they did *not* do or say. Why did one of the women not cry out or yell, for instance, when there were people around who could have helped her? Why didn't she explicitly tell the man that she did not want to have sex with him, rather than saying merely that she had a class in the morning and he had better leave? (Ehrlich 2001: 79, 86–7). Ehrlich concludes that the utmost resistance requirement is still discursively present, even if no longer explicitly required by law (2001: 92).

Yet it seems that as long as consent remains an element of rape law, we will have to use logical inferences to decide the woman's state of mind. The fact that a woman does not scream or yell or try to leave is at least somewhat relevant in this endeavour; these facts support an inference that she consented. In a situation where there is little coercion, where the man is not intimidating, the door is unlocked, he has no weapons and makes no threats, and there are other people nearby, it seems natural to draw a fairly strong inference of consent if a woman does not scream, yell, say "stop," or try to leave. As the environment becomes more coercive, that inference becomes correspondingly weaker or disappears entirely. If a man is holding a gun to a woman's head, it seems ludicrous to infer consent from her failure to cry out.

That we use inferences to determine consent is unavoidable. What is often objectionable is that in the context of rape law, these inferences may rest on questionable or offensive (some would say patriarchal) assumptions. These include the fact that a woman was hitchhiking, wore sexy clothing, invited the man to her room, was sexually experienced, and so forth (Estrich 1987: 121–48). A particularly egregious example is a recent case in which a Texas judge determined that a woman's request that a man use a condom was evidence of consent, despite the fact that he had threatened her with violence (see Da Luz and Weckerly 1993).

One solution to the problem is to limit the jury's access to facts from which questionable inferences could be drawn. Rape shield laws are an example: they typically exclude certain facts from evidence. This is a rather paternalistic response, of course, because it suggests that the jury cannot be trusted with the information. And the suspicion that relevant evidence is being withheld from them may make the jury speculate about what they are missing. Nonetheless, it is not the only type of information that is withheld from jurors, and in the case of rape shield laws it seems like the right thing to do.

A somewhat different approach is to admit the facts into evidence, but to warn the jury to be cautious in drawing an inference from them. Following the notorious "condom" case in Texas, the California legislature enacted a statute that provided as follows: "evidence that the victim suggested, requested, or otherwise communicated to the defendant that the defendant use a condom or other birth control device, without additional evidence of consent, is not sufficient to constitute consent."[3] Nonetheless, although such rules of evidence are helpful, they cannot solve the many uncertainties surrounding consent. There are just too many inferences that can be drawn from too many differing factual situations.

A final observation that I would like to make about consent is that it can be either voluntary or involuntary. At first, the notion of involuntary consent might seem to be an oxymoron. Isn't consent voluntary by definition? Most of us have the notion that consent at least *ought* to be a matter of free will, uninfluenced by force, intimidation, or other pressure. That is certainly the ideal. But sometimes we can, by the exercise of our free will, consent to have something happen that we would rather not have happen. We do so because preventing the undesirable act would have even worse consequences than allowing it. In that case, we might say that although we consented, it was not really voluntary. And if the event or state of affairs that induced us to consent was coercive or illegal, we could later argue that our consent should not be considered valid.

Lest this discussion seem a bit esoteric, let me give an actual legal example: consent to search. In the United States, police may search a person or a person's car or house only under specified circumstances. Otherwise the search would be illegal. If the police have no legal basis for a search, they can request consent to search. If the person consents, what would otherwise be illegal is now acceptable, and any evidence found during the search is admissible.

The obvious danger with consensual searches is that people may consent because they believe they have no real choice in the matter, especially if a uniformed police officer requests their permission alongside a busy highway in the middle of the night. The United States Supreme Court has addressed this concern by holding the government must show that the consent was voluntary. Elsewhere, Lawrence Solan and I have discussed some of the linguistic problems raised by consensual searches and the voluntariness requirement (Tiersma and Solan 2004). My point here is merely that the legal system recognises that consent can be either voluntary or involuntary.

Of course, whether someone consents involuntarily, or does not consent at all, can be a subtle distinction. It might even seem to be a trivial distinction. Normally, it does not matter whether a driver refuses to consent to a search, for instance, or consents involuntarily. In either case, the subsequent search is invalid.

But sometimes the distinction between nonconsent and involuntary consent matters. An illustration is the distinction between robbery and extortion. The prototypical robbery occurs when the perpetrator stops someone on the street and threatens that person with violence unless the person gives the perpetrator money or some other item of value. Extortion, on the other hand, usually takes place in private and involves the perpetrator threatening to expose a secret about someone unless that person gives the perpetrator money or some other item of value. These crimes closely resemble each other, but there is an interesting difference with respect to consent. The California Penal Code defines robbery as "the felonious taking of personal property in the possession of another, from his person or immediate presence, and *against his will*, accomplished by means of force or fear."[4] California law defines "against a person's will" as "without consent."[5] Extortion, on the other hand, is defined as "the obtaining of property from another, *with his consent*, or the obtaining of an official act of a public officer, induced by a wrongful use of force or fear, or under color of official right."[6] Thus, robbery involves obtaining property from someone *without consent*, whereas extortion involves obtaining property *with consent*.

Rape and other sexual crimes are almost universally defined as being "against the will" of the woman or "without her consent." Thus, while the law in other areas distinguishes between acts done *without* the consent of the victim, and acts done with the *involuntary* consent of the victim, the law of rape has traditionally not drawn this distinction.

To summarise our discussion so far, consent (at least in rape law) is essentially a mental state, not a speech act. Because what goes on in a person's mind is not directly observable, a person's mental state must be determined by inferences based on the person's speech and conduct. The inferences that people draw are dependent on their beliefs about how people act or should act in specific situations. In the context of rape law, such inferences may be based on incorrect information or might be objectionable for other reasons. As a consequence, the law's dependence on consent, which persists even after widespread reform, is problematic. Finally, I have argued that consent can be either voluntary or involuntary.

Despite all these difficulties, we cannot eliminate consent completely, it seems to me, because consent is ultimately what distinguishes a very ordinary human activity from a serious crime. I will therefore suggest that the legal system should acknowledge that consent is critical, rather than try to avoid it, but at the same time redefine the crime of rape so that consent plays a very different role.

## Managing Consent

Part of the traditional definition of rape is that the woman did not consent to the intercourse. In cases of sexual violence, especially by a stranger, it seems to me that this is the correct assessment. To the extent that a man physically forces himself on a woman, it is perverse to say that she consented. This is true even when she does not actively resist. In the face of imminent violence, there is no time to think and reach a mental state that we would rationally label "consent."

In the typical date rape scenario, however, the threat—although it may be just as real—may be less immediate. Consequently, it seems to me that a woman who submits to a man in this situation is often consenting—not because she wants to, but because it seems like the best choice under the circumstances. She has weighed her options, and the threat of violence if she refuses, or the possibility that her boss might retaliate against her, or whatever other coercive circumstance exists, leads her to decide that she should consent rather than resist. Yet as in the case of extortion, her consent is involuntary.

The result is that in cases where a woman involuntarily submitted or involuntarily consented to intercourse, her consent is no longer an issue. The prosecution does not need to prove that the woman did not consent; it can concede that the woman consented. Any evidence that relates to the woman's consent or nonconsent should be irrelevant. The only thing that matters would be the amount of force, threat of force, or other coercive device that the defendant used and whether this rendered her consent involuntary. Because the fact of consent could be taken for granted, this approach would help focus the inquiry on the perpetrator's conduct, which is where it properly belongs.

However, there is an additional problem with rape law as presently constituted: all of the emphasis is on the woman's mental state, not the man's. It seems to me that consent, and particularly the voluntariness of consent, are very relevant to rape law. The critical question, however, is not whether the *woman* failed to consent, but rather whether the *man* knew or should have known that this was the case. Virtually all crimes require not only that the defendant have done some act (the *actus reus*), but also that he have had a particular intent or state of mind while performing the act (the *mens rea*). As Susan Estrich has pointed out, rape may be unique in not requiring that the perpetrator have a particular intent.[7]

I would therefore redefine the crime of rape as follows. First, as with current law, there must be a specified sexual act. In addition, I would require that either:

(1) the defendant knew, or reasonably should have known, that the woman did not voluntarily consent to the sexual act; or

(2) the defendant knew, or reasonably should have known, that the woman consented to the sexual act only because of threats, intimidation, or fear caused by the defendant.

The second option could be expanded to include situations where a woman consents because of misrepresentations the man made, for example, or where the man knew or should have known that a woman was not mentally competent.

Rather than avoid consent, my proposal takes it on directly. In cases where a woman resists or says "no," she clearly does not consent, and the man should know it. The fact is that often enough, women *do* resist or refuse to submit voluntarily. Or they make it clear in words that they do not consent. In those cases, consent should not be a major issue and a prosecutor should not normally have trouble convincing a jury to convict. In addition, it reaffirms that where a woman resists or communicates to a man that she is not interested in sex, her actions should count for something in the legal system.

On the other hand, there are situations where, in the face of a man's sexual aggression, a woman is intimidated into doing nothing, or passively goes along with the defendant's wishes because she fears the consequences if she resists or says "no." My proposal essentially neutralises the issue of consent in this context, where it has traditionally been most problematic, by simply admitting the woman consented. It also strikes me as the best description of what is actually happening. Essentially, women in this situation often make a rational choice: that it is better to submit to the defendant's aggression than to risk the possibility of a more severe injury if they refuse. In such cases, it does not matter that she did things that the defendant might argue seemed to him like consent. The critical issue would be whether he reasonably should have known that she consented because of fear or intimidation.

The other advantage to my proposed reformulation is that it directs the inquiry not to what was going on in the woman's mind, but on what the defendant knew or believed, a point also made by Estrich. Not only is this more consistent with other crimes, but it potentially has some other advantages. Issues regarding the victim's credibility continue to be a major concern in this area of the law.[8] At least in theory, requiring that the man, have a certain mental state, rather than the woman, should focus more attention on the man's credibility, and less on the woman's. Finally, my proposal might make men more careful in ambiguous situations. If the issue is what the man knew, or reasonably should have known, men will have a greater incentive to make sure that their potential sexual partner is in fact acting voluntarily, rather than blithely assuming that as long as a woman isn't physically resisting him, he can, in the words of the prosecutor in *Regina v. Doe*, "have his way" with her.

## Notes

1. Westlaw search for the words "written consent" conducted on the database CA-ST on June 26, 2003.

2. It may be possible to do so in more cohesive communities, as has happened at Antioch College in Ohio. See Francis, 1996: 135.

3. Cal. Penal Code sec. 261.7. The same is true of evidence regarding a "current or previous dating relationship." Id., sec. 261.6.

4. Calif. Penal Code § 211 (emphasis added).

5. Calif. Jury Instructions, Criminal, 9.40 (1996).

6. Id., § 518 (emphasis added).

7. See Estrich (1987: 92–104). Estrich argues that the intent of the man should matter, although the exact standard she would propose is not entirely clear to me.

8. See, for example, Matoesian (1993) and Taslitz (1999).

## References

da Luz, C. M. and Weckerly, P. C. (1993) The Texas "Condom-Rape" Case: Caution Construed as Consent, *UCLA Women's Law Journal*, 3: 95–104.

Ehrlich, S. (2001) *Representing Rape: Language and Sexual Consent*. London and New York: Routledge.

Estrich, S. (1987) *Real Rape*. Cambridge, Mass.: Harvard University Press.

Francis, L. (1996) *Date Rape: Feminism, Philosophy, and the Law*. University Park, Pa.: Penn State University Press.

Remick, L. A. (1993) Read Her Lips: An Argument for a Verbal Consent Standard in Rape, *University of Pennsylvania Law Review*, 141(3): 1103–1151.

Tiersma, P. M. and Solan, L. M. (2004) Cops and Robbers: Selective literalism in American Criminal Law, *Law and Society Review*, 38: 229–66.

Wierzbicka, A. (1987) *English Speech Act Verbs*. Sydney: Academic Press.

22

# "Inferring" Consent in the Context of Rape and Sexual Assault

Susan Ehrlich

In spite of widespread reform to rape and sexual assault statutes in the United States and Canada over the last four decades, many theorists have pointed to the "androcentric cultural stereotypes" (Sanday 1996: 285) or the "traditional cultural mythologies about rape" (Comack 1999: 234) that can shape "discretionary decision making" (Caringella 2009: 97–98), often undermining the goals of rape law reform. Peter Tiersma's work (1995, 2007) on consent within the context of sexual assault and rape law has made an invaluable contribution to our understanding of this disjunction between what sociolegal scholars have termed "law on the books" vs. "law in action." In particular, Tiersma (2007: 95) argues that because consent is a mental state and not a speech act, it can only be determined on the basis of inferences, not direct observation. In other words, Tiersma contends that the meaning of consent is underdetermined by linguistic forms alone (i.e., it is not a speech act) and is thus dependent for its full interpretation on inferential processes. And, as McConnell-Ginet (2011, 2014) has demonstrated, ideological assumptions about gender and sexuality can play an important role in the processes that give rise to inferred meanings. In Tiersma's words, "that we use inferences to determine consent is unavoidable. What is often objectionable is that in the context of rape law, these inferences may rest on questionable or offensive (some would say: patriarchal) assumptions" (Tiersma 2007: 93).

In the remainder of this essay, I draw upon data from a Canadian rape trial, *R. v. Ewanchuk*, 1995, as a way of exemplifying how adjudicators in rape trials can "infer" consent based on a complainant's linguistic and non-linguistic conduct. What is particularly interesting about this case vis-à-vis Tiersma's argument is the lower courts' explicit use of the language of inference and implication in determining whether the complainant had consented or not. The two lower courts in the *Ewanchuk* case (the trial court and the Alberta Court of Appeal) acquitted the accused of sexual assault, after which the Supreme Court of Canada overturned this acquittal and convicted him. Significant about the initial acquittal is the lower courts' opinion that the complainant had "implied consent" through what they termed her "conduct." Indeed, the Alberta Court of Appeal, in upholding the trial court's decision, defined "implied consent" as "consent by conduct." Thus, while both lower courts found the complainant to be credible and her fear of the accused to be genuine, they at the same time determined that she had not communicated her fear to the accused. As the trial judge (i.e., the lowest court) said in his ruling:

> All of B's [the complainant's] thoughts, emotions and speculations were very real for her. However, she successfully kept all her thoughts, emotions, and speculations deep within herself. She did not communicate most of her thoughts, emotions and speculations … Like a good actor, she projected an outer image that did not reflect her inner self. B did not communicate to A [the accused] by words, gestures, or facial expressions that she was "frozen" by a fear of force. B did not communicate that she was frozen to the spot, and that fear prevented her from getting up off the floor and walking out of the trailer. (from Reasons for Judgment (Moore, J., C.Q.B.A.), November 10, 1995)

In Ehrlich (2007), I suggest that the picture emerging from this description of the complainant is one of passivity: that is, a woman who keeps all her thoughts and emotions "deep within herself" and does not "communicate most of her thoughts, emotions and speculations" is clearly not initiating sexual activity nor, arguably, is she responding in any active way to the man's sexual advances. However, as indicated above, it was this kind of conduct on the part of the complainant that led the two lower courts to conclude that she "implied consent" to the accused. Tiersma's (1995: 33) comments about how silence (and passivity) acquire meaning are relevant here: he argues that "drawing inferences from silence depends heavily upon the observer's knowledge and experience" and on "social norms." Put somewhat differently, in understanding how consent can be inferred from passivity and silence, it is useful to consider the cultural assumptions or sense-making frameworks upon which such inferences rely. In Ehrlich (2007), I make the argument that culturally normative ideas about women's passive, acquiescing sexuality (Gavey 2005) seemed to be "in play" when the lower courts ruled that a woman who is emotionless and "frozen" in her demeanor *implies* consent. In other words, the trial judge and the Alberta Court of Appeal judges seemed to view sexual passivity as appropriately feminine and, as a result, what the complainant described as submitting to sex out of fear became intelligible to these courts as consenting to sex, or at the least, implying consent to the perpetrator. While the Supreme Court of Canada ultimately overturned the decisions of the two lower courts, arguing that submission or compliance on the part of the complainant did not constitute consent,[1] the kind of "logic" employed by the lower courts is not unusual in the judicial opinions of sexual assault cases more generally (see, for example, Bogoch 2007; Coates 1997; Coates, Bavelas, and Gibson 1994; Coates and Wade 2004) and is revealing of the "questionable or offensive" (Tiersma 2007: 93) cultural assumptions that can underlie such opinions. Moreover, as the work of Ehrlich (2001) and Matoesian (2001) demonstrates, the power of such cultural mythologies is not lost on defense lawyers in rape trials who strategically invoke them in their questioning as a way of undermining the credibility of complainants.

## Note

1. The Supreme Court of Canada held that Canadian law does not recognize consent implied by conduct. Either the complainant consented or she did not. It held further that the law does recognize a defense to rape that the accused mistakenly believed that the complainant had consented. However, this mistake must be grounded in an actual expression of consent—not in the complainant having given up her fight out of fear and resignation. Since the evidence was that she had said "no" to each of the defendant's advances as the assault proceeded, and since, after that, she never affirmatively expressed her consent, the Supreme Court made the unusual move of imposing a judgment of conviction, rather than ordering a new trial. The relevant facts had already been uncovered.

## References

Bogoch, Byrna (2007) The Victim as "Other": Analysis of the Language of Acquittal Decisions in Sexual Offences in the Israeli Supreme Court. In Janet Cotterill (ed.) *The Language of Sexual Crime*, 159–179. Basingstoke, Hampshire: Palgrave Macmillan.

Caringella, Susan (2009) *Addressing Rape Reform in Law and Practice.* New York: Columbia University Press.

Coates, Linda (1997) Causal Attributions in Sexual Assault Trial Judgments. *Journal of Language and Social Psychology*, 16: 278–296.

Coates, Linda, Janet Bavelas, and James Gibson (1994) Anomalous Language in Sexual Assault Trial Judgments. *Discourse & Society*, 5: 189–206.

Coates, Linda and Allan Wade (2004) Telling It Like It Isn't: Obscuring Perpetrator Responsibility for Violent Crime. *Discourse & Society*, 15: 499–526.

Comack, Elizabeth (1999) Theoretical Excursions. In Elizabeth Comack (ed.) *Locating Law: Race/Class/Gender Connections*, 19–68. Halifax, Nova Scotia: Fernwood Publishing.

Ehrlich, Susan (2001) *Representing Rape: Language and Sexual Consent*. London: Routledge.

Ehrlich, Susan (2007) Legal Discourse and the Cultural Intelligibility of Gendered Meanings. *Journal of Sociolinguistics*, 11: 452–477.

Gavey, Nicola (2005) *Just Sex?: The Cultural Scaffolding of Rape*. London: Routledge.

Matoesian, Greg (2001) *Law and the Language of Identity: Discourse in the William Kennedy Smith Rape Trial*. New York: Oxford University Press.

McConnell-Ginet, Sally (2011) *Gender, Sexuality, and Meaning: Linguistic Practice and Politics*. New York: Oxford University Press.

McConnell-Ginet, Sally (2014) Meaning-Making and Ideologies of Gender and Dexuality. In S. Ehrlich, M. Meyerhoff, and J. Holmes (eds.) *The Handbook of Language, Gender and Sexuality* (2nd edition), 316–334. Malden, Mass.: Wiley-Blackwell Publishers.

Sanday, Peggy (1996) *A Woman Scorned: Acquaintance Rape on Trial*. New York: Doubleday.

Tiersma, Peter M. (1995) The Language of Silence. *Rutgers Law Review*, 48: 1–99.

Tiersma, Peter M. (2007) The Language of Consent in Rape Law. In Janet Cotterill (ed.) *The Language of Sexual Crime*, 83–103. Basingstoke, Hampshire: Palgrave Macmillan.

**Cases Cited**

R. v. Ewanchuk (November 7, 1995) Alberta Court of Queen's Bench, Edmonton, Alberta.

23

# Felicitous Consent

Tim Grant and Kerrie Spaul

Within the volume *The Language of Sexual Crime* (2007) edited by Janet Cotterill, Peter Tiersma published a thoughtful paper, The Language of Consent in Rape Law, focusing on the nature of consent in the context of rape and sexual crime. His paper begins with the description of a rape trial at the Old Bailey in London and from this starting point, Tiersma argues for the proposition that "Consent (at least in rape law) is essentially a mental state, not a speech act" (95). He also proposes a reformulation of the law on rape that attempts to shift the focus of the rape trial from the mental state of the victim to the *mens rea* of the accused.

In this brief paper we take issue with Tiersma's contention that consent is in itself a mental state and argue that felicitous consent must be in some way communicated. For Tiersma the communication of consent is a matter of evidence of the mental state, whereas for us the communication is a necessary constitutive element of consenting. Such a communication may fall between a traditional performative speech act and a communicative behaviour, but drawing on the medical literature on presumed consent, we argue that felicitous consent requires some form of communicative act.

Tiersma's criteria for consent as a mental state might be articulated thus:

- ¤ Consent is a response to another's plan.
- ¤ Consent involves submission to that plan.
- ¤ Consent is a mental state and thus may or may not be articulated.
- ¤ Consent may be voluntary, or (under coercion) involuntary. [Tiersma uses the example of robbery, in which involving the threat of violence is not consensual, contrasting this with cases of extortion, in which involuntary consent occurs when the goods are handed over.]

In contrast Cowart (2004) provides an extended discussion of consent as a speech act. Her briefest formulation (520) is intentionalist and contends that consent is

> The giving of permission in response to a request by H to do X, that H does not have a right to perform without permission, but if granted will be performed by H.

Cowart disagrees with Tiersma in two important respects. First, she argues that although the request must be articulated through language, a consenting or refusing response might be made linguistically or through gesture or behaviour. There is, though, a further condition that any such behaviour needs to be a clear indication of permission or refusal. Second, Cowart (2004: 522) rejects the idea of involuntary consent, arguing that

> if she is forced to give permission, especially in instances of coercion or threats, then she is not consenting, but either complying, obeying, surrendering or acquiescing (depending upon the specifics of the situation). However, it is clear that SHE IS NOT CONSENTING.

Tiersma's argument that "consent can be used in either a descriptive or performative sense" rests on "the critical point that a person can consent without saying so" (91). He cites the adage that "silence is consent," (91) which originates with Thomas More. In 1535 More was on trial for high treason and is said to have been asked why, when questioned, he failed to verbally acknowledge Henry VIII's supremacy and authority over the Church. More's response in Latin was *qui tacet consentire videtur*, he who is silent seems to consent (Simpson, 1993).

Tiersma's argument does not rest upon Thomas More, but rather upon a contrast of "consenting" with "promising." Promising, Tiersma argues, requires a verbal component, whereas consenting does not. Thomas More's situation, however, is instructive in the consideration of consent. More was questioned, an adverse inference was drawn from his silence, and his defence was thus harmed. As Kurzon (1998) argues, silence in response to a question is strongly marked as intentional and will typically be interpreted as containing some meaning. Silence in practice may be an inadequate or dangerous response to prosecutorial questioning because it does not constrain any potential meaning and allows prosecutors to select the most damaging possible interpretation available to them.

We agree with Tiersma that persons can consent without saying so, but would argue that some kind of communication of their consent is necessary, and this might amount to something like a non-verbal speech act. In medical contexts, silence in the right circumstances may be constructed as presumed consent. For example, if a medical professional requests a blood sample, an individual might respond by silently rolling up her sleeve and offering her arm. Such a behaviour is communicative in the sense that it helps the practitioner understand the meaning of the patient's silence and it will be understood as indicating consent. Presumed consent in medicine cannot be made where there are no grounds to believe a patient might consent. Pierscionek

(2008) argues that medical-legal "presumption" is "an inference that is made on available facts or evidence." The evidence one provides when asked for blood is communicative behaviour, and so rolling up one's sleeve is unproblematically taken to indicate consent. If, in contrast, one just thinks her consent, sitting silently and without gesture, that is to say, if a person keeps her consenting mental state private from the medical practitioner, then there is no evidence or legal ground upon which to presume her consent. Further to this we would argue that this individual has not consented; uncommunicated consent is no consent at all, but just as speech can be acts, so, too, behaviours can be communicative.

As we've seen, Tiersma and Cowart offer differing contrasts in arriving at their positions on consent: Tiersma contrasts consenting with promising, Cowart (in her consideration of coercion) contrasts consenting with "complying, obeying, surrendering or acquiescing" (522). We would argue that complying, obeying, surrendering, or acquiescing may not require communication on the part of the individual but that in both consenting and promising the communicative aspect is a crucial element.

We are in agreement with both Tiersma and Cowart that "consent" is reactive to another's plan or proposition, but would add a further observation. Consent, we would argue, is socially required only when there is some likelihood of it not being given. In a dating situation some of the potential awkwardness can be explained by the fact that neither party can be sure of the other's response to a sexual advance. Each party believes there is a reasonable possibility that their approach may be turned down and privately knows that such a response is within the range of socially expected responses. In the medical domain treatments may be invasive and the law around medical consent is based upon the autonomy of patients; the act of asking for consent presupposes that some proportion of competent patients is expected to refuse a recommended treatment. In broader contexts, consent is not at issue unless there is some likelihood of refusal. Consent is an expression of a real choice between permission and refusal of someone else's plan and as this choice involves an external agent, it requires an external expression of which option has been selected. On this ground also, we argue that unexpressed or uncommunicated consent is not consent at all, but we continue to maintain that such an expression may be behavioural.

The contrasts between the positions here can be illustrated through consideration of three possible assertions[1]:

[1] She consented to his proposals but did not communicate her consent.
[2] She did not consent to his proposals but communicated her consent.
[3] She did not want to consent to his proposals but communicated her consent.

Our understanding is that Tiersma would argue that all three statements represent coherent positions. Our view (and we believe it to be Cowart's as well) would be that statements [1] and [2] are both incoherent. In accordance with our belief in the incoherence of statement [1], we believe Thomas More's response was incoherent and his prosecutors made a reasonable inference from his lack of communication. More's silence did not indicate his consent to Henry VIII's supremacy over the Church because consent requires active communication. Statement [2] is incoherent in the sense that she has indeed consented—the communication constitutes the consent (which is not to say she cannot change her mind and communicate her withdrawal of that consent).

Furthermore, we argue that statement [3] is importantly different from statement [2]. In some circumstance this might represent involuntary consent (for Tiersma), or compliance (for Cowart). Our view here is probably closer to Cowart's, but the important distinction is that we see [3] as a coherent statement and [2] as incoherent. If consent comprised just the mental state, [3] becomes a matter of internal conflict of having an unwanted mental state (and this might be Tiersma's position). In our interpretation, however, the unease caused is a result of the mismatch between the mental state and the external communication. In either case, it is a coherent statement. Tiersma's solution to the issue of judging consent is to shift the focus of the trial onto the defendant—he suggests a new clause on consent, that

> the defendant knew, or reasonably should have known, that the woman did not voluntarily consent to the sexual act. (2007: 96)

The UK Sexual Offences Act 2003, published a couple of years before Tiersma's article but after the time of the trial that he observed at the Old Bailey, seems to be in agreement with his analysis. The section on rape provides that

(1) a person A commits an offence if
    (a) he intentionally penetrates the vagina, anus or mouth of another person (B) with his penis,
    (b) B does not consent to the penetration, and
    (c) A does not reasonably believe that B consents
(2) Whether a belief is reasonable is to be determined having regard to all the circumstances, including any steps A has taken to ascertain whether B consents.

Clauses (1c) and (2) were new in 2003 and echo Tiersma's analysis, but sadly for victims of sexual crime, this shift in UK law has done little to improve conviction rates.

Our concern here has been to maintain that consent is more than a mental state. It involves an act that may be non-verbal but must be communicated. We do not believe that communication of consent requires articulation of consent and whilst we would recognise interpretation of behavioural communication produces complications at law, we feel it reflects the reality of complicated human social and sexual behaviour. Uncommunicated consent is not felicitous consent.

The practical differences between the two approaches may surface only in the unusual case in which the person alleging rape communicated nothing at all. In that situation, Tiersma's approach would result in there being no evidence of non-consent. Cowart's, in contrast, would by definition not regard there having been any consent. Whichever policy one prefers, the debate is one well worth having, demonstrating how the serious study of language issues in legal contexts can put important societal questions in clearer focus.

## Note

1. These examples were inspired by interesting and provocative responses of the reviewers, to whom we extend our thanks.

## References

Cowart, Monica R. (2004) Understanding Acts of Consent: Using Speech Act Theory to Help Resolve Moral Dilemmas and Legal Disputes, *Law and Philosophy* 23: 495–525.

Kurzon, Dennis (1998) *Discourse of Silence*. Amsterdam: John Benjamins.

Pierscionek, Barbara K. (2008) What Is Presumed When We Presume Consent? *BMC Medical Ethics* 9:8 doi:10.1186/1472-6939-9-8.

Simpson, John A. (1993) *Oxford Dictionary of Proverbs*. Oxford: Oxford University Press.

Tiersma, Peter M. (2007) *The Language of Consent in Rape Law* in J. Cotterill (Ed), The Language of Sexual Crime 83–103.

UK Sexual Offences Act 2003; http://www.legislation.gov.uk/ukpga/2003/42/contents. Accessed 20/02/2015.

24

# Reflections on Peter Tiersma's "The Language and Consent in Rape Law"

Gregory M. Matoesian

Peter Tiersma, either solely or with his longtime collaborator Larry Solan, has written extensively on some of the most crucial issues in the field of language and law, or what we now call forensic linguistics. Moreover, his books, articles, and edited volumes, such as the classic *Legal Language* (1999), are required reading for scholars in the field, not just for understanding how language functions in the legal system but for broader social problems the law deals with on a mundane basis. One of these social problems concerns sexual assault and how rape cases are handled in the courtroom. In this chapter I discuss Tiersma's analysis of "The Language of Consent in Rape Law," (2007)—doubtless one of the most vexing social and legal problems confronting those of us interested in language, law, and legal policy. In doing so, I hope to elaborate, expand, and re-specify key points relevant in thinking about consent.

The case under consideration here represents the most common type of sexual assault charge that goes to trial—date or acquaintance cases—so Tiersma's analysis does not apply to the less-frequent stranger rapes, only to the prototypical "he-said-she-said" case where the issue of consent becomes relevant. Who wins the "war of words"? Tiersma demonstrates the inherently problematic nature of consent (he is only dealing with heterosexual cases where the male is the defendant and the female is the complainant) along numerous dimensions. I will address only several here. First, how do we determine the woman's mental state, the locus of consent? Second, how do various patriarchal assumptions inform determination of consent? Finally, how does aggressive cross-examination by the defense attorney revictimize the complainant and "cloud" interpretation of consent? While these may appear as distinct questions, they interrelate along several lines.

To address these questions in this brief essay, let me provide a piece of data from an actual date/acquaintance rape trial and move on from there. The following question and answer sequence consists of the defense lawyer (DL) and complainant (C) (edited).

DL: You were attracted to Bruce weren't you?

C: I thought he was a nice, clean looking man.

DL: He was attractive looking correct?

C: Yes.

DL: And basically when you left the parking lot that night all you knew about him was that he was a good looking man?

When discussing the legal issue of consent, we might want to start off with a strange question. What does the woman consent or not consent to? As Tiersma mentions, while legal consent rests in the complainant's state of mind, its proof rests in her speech and conduct. But still, what does she consent or not consent to? Sex? Of course, the defense will say that she did consent and the prosecutor will say that she didn't consent—with consent referring to the specific acts that constitute the crime of rape in this case. And as Tiersma further mentions, if the defense attorney is aggressive enough and his language is patriarchal enough (in terms of the typical stereotypes such as clothing, credibility, etc.), then consent is typically interpreted from the defense perspective so that the defendant "walks," as his case study of *Regina v. Doe* at the Old Bailey demonstrates.

However, what if the object of consent is not sex? What if the defense attorney's first question involves more than mere aggressive questioning and patriarchal assumptions about sexual access? In the above example, the defense attorney's question is a product of the sexual ideology that if a woman is "attracted" to a man, then she is attracted the same way men are attracted to women: sexually. The defense attorney's implicit assumptions erase the woman's sexual culture and personal experience, and we can feel a sense of caution in her response. Her rather neutral assessment of Bruce's looks is symbolic of the status of their more-or-less impersonal relationship. Unable to get her to agree to this ideology of "attraction," the defense attorney takes the back door route, a logical process that unfolds as follows: Since the defendant was attractive, she must have been attracted to him and if she was attracted to him, then she was "attracted" the same way that men are attracted to women: sexually. That is, she consented not to sex but to those patriarchal assumptions Tiersma describes.

But this logic is neither patriarchal nor adversarial—at least not just that. Much more powerfully, at key moments patriarchal logic appropriates the adversary system as the adversary system co-opts patriarchal logic in a way that something novel emerges, something concealed and naturalized as the adversary system, and gender neutrality in the process.

More theoretically, both the adversary system and patriarchal assumptions converge and merge into what I refer to, for lack of a better term, as the patriarchal logic of sexual rationality, a linguistic ideology that conceals and naturalizes male standards as commonsense reasoning embodied in key moments of legal inconsistency, impeachment, credibility, and so on—moments that are key when it comes to determining the legal fact of consent (see Matoesian 2001).

In fact, we may find more in legal language than just language: our sociocultural practices in the contextualization of meaning and reproduction of hegemonic structures. If this is so, then seeking solutions to consent through, for example, Tiersma's recommendations on rape shield legislation, may fail to offer a viable avenue for change. I have no workable solutions to the quandary either, so I won't pretend to offer one. More forcefully, if we expand Tiersma's ideas on aggressive questioning in the adversary system and patriarchal assumptions, along the lines I've indicated here, then we can envision why the problem of consent will, as he puts it, "never go away."

### References

Matoesian, Gregory M. (2001) *Law and the Language of Identity: Discourse in the William Kennedy Smith Rape Trial.* New York: Oxford University Press.

Tiersma, Peter M. (1999) *Legal Language.* Chicago: University of Chicago Press.

Tiersma, Peter M. (2007) The Language of Consent in Rape Law, in Janet Cotterill (ed.), *The Language of Sexual Crime.* Houndmills: Palgrave, 83–103.

25

# Speaking of Consent

Gail Stygall

Peter Tiersma's work on silence, nonverbal communication, and consent presents a thoughtful yet provocative set of ideas about these ways of "communicating." I am choosing to concentrate on his chapter,"The Language of Consent in Rape Law," in Janet Cotterill's *The Language of Sexual Crime* (2007). Tiersma begins his exploration of sexual consent by considering a trial in London—a rape trial. The defendant and the victim at one time had a relationship. Sometime later, after she had joined an evangelical church, the victim visited the defendant at his dwelling. On that occasion, the victim said he raped her. The defendant said that it was consensual sex. The lawyers for each side made extensive arguments about whether the victim had consented. Unlike most other crimes, in a rape case the prosecutor must not only prove that the defendant did the act that constituted the crime, but also that the victim did not consent to it, thus making it acquaintance rape—especially when the defendant and victim had a previous relationship—a particularly difficult case for the prosecution. In other crimes—a beating, for example—we don't ask if victims have consented to be beaten. But in a rape case, proving that the victim did not consent is required for a conviction.

Tiersma examines various reform efforts advocated and implemented that were intended to make rape prosecutions fairer to victims. Rape shield laws, for example, generally prevent the victim from having to testify about prior sexual conduct or relationships. However, those rape shield laws are not absolute protections. One loophole in them allows the victim to be questioned about any prior sexual relationship she may have had with the defendant. Another rape law reform concerns the traditional rule in some states that, to obtain a rape conviction, it is necessary to demonstrate that the woman had actively resisted her attacker. Under the reformed legal rules, the requirement that the victim had resisted with the "uttermost exertion" was eliminated. Instead, the reformed law substitutes a requirement that the victim had experienced the act of intercourse "against a person's will by means of force, violence, duress, menace or fear of immediate and unlawful bodily injury on the person or another" (Tiersma 89). Of course, even under these reformed rape rules, consent is still part of the prosecution's burden to disprove. Some states went further—Michigan, for example, changed its rape statute so that non-consent was presumed, and the defense had to raise and prove consent as an affirmative defense.

In considering the role of consent in rape cases, Tiersma compares generally the nature of the speech acts of consenting and promising. To promise, on the one hand, there must be some explicit communication that conveys a commitment to the person who is being promised something. Consent, on the other hand, can be used to describe a state of mind: thinking or believing without ever explicitly communicating with the conversational partner. The speech act of consenting assumes that the other party to the interaction has initiated the proposal, which the consenting party then agrees to. The related speech act of "agreement," in contrast, need not imply which party is the initiator of the proposal and which the acquiescent party (Wierzbicka, (1987: 112–20)), cited in Tiersma, suggests that "consent" implies a dependent relationship of the parties, while "agreeing" implies a more active role in endorsing the suggested action. In addition, Tiersma points out that what is called "consent" can be either voluntary or involuntary. As a result of ignoring that fact, Tiersma suggests, the law has been conceptualizing consent inappropriately in the case of the crime of rape. When a woman involuntarily submits to a rape, consent shouldn't be the issue, since that consent is not voluntary. Instead, the focus in those cases should be "whether the man knew or should have known" that the woman did not consent (96). Although, as Tiersma acknowledges, this approach raises some issues of its own and most importantly he has shifted the locus of the legal inquiry from the victim's state of mind to the defendant's actions.

Tiersma's article leads me to consider what might happen if the concept of consent is re-conceptualized in a different legal context—the enforcement of so-called contracts of adhesion. A contract of adhesion is a standard printed form contract, in which perhaps a few blank terms can be filled in, or often none at all. The contract of adhesion is presented by the drafting party to the other party on a "take it or leave it" basis. Consent is an issue in contracts of adhesion at least in part because there is no real negotiating between the parties. Often, these contracts are presented to a consumer who usually stands alone without legal counsel, while the contract of adhesion was drafted by a powerful, well-counseled corporation. Contracts of adhesion often occur in transactions such as obtaining a mortgage to purchase a house, applying for a credit card, or in purchases made by visiting online websites. These contracts are nothing like those assumed under classical contract law, in which participants with relatively equal bargaining power negotiate toward a satisfactory outcome for both. In cases of contracts of adhesion, the law has rarely addressed the question of consumer consent to the contract terms. Instead, the consumer's consent to the terms is assumed or taken for granted. As Margaret Radin (2013) describes the position taken by law and economics scholars on this matter, consumers are assumed to be satisfied with these contracts because, according to law and economics theorists, consumers thereby save money. Radin notes, "recipients are compensated for the loss of their legal rights by lower prices charged by the firm, and that recipients "would" (or hypothetically "do") choose this trade-off" (162). Radin expresses concern about consumers in a sense selling their rights in this way, without being given a meaningful choice in the matter.

Consent in contracts of adhesion is elusive. Let me demonstrate with excerpts from two cases. In *Applebaum v. Nissan*,[1] a case heard in the US Court of Appeals for the Third Circuit, Applebaum could not understand the contract language describing how the residual value of his leased automobile was figured. Although the Court agreed that Regulation M in effect at the time required "that disclosures be in reasonably understandable form" (218), this rule didn't require that the consumer actually understand the terms. In other words, actual consent of this consumer wasn't really necessary. Instead, the Court settled for a distant approximation of true consent: "Thus the [regulations] require disclosure in a form that is 'reasonably understandable' in light of the inherent difficulty or complexity of the method described; they do not necessarily demand disclosure in a form that the average consumer can understand" (220). Consent to the terms of this contract turned out not to require actual understanding. Yet consent without understanding cannot really be considered consent at all.

Another case in which the consent of the consumer to the terms of the contract is questionable is one of the so-called "clickwrap" cases, *ProCD v. Zeidenberg*.[2] Zeidenberg purchased a CD-ROM without having the opportunity to read the terms of use. The CD contained a telephone number database, and the terms of use prohibited the purchaser from selling items from the database. The court ruled for ProCD that the restriction was enforceable, reasoning that the purchaser accepted the terms when the license agreement appeared on the screen as he installed the software. The court reasoned that the situation was nothing more than ordinary contract assent, in which "a buyer may accept by performing the acts the vendor proposes to treat as the kind of conduct that constitutes acceptance" (1452). So this consumer's consent was presumed by his installing the software and clicking through the license agreement in that installation. Nothing more.

Rather than the consumer having the burden of proving that he or she didn't understand the form contract, or rather than presuming that a "click" should have the same legal effect as a signature, Tiersma's analysis of consent in the rape context suggests that consent should not be presumed from bare acquiescence to the demands of the more powerful party. A corporation using a form contract, a contract of adhesion, should have to show that ordinary consumers can and do understand the terms of the contract. This showing could be demonstrated by linguistic analysis of the documents and empirical testing of prototypical consumers. Requiring true consumer understanding of the terms of these contracts and informed consent to those terms makes a fairer contract and a better contract law.

## Notes

1. 226 F.3d 214 (3rd Cir. 2000).
2. 86 F.3d 1447 (7th Cir. 1996).

## References

Radin, Margaret Jane (2013) *Boilerplate: The Fine Print, Vanishing Rights, and the Rule of Law*. Princeton, N.J.: Princeton University Press.

Tiersma, Peter M. (2007) The Language of Consent in Rape Law, in J. Cotterill (ed.), *The Language of Sexual Crime*, 83–103. Hampshire, U.K.: Palgrave Macmillan.

Wierzbicka, Anna (1987) *English Speech Act Verbs*. Sydney: Academic Press.

# Defaming

26

# Defamatory Language and the Act of Accusing*
Peter M. Tiersma

This Article has argued that defamation should be defined not only in terms of the effect on the target or his reputation, but also in terms of the act of the speaker. Defamatory language requires—or ought to require—that the speaker perform the illocutionary act of *accusing*. An utterance has the force of an accusation when it attributes responsibility to someone for an act or state of affairs. An accusation's force is most explicit when a speaker states, "I accuse *P* of *A*," using a performative phrase in the first person, present tense. In addition to having this particular force, an accusation must have a specific propositional content; it must attribute responsibility to a specific person for a discreditable or blameworthy act or state of affairs.[1]

Support for the notion that defamatory language is accusatory can be found in judicial opinions. Not infrequently, judges use words such as "accuser" and "accusation" in describing libelous or slanderous communications. In dissenting from a denial of certiorari in *Dun & Bradstreet, Inc. v. Grove*, Justice Douglas stated that the libeled may rebut "their accusers."[2] In *Gertz v. Robert Welch, Inc.*, the Court referred to the "accusations" made in the offending article.[3] Other instances of the use of "accuse" (and its morphological variants) in describing defamatory language are not unusual.[4]

While judges and others often use the verb "accuse" to describe charges made against another, accusers seldom overtly state this word in their accusations. Unlike a judge, who often takes pains to preface explicitly the holding of an opinion with "we hold," an accuser does not normally announce the force of an accusation with "I accuse." For this reason, it is necessary to inquire into the speaker's intent in making the utterance: whether she is attempting to attach responsibility to someone

---

* Excerpt from Peter Meijes Tiersma, The Language of Defamation, *Texas Law Review* 66: 303. 314–22 (1987).

for a discreditable act or state of affairs. For example, suppose a store manager says to a police officer, "That fellow took a radio without paying for it." This utterance is not a casual statement or report, but an accusation of theft. It is equivalent to "I *accuse* that fellow of taking a radio without paying for it." In a recent case, an insurance agent asked a woman whose house had burned down, "How did you set the fire?" The true force of his utterance was not a question, but an accusation of arson.[5] The essential question is whether an utterance is expressible with an explicit performative phrase ("I accuse") or its semantic equivalent.[6]

The illocutionary act of accusing is closely related to confession and blame. When a person confesses, she essentially attributes responsibility for a bad act to herself. Like accusing, the act of confession is done publicly—one must confess before witnesses.[7] In contrast, blaming usually entails an uncommunicated attribution of responsibility. I can blame myself or someone else for a reprehensible act, but this attribution is primarily a mental process (although I could, of course, make it public by announcing my mental state of blaming someone). Also similar to accusing is alleging, at least in the popular use of the word. The main distinction between them is that allegations do not refer exclusively to reprehensible acts, but rather to factual or legal claims that do not necessarily involve blameworthy conduct. In addition, the claims of an allegation remain to be proved, thus its force is weaker than that of an accusation.

More distantly related to accusation is insult. An insult is usually directed at the victim. An accusation, on the other hand, is often addressed to someone else, although its ultimate target is the reputation of the victim. Both insults and accusations involve negative characterizations of a person's actions, character, or physical attributes. But accusations, along with blame and confession, are appropriate only when the act is blameworthy or discreditable—a person cannot accuse someone of having a big nose, though this is a perfectly acceptable insult and might well subject the victim to painful ridicule.

### The Propositional Content: Blameworthy Conduct or State of Affairs

Every illocutionary act such as accusing also has a proposition. For example, I can explicitly indicate the force of a promise by beginning my utterance with "I hereby promise." But then I must promise *something* to *someone*. This is the proposition. With a promise, the proposition must be an act that I will perform or cause someone else to perform in the future. I obviously cannot commit myself to do something that is already done.[8]

In an accusation, the proposition is that someone has done or is doing something blameworthy or discreditable. This proposition requires moral judgment and presupposes a community with a shared set of values. The law will not provide a remedy if the accusation relates to moral standards that are considered antisocial[9] or are held by too small a group of people,[10] even if the harm to the victim is very real. This limit is obviously an artificial one. For a drug dealer, the worst possible accusation would be that he is an undercover narcotics agent. It could ruin his business and cause his friends and acquaintances to shun him or even kill him. On the other hand, a newspaper article reporting that he is the largest drug dealer in the state might, if inaccurate, lead to a large damage award even though in the eyes of the victim's community it was not reprehensible, but enhanced his reputation.[11]

One reason that the definition of defamatory language has been so elusive is that community standards often vary widely according to time, geography, and social status.[12] Community moral standards, of course, may differ depending upon the target of the accusation. One might not accuse a sailor or steel mill worker of having been drunk or kissing the barmaid the night before, but one might well accuse a priest of the very same act.[13] And although driving five miles over the speed limit is not especially blameworthy, it might be for the chief of police to do so while off duty. In this case, we could properly accuse the chief, not for driving too fast per se, but for being a hypocrite by disobeying the very rules he enforces against others.

Additionally, an utterance has the propositional content of an accusation only if the audience, according to the values of the community, would find the conduct discreditable. Prevailing values, however, often differ from one community to another. Homosexuality is apparently still morally reprehensible in many areas,[14] and to impute this to someone would be an accusation.[15] It is less likely that one can accuse someone of being gay in certain districts of San Francisco. Whether the utterance "Bill is gay" is an accusation depends on the standards of his community.

We can categorize defamation cases by the propositional content of the accusations. Any conduct that violates community moral standards can form the propositional content for an accusation. Because moral standards often correlate to the criminal law, serious violations of the law generally constitute blameworthy conduct sufficient for an accusation. Sexual misconduct and business impropriety also frequently serve as the propositional content of an accusation.[16] Imputation of a loathsome disease describes another traditional category of accusations in defamation cases.[17] The unifying element for all categories is a violation of community norms: the accuser must charge his target with violating community norms to make a true accusation.

To charge someone with the commission of a crime is one of the most damaging forms of accusation.[18] This characterization is particularly appropriate when the charge is the commission of a significant crime, but less so when the infraction is minor. Driving five miles over the speed limit is unlikely to be the proposition of an accusation because the conduct probably does not violate community moral standards. When the infraction is more serious, a perpetrator may be subject to community censure, and attributing responsibility for the infraction may indeed be an accusation. Interestingly, although imputation of a crime is one of the categories of slander per se, courts generally hold that only crimes involving "moral turpitude" will qualify.[19] In a legal setting a prosecutor might formally accuse someone of lesser crimes, but the speech community would probably not speak of an accusation in such cases. Limiting defamatory language to accusations, as defined here, accommodates the law's refusal to treat imputations of crimes without moral turpitude as the bases of defamation actions.

Another common type of defamation is a charge of unchastity. This imputation fulfills the requirement of the propositional content rule—an accuser attributes responsibility for a blameworthy or discreditable act. For instance, in *Time, Inc. v. Firestone*, the Supreme Court quoted a *Time* article that stated that the plaintiff's divorce was granted "on grounds of extreme cruelty and adultery ... The 17-month intermittent trial produced enough testimony of extramarital adventures on both sides, said the judge, 'to make Dr. Freud's hair curl.' "[20] The plaintiff based her libel claim on the implicit accusations in the article.[21]

As a general principle, it appears that one can accuse only a woman of mundane varieties of unchastity;[22] charges of unchastity regarding men must often be more serious or even criminal to be defamatory.[23] Indeed, in England charges of unchastity were regulated by legislation entitled the Slander of Women Act.[24] This sex-based distinction reflects what is morally reprehensible according to community standards and is to a large extent still prevalent today.[25]

Charges tending to injure someone in her trade or business are also a common type of defamation.[26] If these charges involve blameworthy conduct, then imputations of such conduct would be accusations. One commentator writes of accusing a lawyer of being ignorant and unqualified to practice law, or a merchant of being insolvent.[27] Of course, being insolvent or ignorant is not inherently blameworthy. But not knowing the tax code, while not an accusation in reference to the man on the street, might well be so with respect to a tax attorney. In part, the morally reprehensible nature of these acts is not the lack of qualification for a particular trade. Rather, it is the deception that is implicit when a lawyer takes money from people who innocently assume that she knows the law, or when a merchant accepts goods from people who innocently assume that she is solvent. Characterized in this way, the charges are indeed accusations.[28]

The following hypothetical cases further illustrate that defamation requires or should require an imputation of blameworthy conduct, rather than simply a statement that tends to injure someone in his trade or business. Suppose that a newspaper published a consumer group's ranking of local lawyers and that the lowest ranked lawyer in the newspaper's report had in fact been two notches higher in the original survey. The false statement indeed might injure the lawyer in his trade. But as long as the report does not suggest that any of the lawyers are unqualified to practice law, it will not impute blameworthy conduct. Otherwise, every list of this nature technically would defame those in the bottom half of the rankings, with only the defense of truth to protect the publisher of the list.[29] Nor is it appropriate to speak of the newspaper accusing half of the lawyers of being below average or at the bottom of the survey, because being below average is not blameworthy.[30]

Another traditional category of defamation is an imputation of a loathsome disease. This category generally is limited to an "existing venereal disease" or another "loathsome and communicable disease."[31] Of course, merely having a disease, even a communicable one, is not reprehensible. A person does not accuse someone of having influenza or smallpox. Imputation of disease does not seem, at first glance, to meet the propositional content requirements of an accusation.

Defamation necessarily involves the notion of disgrace—something that reflects upon the character of the person defamed.[32] Imputation of disease, therefore, can be disgraceful, or in the terms used here, an accusation of blameworthy or discreditable conduct, in several ways. To be defamatory, the imputation must be of a disease that is not only contagious but also loathsome.[33] The diseases associated with defamation are apparently not those that inspire sympathy or that cause others to maintain a respectful distance. Rather, they seem to be diseases which, like venereal disease, imply that the victim has engaged in promiscuous or commercial sexual activity,[34] or imply that the victim lives in poverty or unsanitary conditions. The latter implication serves as an explanation for why leprosy is the only disease that Prosser and Keeton mention in addition to venereal diseases.[35] The World Health Organization has labeled leprosy the "most stigmatizing of all diseases," although it is not especially contagious.[36]

The imputation that someone has a contagious disease may constitute an accusation because of moral reprehensibility in another sense: if the disease is truly contagious, the target may be exposing others to it. Many people consider it irresponsible to venture into public with a cold; this belief certainly will be much stronger with more serious diseases. Perhaps for this reason, one commentator speaks of accusing someone of being a typhoid carrier,[37] which does not emphasize the plight of the ill person (which should arouse only sympathy), but condemns the carrier for exposing others.

## Notes

1. Although an accusation must relate to a discreditable act, obviously not every reference to such an act is an accusation; one can, for example, *state* or *allege* that someone has engaged in blameworthy conduct.

2. 404 U.S. 898, 901 (Douglas. J., dissenting), *denying cert. to* 438 F.2d 433 (3d Cir. 1971).

3. 418 U.S. 323, 332 (1974).

4. *See, e.g.,* Polygram Records, Inc. v. Superior Court, 170 Cal. App. 3d 543, 550, 216 Cal. Rptr. 252, 256 (1985) (stating that "false statements simply indicating that plaintiff's business goods 'were of inferior quality,' though conceivably tortious as injurious falsehoods, do not accuse plaintiff of dishonesty, lack of integrity or incompetence or even imply any reprehensible personal characteristic, and are therefore not defamatory."); 1 E. Seelman, THE LAW OF LIBEL AND SLANDER IN THE STATE OF NEW YORK 16 (1964) (defining libel as "an accusation in writing . . . against the character of a person."). In a recent defamation case, the Supreme Court spoke of letters to the president that "falsely accused" the respondent of violating the civil rights of various individuals while he was a Superior Court judge, as well as of fraud and conspiracy to commit fraud, blackmail, and violations of professional ethics. McDonald v. Smith, 472 U.S. 479, 481 (1985). In a similar case, a newspaper columnist was said to have "accused" someone of lying about a fracas during a wrestling match. Lorain Journal Co. v. Milkovich, 449 U.S. 966, 966 (Brennan, J., dissenting), *denying cert. to* 65 Ohio App. 2d 143, 416 N.E.2d 662 (1980).

5. Hunt v. Gerlemann, 581 S.W.2d 913, 914 (Mo. Ct. App. 1979).

6. Austin suggests that the test is whether an utterance is "reducible, or expandible, or analysable" as an explicit performative. J. L. Austin, HOW TO DO THINGS WITH WORDS 61–62 (2d ed. 1962); *see also* Peter Meijes Tiersma, Comment, *The Language of Offer and Acceptance*, 74 CALIF. L. REV. 189, 201 (1986) (applying a similar analysis to offer and acceptance by stating that the essential question is whether the words or actions are equivalent to an offer or acceptance). Determining the true force of an utterance is also a concern of the law and jurisprudence in general. H. L. A. Hart has discussed and criticized the notion that law is really a series of commands. This notion requires that a law be viewed as the equivalent of an imperative, even though laws are not always in explicit imperative form. *See* H. L. A. HART, THE CONCEPT OF LAW 18–19 (1961).

A very interesting example of this problem confronted the Supreme Court in Rhode Island v. Innis, 446 U.S. 291 (1980). A suspect arrested for murder had asked for counsel to assist him. The rules developed in *Miranda v. Arizona* and subsequent decisions held that police officers could not question the suspect on the way to the police station. *See* Miranda v. Arizona, 384 U.S. 436, 444–45 (1966). The officers who drove the suspect were, nonetheless, quite interested in persuading him to divulge the location of the murder weapon, a shotgun. One officer said to the other that a school for handicapped children was in the area, and "God forbid" that one of the children find the weapon with shells and hurt herself. The suspect at that point offered to take the officers to where he had hidden the gun. The issue for the court was to determine the *force* of the officer's statement—whether it was the equivalent of questioning. The majority held that it was not, defining interrogation as "words or actions on the part of police officers that they *should have known* were reasonably likely to elicit an incriminating response." 446 U.S. at 302. In contrast, the dissent by Justice Stevens was linguistically more sophisticated. He posited that any statement that would be understood by the average listener as calling for a response is the functional equivalent of a direct question, whether or not it is punctuated by a question mark. *Id.* at 309 (Stevens, J., dissenting).

7. Religious confession operates somewhat differently, unless God is viewed as a witness.

8. Of course, "promise" is sometimes used colloquially in the sense of "swear," and in this instance, it can have a proposition in the past ("I promise I did not do it"). This Article uses "promise" to mean the creating of an obligation.

9. *See, e.g.*, Heimerle v. Charter Books, 11 Media L. Rep. (BNA) 1278, 1279 (N.Y. Sup. Ct. 1984) (dismissing a claim for slander based on defendants' statement that plaintiff was an informer who turned defendants in for diamond smuggling); Connelly v. McKay, 176 Misc. 685, 687, 28 N.Y.S.2d 327, 329 (Sup. Ct. 1941) (noting that statement is not defamatory if the act accused of serves the public interest); Rose v. Borenstein, 119 N.Y.S.2d 288 (N.Y. City Ct. 1953) (finding defendant's action in identifying plaintiff as an informer not defamatory).

10. Courts have held, for example, that to be actionable a communication must be defamatory in the eyes of a "considerable and respectable class in the community." Peck v. Tribune Co., 214 U.S. 185, 190 (1909). Or it must be defamatory in the eyes of "society . . . taken as it is." Van Wiginton v. Pulitzer Publishing Co., 218 F. 795, 796 (8th Cir. 1914).

11. *See* W. Keeton, D. Dobbs, R. Keeton & D. Owen, Prosser and Keeton on the Law of Torts § 111, at 777–78 (5th ed. 1984) [hereinafter Prosser & Keeton]. As Justice Black stated in his concurrence to *New York Times Co. v. Sullivan*, "instead of being damaged [the plaintiff's] political, social, and financial prestige has likely been enhanced by the Times' publication." 376 U.S. 254, 294 (1964).

So far the discussion of the proposition has concentrated on the predicate—>what the accused did. A second element of the proposition is *reference* —the communication must refer to the plaintiff. Problems arise when the accusation refers to a group. The question then becomes whether the accusation implicates a particular member of the group. *See, e.g.*, Barger v. Playboy Enters., 564 F. Supp. 1151, 1153–55 (N.D. Cal. 1983) (stating that when the group is large, as in over 25 persons, the courts presume that no reasonable reader would take statements literally to apply to each individual member when directed at the group as a whole). Although this issue is interesting, it exceeds the scope of this Article.

12. *See* Prosser & Keeton, *supra* note 11, § 111, at 771–73.

13. *Cf.* Cobbs v. Chicago Defender, 308 Ill. App. 55, 58, 31 N.E.2d 323, 325 (1941) (holding libelous a false newspaper report suggesting that a clergyman had engaged in misconduct).

14. *See, e.g.*, Tex. Penal Code; Ann. § 21.06 (Vernon 1974) (prohibiting "homosexual conduct"); *cf.* Bowers v. Hardwick, 106 S. Ct. 2841, 2846 (1986) (noting "the presumed belief of a majority of the electorate in Georgia that homosexual sodomy is immoral and unacceptable").

15. *See, e.g.*, Manale v. New Orleans Dep't of Police, 673 F.2d 122, 125 (5th Cir. 1982) (allowing police officer to recover damages resulting from sergeant's statements that he was a "fruit"); Schomer v. Smidt, 113 Cal. App. 3d 828, 835, 170 Cal. Rptr. 662, 666 (1980) (false imputation of the commission of a homosexual act is slanderous per se).

16. *See* P<small>ROSSER</small> & K<small>EETON</small>, *supra* note 11, § 111, at 774–75.

17. R<small>ESTATEMENT</small> (S<small>ECOND</small>) <small>OF</small> T<small>ORTS</small> § 572 (1976); P<small>ROSSER</small> & K<small>EETON</small>, *supra* note 11, § 112, at 790.

18. *See* Stevens v. Wilber, 136 Or. 599, 602, 300 P. 329, 330–31 (1931); Blake v. Smith, 19 R.I. 476, 34 A. 995 (1896), *cited in* P<small>ROSSER</small> & K<small>EETON</small>, *supra* note 11, § 111, at 789 n.46.

19. *E.g.*, Cinquanta v. Burdett, 154 Colo. 37, 39–40, 38 P.2d 779, 780 (1963); Morgan v. Kennedy, 62 Minn. 348, 355–56, 64 N.W. 912, 914 (1895); *see also* R<small>ESTATEMENT</small> (S<small>ECOND</small>) <small>OF</small> T<small>ORTS</small> § 571 comment f (1976) (unless the imputed crimes are regarded "as involving moral turpitude, the accusation of their commission is not actionable per se."). 

20. 424 U.S. 448, 452 (1976).

21. *Id.* The Supreme Court affirmed a $100,000 damages award for the plaintiff, *id.* at 460–61, but then remanded the case to try the issue of fault, *id.* at 464. Strangely enough, in Yousoupoff v. Metro-Goldwyn-Mayer Pictures, Ltd., 50 T.L.R. 581, 587 (C.A. 1934), the charge that a woman had been raped by Rasputin was held defamatory. This charge should evoke only sympathy and hardly seems to be an accusation. "Right-thinking" individuals should not think less of someone who is the victim of rape. But perhaps the court, reflecting community prejudices, felt that to accuse a woman of being raped was to accuse her of having tempted her assailant to rape her. Only this distasteful account, which comports with the notion that often the victim of rape is as much on trial as the perpetrator, would allow one to *accuse* a woman of having been raped.

22. *See, e.g.*, Memphis Publishing Co. v. Nichols, 569 S.W.2d 412, 419 (Tenn. 1978) (article merely stating that man and woman were present at time of shooting was sufficient to infer unchastity on part of woman).

23. *See, e.g.*, Jelly v. Dabney, 581 P.2d 622, 625 (Wyo. 1978) (holding that to accuse a man merely of having an affair was not actionable, and stating in dictum that to accuse a woman of the same thing would be actionable).

24. 1891, 54 & 55 Vict., ch. 51, *cited in* P<small>ROSSER</small> & K<small>EETON</small>, *supra* note 11, § 112, at 793.

25. Prosser and Keeton suggest that the rule might now apply to serious sexual misconduct of either sex. P<small>ROSSER</small> & K<small>EETON</small>, *supra* note 11, § 112, at 793. The alleged womanizing that caused presidential aspirant Gary Hart to withdraw (temporarily) from the 1988 presidential race shows that adultery is still blameworthy conduct to many Americans, and may now be just as blameworthy for a man as for a woman. But attributing sexual relations to an unmarried man could less clearly be called an accusation, and contemporary language usage suggests that unchastity is still a more serious charge for women. Terms for unchaste women almost universally have an unfavorable (even condemning) connotation in English: slut, whore, tramp, and so forth. Corresponding terms for an unchaste man are, by contrast, largely positive and certainly not accusatory: playboy, casanova, don juan, and ladies' man.

26. R<small>ESTATEMENT</small> (S<small>ECOND</small>) <small>OF</small> T<small>ORTS</small> § 573 (1976); P<small>ROSSER</small> & K<small>EETON</small>, *supra* note 11, § 112, at 790–92.

27. R. S<small>ACK</small>, L<small>IBEL</small>, S<small>LANDER</small>, <small>AND</small> R<small>ELATED</small> P<small>ROBLEMS</small> 95 n.24 (1980).

28. A New York court held that it is slander per se to say of a merchant, whose business involves giving credit, that he keeps false books. The same is not true of a lumber sawyer, in whose business keeping books is unnecessary if credit is not given. 2 E. S<small>EELMAN</small>, *supra* note 4, at 893–94 (citing Rathbun v. Emigh, 6 Wend. 407 (N.Y. Sup. Ct. 1831)). The difference seems to lie in the implication that the merchant is defrauding the community.

29. *Cf.* Blatty v. New York Times Co., 42 Cal. App. 3d. 1033, 232 Cal. Rptr. 542, 728 P.2d 1177 (1986) (holding that both state and federal constitutions preclude a cause of action against a newspaper for negligently or intentionally failing to include an author's book on the bestseller list).

30. The *Restatement* suggests that an imputation that a doctor's patient died because of unsuccessful treatment is not actionable without proof of special harm, because even the best physician can make a mistake. But to charge that a doctor's treatments are repeatedly unsuccessful, or that the doctor lacks the expected professional skills, is actionable. RESTATEMENT (SECOND) OF TORTS § 573 comment d (1976). *Compare* Camp v. Martin, 23 Conn. 86, 91 (1854) (charging a physician with mismanagement in the treatment of a case is not, of itself, actionable) *and* Lynde v. Johnson, 39 N.Y. 12, 17 (1896) (words spoken of a physician in reference to a particular case are not actionable unless they have an import and meaning that reaches beyond the particular case) *with* Amick v. Montross, 206 Iowa 51, 61, 220 N.W. 51, 55 (1928) (a charge of drunkenness against a physician is actionable per se). Publication of either allegation might cause patients to avoid the doctor, but only the latter allegation is an accusation. A single unsuccessful treatment is presumably accidental, hence not necessarily blameworthy.

31. RESTATEMENT (SECOND) OF TORTS § 572 (1976); *see also* Atkinson v. Equitable Life Ins. Soc'y, 519 F.2d 1112, 1118 (5th Cir. 1975) (stating that in most jurisdictions, oral communication is actionable per se if it imputes to another a presently existing venereal or other loathsome or communicable disease); Kirk v. Village of Hillcrest, 31 Ill. App. 3d 1063, 1065, 335 N.E.2d 535, 537 (1975) (noting that imputing a communicable disease to another constitutes slander per se).

32. PROSSER & KEETON, *supra* note 11, § 111, at 773–74.

33. RESTATEMENT (SECOND) OF TORTS § 572 (1976). The *Random House Dictionary* defines "loathsome" as "disgusting; revolting; repulsive. . . ." RANDOM HOUSE DICTIONARY OF THE ENGLISH LANGUAGE 840 (unabridged ed. 1973).

34. Holdsworth speaks of an "accusation" of having syphilis. W. Holdsworth, *Defamation in the Sixteenth and Seventeenth Centuries* (pt. 2), 40 LAW Q. REV. 397, 399 (1924). He points out that an imputation of syphilis is actionable in part because of the obvious implication as to the sufferer's moral character. *Id.* at 400. Those who currently have AIDS may likewise face such a stigma. Although venereal disease is contagious, this attribute alone does not seem a reason to consider it defamatory. The disease tends to spread only among those who are sexually active with more than one partner. Individuals who do not belong to this group have no reason to shun someone for fear of catching the disease. The avoidance must be a matter of stigma, not of contagion.

35. PROSSER & KEETON, *supra* note 11, § 112, at 790.

36. Harden, *Doctors in Africa Wage Frustrating Battle Against Horrors of Leprosy*, L.A. TIMES, Jan. 12, 1986, pt. 1, at 4, col. 1. In a leprosy defamation case at the beginning of this century, the defendant asked to prove that leprosy was not contagious, but hereditary, and that the imputation was no longer slanderous per se. The court rejected this as irrelevant, stating that people would shun the plaintiff regardless of whether the disease was considered contagious. Simpson v. Press Publishing Co., 33 Misc. 228, 229, 67 N.Y.S. 401, 402 (Sup. Ct. 1900).

37. R. SACK, *supra* note 28, at 95 n.242. Consider "Typhoid Mary," whose name even today evokes scorn.

27

# Defamation as Speech Act

A THEORY THAT WORKS

John M. Conley

Peter Tiersma's 1987 *Texas Law Review* article, "The Language of Defamation," is one of his earliest law-and-language pieces and, to me, still one of his most interesting. Remarkably, he wrote it (and a related piece (Tiersma 1986) on "The Language of Offer and Acceptance") when just out of law school and working as a law clerk for the California Supreme Court and then a litigation associate in a law firm. I say "remarkably" because survival as a new associate depends very heavily on how many hours one can bill, and I doubt Tiersma's firm had a billing code for linguistics.

"The Language of Defamation" reflects Tiersma's early and perspicacious realization that while many significant problems that lawyers and judges confront are fundamentally linguistic, their approaches to these problems usually ignore linguistic learning that might be helpful. Here, Tiersma chooses defamation—a civil tort that consists of an utterance and its consequences—as an example of how the law might be made both more predictable and more just by the application of linguistic sensibility. This is not an easy task; as his longtime collaborator Lawrence Solan (1993: 186) wrote a few years later when analyzing judicial opinions, "Interpretive principles do not make good legal principles." But Tiersma overcomes this inherent difficulty and largely succeeds in adding value through linguistics.

As Tiersma recounts, early Anglo-American cases defined defamation (written libel and oral slander) primarily in terms of its effect on the victim, in particular its capacity to diminish the victim's reputation. In some cases simply ridiculing the victim was enough. The defendant's intent had little or no relevance, as long as the defendant was in some sense responsible for the utterance. Contemporary law further requires that the statement itself be "false and defamatory," which means that it must "lower [the victim] in the estimation of the community," and specifically "in the eyes of a 'substantial and reputable minority'" (Tiersma 1987: 311 [quoting *Restatement (Second) of Torts* § 559]). But while the newer formulation sharpens the definition of the requisite effect, it still "sheds little light on the nature of the communication itself" (Tiersma 1987: 311).

More specifically, Tiersma argues plausibly that the law of defamation has been both over- and under-inclusive. Quoting from the iconic Prosser and Keeton treatise on tort law, he points to the "anomalies and absurdities" of defamation law, including "a strict liability imposed on innocent defendants, as rigid and extreme as anything found in the law, with a blind and almost perverse refusal to compensate the plaintiff for very real and serious harm" (Tiersma 1987: 304 [quoting Keeton et al. 1984: 771–772]). How can linguistics help?

Enter speech act theory. From a legal perspective, as Tiersma notes, every tortious act, including a defamatory statement, "has at least two components: an act or failure to act by a tortfeasor, and a resultant harm to a victim" (Tiersma 1987: 307). Where the tort consists of the use of language, these two legal elements have linguistic parallels: the *illocutionary force* of the utterance, "which reflects a speaker's intent," and the *perlocutionary act*, which "identifies the effect that an utterance has on the feelings or actions of the hearer" (Tiersma 1987: 305). While illocutionary force is sometimes made explicit by a preamble such as "I assert" or "I warn," it is usually implicit and indicated by context. Perlocutionary effect is generally caused by illocutionary force—speakers usually achieve the effect they intend, whether it is to warn, to assert a fact, or, sometimes, to defame.

Tiersma sees the application of these two features of speech act theory as a way out of the "anomalies and absurdities" that plague defamation law. He argues that the law has focused almost exclusively on the *effects* of defamatory speech, in particular its capacity to damage the reputation of the victim—that is, on the perlocutionary element. He then contends that defamation law could be made both fairer and more predictable if equal attention were given to the "specific kinds of communicative action by the defamer" that produce such effects—the illocutionary force of the defamatory utterance (Tiersma 1987: 310). He distinguishes, for example, speech acts that intended to *report* from those intended to *accuse*. He further subdivides the reporting category into reporting the facts, reporting or spreading another's accusation, neutral reportage, and reporting state of mind or opinion.

Tiersma's overall conclusion is that "[d]efamatory language is best described as the illocutionary act of accusing" (Tiersma 1987: 349). The reporting-accusing dichotomy also provides a template for awarding damages. Since "accusing most clearly constitutes an intentional act aimed at causing" injury, damages are presumptively appropriate for both compensation and deterrence. Where reporting damages the plaintiff's reputation, a corrected report will usually suffice; where compensatory damages seem necessary, the plaintiff should be required to prove specific harm.

In evaluating this chapter's contribution to the law, two things strike me. The first is that Tiersma's speech act approach seems to work. The focus on illocutionary force, and in particular the accusing-reporting distinction, accounts for every category of case I can think of, producing results that are both coherent and fair. As I read the paper, most of my marginal notes were in the form of "but what about . . .?" However, in every such case, I read on for a page or two and found that he had dealt with my concern. Prime examples include liability for republishing a false report (depends on whether the illocutionary force was to renew the underlying accusation) and liability for injurious opinions (reporting a state of mind can almost always be distinguished from making a fact-based accusation).

The second reaction relates to my earlier point that "while many significant problems that lawyers and judges confront are fundamentally linguistic, their approaches to these problems usually ignore linguistic learning that might be helpful." I do not mean to ignore the fact that courts have often made use of case-specific linguistic evidence. One need go no further than the distinguished career of Roger Shuy to establish that proposition. Forensic linguists such as Shuy have provided expert evidence in a wide array of contexts ranging from trademark to criminal law.

My point, rather, is that the law has rarely if ever recognized linguistic *theory* as a challenge to its own historically ingrained methods of analysis. This has been true even when the legal subject matter is linguistic, as in the case of defamation. This is partly because linguistic theorists have rarely offered the law a rationale and a roadmap for doing so. Tiersma's article is the rare exception. In fact, much of his work—some solo, some in collaboration with Solan (e.g., Solan and Tiersma 2005)—is of this unusual sort. The next step is to get the legal world to pay attention.

### References

Keeton, W. Page et al. (1984) *Prosser and Keeton on the Law of Torts*. 5th ed. St. Paul, MN: West Publishing.

Solan, Lawrence M. (1993) *The Language of Judges*. Chicago: University of Chicago Press.

Solan, Lawrence M. and Peter M. Tiersma (2005) *Speaking of Crime*. Chicago: University of Chicago Press.

Tiersma, Peter Meijes (1986) The Language of Offer and Acceptance. *California Law Review* 74: 189–242.

Tiersma, Peter Meijes (1987) The Language of Defamation. *Texas Law Review* 66: 303–350.

# Applying Tiersma's Defamation Theory to Defamation Cases

Roger W. Shuy

A law professor friend once told me that lawyers practice linguistics without a license. No doubt it's true that lawyers often have to make linguistic decisions, whether trained in the field or not. It's equally true that linguists who work in the legal arena have a lot to learn about law. Since it's rare that law professors are also trained linguists, we can be very grateful to Peter Tiersma for using his considerable linguistic background and knowledge to help bridge the gap between linguistics and law in his many excellent books and articles. A prime example is his work on defamation (Tiersma 1987), in which he applies his linguistic expertise in speech acts to defamation statutes, producing results that are important to both fields.

In his article Tiersma points out that defamatory statements do considerably more than cause harm to persons' reputations and lower their esteem in the minds of the larger community. He explains that this conventional understanding of defamation sees only one side of the communicative event. It relates only to the effects of defamatory utterances but not to their causes. Looking at half the picture fails to recognize the more important substance in defamatory communication because it deals with the experience of the receiver of the message but ignores its sender. Tiersma pointed out that this important missing substance can be found in the sender's actual language used to defame.

Tiersma also explains that while senders seldom use the performative word "accuse" in their messages, those who follow the conventional perception of defamation overlook the important illocutionary speech act of accusing, which attributes responsibility to the sender of alleged defamatory messages. He then helpfully distinguishes accusing from other speech acts such as blaming and alleging, both of which relate to judgmental claims that are not considered defamatory acts, and points out that differing community standards are addressed in the propositional content of accusations.

Even the major doctrines of defamation, including the fair report privilege that deals with language used honestly about a matter of public interest, the distinction between fact and opinion, and the standard of malice (intentional and reckless defaming), can benefit from understanding the work done by speech acts, an analytical procedure originally introduced by Austin (1962) and Searle (1969) and later expanded and developed by others. The study of speech acts is now regarded as a vital component of linguistics. Recognizing the ways that speech acts operate in language can even provide clues to a person's intentions, which can enable the courts to better distinguish between defamatory accusations and reports that merely inform readers of a state of affairs or opinions about the author's state of mind.

Tiersma's idea is that defamation should be understood not only in terms of the perlocutionary effect that subjects believe an accusation has on their character or reputation but also and more importantly in terms of the illocutionary force of the defamatory language that reflects the *intent* of such language. This turns the conventional understanding of defamation on its head by addressing it not just from the perspective of the recipient, but rather from the abstract mental concept of the sender's intention.

It is not possible to expect statutes to define intentions for us because they can't begin to anticipate and contextualize the intentions underlying all of the many specific real-life situations that arise. In his paper, however, Tiersma suggests that using speech act theory "reflects" the intent of the sender, and this opens the door to linguistic analysis of the speech acts used in defamation cases, where the actual language can be the best (if not the only) window to reflect the intent of what defamers say. As Tiersma points out, people get things accomplished through their speech acts, including accusing. As linguists are well aware, accusing, like all successful speech acts, contains its own felicity conditions in order to count as clear and effective (Searle 1969), a fact suggesting that lawyers might want to enlist the help of linguists in their defamation cases.

I made use of Tiersma's ideas in several of the cases noted in my book, *The Language of Defamation Cases* (2010). In one case a local newspaper wrote several stories describing sixth-grade students' low standardized test scores in one teacher's class, adding that her students "learned nothing" and "ran out of steam," while the teacher "became distraught" and had "management issues." The article cited the complaints of students who claimed they were harmed, and the teacher was placed on leave for the rest of the school year. When the teacher brought a defamation suit, the administrators denied they had made any accusations and the newspaper claimed that its statements were "protected statements of opinion." The teacher brought a successful defamation suit against both the press and the school system in which I was able to show that the language evidence demonstrated that both defendant parties had used the speech act of accusing her.

In another defamation case, the Southern School of Optometry claimed it had been defamed in a research report about the current state of optometry commissioned by Tennessee ophthalmologists who strongly believed that optometrists had harmed their reputation by invading their medical specialization. This research report was the major evidence in the lawsuit. The ophthalmologist's conventional defense focused on the lack of any evidence that Tennessee readers had lowered their esteem for optometrists as a result of reading this report. Following Tiersma's ideas, the optometrists countered with an analysis of the actual text of the report, which was rife with pejorative terms, sarcasm, exaggeration, overgeneralizations, ambiguity, and rhetorical questions, as they accused the school of oversupplying the number of optometrists needed and unethically lowering its admission requirements. Defendants countered that the author of the report was merely giving facts and offering opinions, an argument that failed when it was pointed out that the genre of research reports specifies that they are to provide facts and conclusions stemming from the facts, but that it is not proper for them to offer opinions.

More generally, we can be very grateful to Tiersma for opening the door of speech act analysis to the legal context. After this paper, his creative ideas have stimulated linguists to find other linguistic clues to senders' intentions. For example, we now examine the ways that people introduce topics in a conversation, understanding that newly introduced topics are important enough in their minds to be considered a reflection of their intentions. And when they bring up that same topic more than once (recycling it), it is an even clearer reflection of their intentions. Likewise, the various ways that people respond to topics introduced by conversational partners provide further language reflections of their intentions. They can agree, disagree, produce the feedback marker "uh-huh" that signals many possibilities other than agreement, ignore the topic altogether, or change the subject away from the other person's topic by saying, performatively, "not to change the subject, but," which is a clear signal that they are changing a topic that they very likely have no intention of pursuing (Shuy 2005; 2011). In most human interactions, people bring up and respond to what is on their minds, one of the best available windows of intentionality.

On a personal level as a linguist, I am deeply grateful to Peter Tiersma for this 1987 article on the speech acts relevant to defamation, because he not only stimulated my thinking for my book on the language of defamation (2010), but also for my later books that used his ideas on speech acts and intentionality relating to the language of perjury (2011), sexual misconduct (2012), bribery (2013), and murder (2014), in all of which I relied on and cited Tiersma over and over again.

## References

Austin, J. L. (1962) *How to Do Things with Words.* Cambridge, Mass.: Harvard University Press.

Searle, John (1969) *Speech Acts: An Essay in the Philosophy of Language.* London: Cambridge University Press.

Shuy, Roger W. (2010) *The Language of Defamation Cases.* New York: Oxford University Press.

Shuy, Roger W. (2011) *The Language of Perjury Cases.* New York: Oxford University Press.

Shuy, Roger W. (2012) *The Language of Sexual Misconduct Cases.* New York: Oxford University Press.

Shuy, Roger W. (2013) *The Language of Bribery Cases.* New York: Oxford University Press.

Shuy, Roger W. (2014) *The Language of Murder Cases.* New York: Oxford University Press.

Tiersma, Peter Meijes (1987) The Language of Defamation, *Texas Law Review* 66: 303–350.

# Scarlet Letter or Badge of Honour? Semantic Interpretation in Changing Contexts of Culture

Krzysztof Kredens

On receiving the offer to write for this volume, I reflected on the extent to which Peter Tiersma's work has shaped my thinking about language and law, and concluded I owe him both an interest in, and an understanding of, the ways meaning gets interpreted in legal contexts. He has written extensively about semantic issues in product warning labels, statutory regulations, and perjury cases. The premise of his 1987 paper, "The Language of Defamation," is that defamatory statements, unlike neutral reports and statements of opinion, involve the speaker performing the illocutionary act of accusing: "[w]hile an accusation attributes responsibility for an act, a report simply states that the act has occurred" (1987: 306). Tiersma is here less interested in the low-level semantic interpretation often required to decide whether the linguistic substance under scrutiny accuses or merely reports. This chapter aims to expand on his ideas; I discuss the implications of changing cultural norms for semantic interpretation in defamation cases.

I begin with a necessary platitude: the social, political, and technological advances of the last two or three decades have changed the way in which a lot of people live their lives. New technology in particular has been revolutionizing the ways individuals interact with each other, thus redefining social norms. To describe the resulting social dynamic, the sociologist Zygmunt Bauman coined the term "liquid modernity," referring to "forms of modern life [which] may differ in quite a few respects" but are united by "their fragility, temporariness, vulnerability and inclination to constant change" (2012: viii). There is no doubt that this change is reflected in language at its various levels. An interesting example is the word "geek," which seems to have undergone semantic amelioration; not long ago it referred predominantly to a socially inept computer specialist, but is now increasingly used to describe "a person who is knowledgeable and enthusiastic about a specific subject,"[1] most commonly in the field of information technology. This semantic change arguably reflects the fact that a lot of geeks have been contributing to the technological revolution of recent years and have achieved considerable financial success (and thus social respect) as a result.

The problem of understanding socially driven semantic change takes on an urgency in defamation cases, where it can be key in the resolution of the linguistic problem in question. In the early 1990s, post-communist Poland was experiencing a political transformation from a centrally planned to a market economy. The state was no longer hostile to the pursuit of personal wealth. On the contrary, new legislation encouraged private entrepreneurship, which was once viewed with suspicion by the majority working in state-owned companies, but later began to be associated with industriousness and financial independence. Against this backdrop, a fledgling entrepreneur spoke of the business dealings of the country's then-richest person as "the greatest monkey business of the Third Republic." A lengthy defamation suit followed in which the linguists testifying about the meaning and defamatory potential of "monkey business" (Polish *przekręt*) disagreed in their interpretations, with one contending that in certain contexts, "monkey business" could have positive connotations. This reading seemed to equate *przekręt* with a kind of resourcefulness and ingenuity in circumventing the law, activity that, if not ostensibly encouraged, would arguably be met with at least tacit appreciation in the unfamiliar context of the country's unfettered free-market economy. This case, which ended favourably for the plaintiff, illustrates how telling the difference between the acts of accusing and reporting can prove problematic because of the semantic changes in the context of culture.

Although meaning does not always function as part of a cultural constant, the legal standard of "ordinary meaning" presupposes an established frame of reference, a uniform context of culture. The latter may be a fiction at a time when the possibilities afforded by the Internet have led to a proliferation of idiocultures[2] with their own frames of reference. To be sure, this fragmentation is familiar to an extent; before the advent of mass transportation and mass media, people lived their lives in more or less isolated, culturally self-sufficient communities. However, whereas individuals once had little opportunity to contribute to the cultural mainstream, the Internet is nowadays making it relatively easy to do so.

Yet one characteristic of liquid modernity is that many individuals do not aspire to become part of the mainstream, choosing to self-actualise within their (set of) idioculture(s) instead. Thus, self-actualisation through idiocultures ceases to maintain a hitherto shared system of values. At the same time, the constituents of the cultural mainstream themselves change as well, in part because the very idea of a cultural canon (and thus a common frame of reference) is being redefined, if not in fact abandoned. Individuals no longer read the same books, watch the same television channels, or listen to the same radio stations. The kind of canon previously made up of institutionally endorsed cultural artefacts has been supplanted by "micro-canons," the elements of which are not necessarily shared.

Tiersma (1987: 317) quotes two early-twentieth-century US judicial standards for when a communication can be actionable: if it is "defamatory in the eyes of a 'considerable and respectable class in the community'" (. . .) or "society . . . taken as it is." Such standards would be very difficult to defend today, with the notion of "a reasonable person" used across legal contexts becoming more and more problematic as well. Who is the "average recipient," described in another Polish defamation case as "an ordinary, sensible, rational person of average intelligence, education and knowledge"?[3] In what kinds of idiocultures is s/he immersed?

Among the many game-changing Internet artefacts are publicly accessible websites that give university students the opportunity to assess their lecturers anonymously. Categories such as "helpfulness" and "clarity" (but also "hotness") are provided and various scoring systems used. In 2005 a student allegedly posted her evaluation of a lecturer on one such Polish website and left a comment in which she called him a "sex maniac" (Polish *erotoman*). She was subsequently charged with defamation and insult (two distinct offences under Polish law, the latter having to do with a perceived harm to personal dignity). The case went all the way to the Polish Supreme Court, which in 2008 provided the following opinion:

> It is worth noting that the term "sex maniac", which the applicant found to offend him, was used in a joking context, and the posting was published on an internet portal (. . .) used for evaluating lecturers by students. The evaluations are formulated in unconstrained ways and the posters use student slang, not infrequently accompanied by highly offensive expletives.[4]

The Supreme Court thus seemed to ratify the status of a student Internet forum as a discourse community with its own rules of interaction, an idioculture with its own semantic norms and terms of reference. Also interesting is the Court's decision to gauge the potential of the comment to be insulting by referring to the apparent linguistic standards of the forum, and in so doing dispense with the "ordinary meaning" test:

> The language which the applicant found to offend him, when compared to other posts on the portal (. . .) which often refer to outstanding scholars of international fame (. . .), is in fact quite innocent. In the post in question the applicant is not referred to by expletives, there are no insults. (Ibid.)

The Court did not find "sex maniac" to have been an insult, but nevertheless found the term to have been defamatory.

In 2004 the female shop assistants working at a Polish branch of an international fashion merchandiser were made to wear T-shirts emblazoned with the English word "bitch" in rather large letters on the front.[5] Although they had contractually agreed to wear the company's merchandise while working, they felt the nature of the message was defamatory, and complained it invited sexual innuendo from the customers. The episode did not end in litigation; instead, the shop assistants raised their objections with journalists. The company's spokesperson defended the requirement that the workers wear the shirts by arguing the message was aimed at the brand's target demographic of "bold young women, half-naked, sexy and racy."[6] Assuming an idioculture along these lines existed in the Poland of 2004, the case illustrates perhaps most aptly the normative conflict with its related semantic ramifications of concern in this chapter. Tiersma points out that "[a] public accusation of wrongdoing is a linguistic act that lowers the status of an individual who allegedly has violated community norms" (1987: 304). However, as Tiersma further notes but does not discuss in depth (318), his observation raises the additional question, what *are* the community norms applicable in such cases and, more importantly, which community should we be looking at in the first place? The shop employees clearly saw "bitch" as equivalent to Hawthorne's scarlet letter, whereas conceivably the "bold young women" who bought the T-shirt embraced the term as a badge of honour.

I have argued in this brief chapter that changes in contexts of culture can lead to problems in semantic interpretation in defamation cases. I have drawn on examples from Poland, not long ago a "monocultural" country, where the political, social, and cultural changes have been particularly conspicuous, yet the themes I have raised pertain to many other societies as well. As new frameworks of interaction and reference are being created, the legal fiction of a "reasonable person" is becoming even more elusive and may be difficult to maintain for much longer, as may be the notion of "ordinary meaning." Whatever the future brings, there is no doubt that linguists and lawyers aiming to understand semantic interpretation in the times of liquid modernity will find Tiersma's work instrumental.

### Notes

1. Definition after CollinsDictionary.com, which in December 2013 chose "geek" as its "Word of the Year."

2. Defined by Fine (1987: 125) as "system[s] of knowledge, beliefs, behaviors, and customs shared by members of an interacting group to which members can refer and that serve as the basis of further interaction."

3. Warsaw Appeals Court, I ACa 755/12.

4. Supreme Court of Poland, III KK 234/07.

5. Owing to popular culture influences, the word would arguably have been understood by a large proportion of the customers.

6. Agnieszka Zakrzewska, "Sexy bitch," *Gazeta Wyborcza*, June 26, 2004.

## References

Bauman, Zygmunt (2012) *Liquid Modernity.* Cambridge: Polity Press.

Fine, Gary Alan (1987) *With the Boys: Little League Baseball and Preadolescent Culture.* Chicago: University of Chicago Press.

Tiersma, Peter Meijes (1987) The Language of Defamation, *Texas Law Review* 66:303–350.

# PART IV

# Interpreting Laws

# 30

# Dynamic Statutes*

## Peter M. Tiersma

Writing and especially printing were extremely static processes in the past. Once a book or statute was published, it was quite cumbersome to change anything without reprinting it, which was a costly proposition. Many of us remember the list of errata that might accompany a book or the stickers with corrections that needed to be pasted somewhere within it. More substantial changes required printing a second edition or at least a supplement. Loose-leaf publications in binders, commonly used in the legal profession, made it easier to update topical materials, but this solution was also far from ideal.

Modern technology is rapidly making writing and publication more dynamic. Information that is available online, in the form of a cybertext, can be modified or updated with minimal effort. Someone who maintains a website can almost instantly correct mistakes, add newly found material, or adapt the website to address changes in circumstances. Legal publishers who provide electronic access to statutes take full advantage of this dynamism. As soon as the legislature enacts a new statute, it can be posted online. And when amendments are passed, the changes can very quickly be incorporated into the electronic version of the statute. It used to be necessary to find a statute in a book and then do a further search to see whether it had—after the book was printed—been amended or repealed. If amended, it was usually necessary to photocopy both the original statute and the amendment and then to create the current version of the statute by cutting and pasting. On websites currently maintained by legal information providers, the text is almost always an accurate and current copy of statutes as enacted and amended by the legislature.

The dynamic quality of the Internet can take this process one step further. At present, the official text of a statute is the enrolled bill, which

* Excerpt from Peter M. Tiersma, *Parchment, Paper, Pixels* 169–76 (2010).

is printed on paper or parchment and typically preserved in a government archive. In the American Congress, after a bill is passed by both houses in identical form, it is enrolled, printed on parchment or paper, certified by the clerk of the house where it originated, and signed by the speaker of the House and the president pro tempore of the Senate. After the president signs it, the new statute is preserved in the National Archives.[1] In the United Kingdom, an official copy of enacted statutes is printed on vellum and lodged in the House of Lords Record Office.[2]

In an age when most lawyers and virtually all members of the public will access statutes online, there is always the danger that a law in a commercial legal database, or even on the legislature's official website, differs in some way from the text of the statute as originally enacted. Since most legislatures have official websites, and since the public is increasingly obtaining almost all information online, why not make official the version posted on the legislature's website? The shelves bending under the weight of statute books, which currently decorate many law offices and judicial chambers, could then be replaced by an official online version of statutory law that is by definition completely up to date and authoritative.

Moreover, if the legislature discovers a mistake or ambiguity in the statute, it could be fixed immediately. Placing the official version of statutes on a government website could eliminate the bulky amendment procedure that is presently required for even the most minute corrections and changes. If a new statute is enacted, it could almost instantaneously become the law of the land simply by posting it online. And if a law is repealed, the act of removing it from the website would stop in its tracks any mischief that its continued operation might cause. Currently, it can take many weeks or months for these sorts of changes to take effect.

Perhaps an even more provocative idea is to give judges the power to edit the authoritative statute on the legislature's website. Judges would no longer have to write lengthy opinions explaining what is wrong with a statute. They could simply fix the problem by adding or deleting a word or two or by inserting a definition or clarification. If the statute is unconstitutional, they could remove it from the website entirely. Judges are sometimes accused of rewriting statutes. Why not change this vice into a virtue? Currently, lawyers spend a great deal of time researching whether and how judges might have interpreted a statute, a process that often requires reading numerous judicial opinions. If judges could just edit the statute directly on the legislative website, it would save lawyers and the public a vast amount of time and money.

As exciting as these possibilities may seem, we should probably step back and take a deep breath. Even though the dynamic nature of the Internet is one of its great blessings, it is also in some respects a curse. Useful information that you find on a website can be altered or disappear overnight. In fact, the entire website might vanish or be restructured beyond recognition. One of the great advantages of traditional writing and printing is its relative permanence.

Moreover, textualization and other literary conventions of the legal profession served in the past to guarantee that the intentions of legal actors were preserved in a fixed format that for the most part could not be altered informally. By this means, traditional writing and textualization can lend a great deal of stability and predictability to the legal system, features that promote the rule of law.

Thus, it seems likely that even if statutes become e-law in the future and are preserved only in some kind of electronic format, many of the textual practices of the law will remain in effect. The process of writing and publishing laws by applying ink to paper may well be obsolescent, but my guess is that the advantages of having a relatively fixed text that is enacted with prescribed formalities will prevent statutes from becoming too terribly dynamic. It is more important for the law to be clear and certain than for it to be instantly responsive to every minor change in circumstances.

## Dynamic Authorship (or Wikilaw)

Statutes are the result of collective authorship, a process largely enabled by writing. Modern technology, especially the Internet, also has implications for this process. Many current Internet users are familiar with Wikipedia and perhaps also the "wiki" movement in general.[3] Like many scholars, I have to admit that when I first heard of Wikipedia, an online encyclopedia written collectively by ordinary citizens rather than established scholars, I was quite skeptical. There are, after all, some excellent encyclopedias written by scholars that are available free or at modest cost in various electronic formats. How much trust can you place in an online encyclopedia composed and edited anonymously by anyone who wants to participate? For all we know, some of these articles are written by high school students.

Putting aside some legitimate questions about quality, what is revolutionary about Wikipedia is the way in which the information is gathered and edited. The articles in traditional encyclopedias are composed by scholars who have been commissioned to write them. Wikipedia, in contrast, is a collaborative effort by anyone who wishes to contribute. Anyone can create a new entry in Wikipedia or edit the contributions of others. As a result, its authoritativeness has been questioned, and articles on a few particularly controversial subjects have required those in charge to restrict the ability of people to make changes. Despite such problems, Wikipedia exemplifies a movement that cannot be ignored.

How long Wikipedia will last in its current incarnation is anyone's guess. For our purposes, the more interesting issue is that the wiki software makes it possible for large groups of people to collectively write and edit an online document. Clearly, this process has some very interesting potential implications for the authorship of legislation.

Instead of engaging in lengthy debates over the wording of a proposed law, legislators using wiki software, or something like it, could sit behind their computers and jointly scroll through the text of a bill. One legislator could make an edit to the text. If another legislator objected, by clicking on her "I demand a vote" icon, the software would immediately pose to all legislators the question of whether the edit should be adopted or rejected. And so it would go until they scrolled through the entire bill. That procedure would ensure that all of them had read and approved the entire bill so that the legislators could legitimately be viewed as its authors. In the alternative, the legislators could review and edit legislation individually. If another legislator later objected to a change, the software could automatically call for a vote via e-mail and incorporate the majority's decision.

Perhaps we should go a step further and eliminate the legislature altogether. Recall that in the olden days, it was common for all citizens to vote on laws in a popular assembly. Direct democracy is still practiced in some villages in New England and Swiss cantons. It is not practical for larger states, however, which is why representative democracy developed.

Modern technology could help us give the legislative power back to the people. Many jurisdictions have referenda on important legal issues, where all citizens are allowed to vote on a statute or constitutional provision. The current paper-based procedure is very expensive and time-consuming, however. Although there are security and verification issues that would need to be addressed, allowing referenda by e-mail would allow vastly more laws to be passed by the population as a whole. The function of the legislature could be reduced to proposing laws to the populace, who would then have the power to vote them up or down.

In fact, using some variant of the wiki software, legislatures could become entirely superfluous. Why not let the people also write the laws? Just as ordinary users of the Internet can collectively draft an encyclopedia article, ordinary citizens could collectively author and edit legislation. We could call it *wikilaw*.

How far we will travel along this path is highly uncertain. While the notion of wikilaw may seem intuitively attractive, the enormous complexity of much modern legislation makes it unlikely that enough citizens would take the time to educate themselves on the issues in order to write or edit statutes on a regular basis. If too few people participate, any resulting statute will not have much legitimacy. For the same reason, it seems to me that even the idea of widespread e-referenda is problematic. Of course, it seems probable that many people will be casting votes by e-mail in a number of years. But the average person does not have the time and energy to learn about and vote on every proposed law that comes before the typical legislature.

Thus, while computers and the Internet make direct democracy technologically quite feasible, and while the use of electronic voting is likely to increase, most citizens will probably be content to continue to delegate their lawmaking power to their elected representatives.

## Interpreting Electronic Text

The law's increasing use of computers and the Internet may also have ramifications for interpretation. The exact implications are impossible to predict, of course. So this discussion will necessarily be somewhat speculative.

Suppose that in the future legislators do indeed start to use some type of software that allows them to collectively author the text of legislation. If so, it is likely to make interpretation more textual. This is even more likely if judges begin to edit statutes online. The reason is that the text of statutes will become much more authoritative. The online text would be completely current and accurate, having been vetted by both legislators and judges, who would all have had the opportunity to correct errors or clarify ambiguities in the language. The trend historically has been that as drafters take more time to write precise and detailed statutes, and as more authoritative copies become available, interpreters are inclined to treat the text with increasing reverence.

At the same time, there are also ways in which e-laws might promote a more intentionalist method of interpretation. Scholars posit that writing has become more speech-like during the past century or two, and that the Internet is intensifying this trend. If so, it should surprise no one if judges come to adopt a somewhat more oral approach to interpretation. When processing speech, we do not hesitate to access background information, including what we know about the speakers and their intentions. We concentrate more on the speaker's meaning and less on the meaning of the words. This, of course, is exactly what intentionalist judges do when they refer to evidence of legislative intent.

Modern technology has resulted in legislative history and other indications of intent (linguistically speaking, context and background) being much more accessible than before. A major reason that judges did not use such sources in the past is that they were difficult or impossible to access. Just as it's hard to be a textualist without accurate copies of the text, it's hard to be an intentionalist without accurate information about the intentions of the legislature. There are currently commercial services that can provide lawyers with materials relating to state or federal legislative history.[4] But they are quite expensive. In fact, the time and cost of researching legislative history is one of the main reasons Justice Scalia opposes its use.[5]

With the rise of the Internet, the practical impediments to finding such historical resources are fast disappearing. Many legislatures currently make a large amount of information available to the public on their websites at absolutely no cost. Searching this material is also easier than ever. When such a wealth of knowledge is available at the click of a mouse, why not use it? After all, a key to understanding just about any text is its purpose. Often enough the totality of a statute will reveal the purpose of its individual parts, but when the purpose is not obvious, and there is no preamble, evidence of legislative history might reveal it. Persuading lawyers and judges to ignore such evidence will not be easy if it is so readily accessible.

At the same time, consider the massive amount of information that is available to us electronically, the difficulties that many of us have in managing it, and the questions that often arise about its reliability. Concerns that Scalia and other textualists have expressed about the arbitrariness of choosing one source of legislative history over another, and even of the possibility of a group of legislators producing or manipulating such history to serve their purposes, are likely to increase when the information resides somewhere on the wild world of the Internet.

Such concerns are legitimate, that there is a way to balance respect for the text with the need to determine the intent and purpose of the legislature as a key to understanding what the text means. Although I have argued that the law at times overuses textualization, it seems to me that this is an issue that textualization can help solve. Specifically, I propose that when enacting statutes, legislatures should textualize their intentions.

## Official Summaries

In the past, legislation typically began with a statement of a statute's background and purpose in the form of a preamble. Preambles were often used as an aid to interpretation. It was not uncommon for the preamble to be as long as the statute proper. Today, preambles or statements of legislative purpose are less common, perhaps because courts have become accustomed to consulting committee reports, records of debates, and other sources of legislative intent.

An important advantage of the traditional preamble is that it is enacted into law as part of, or along with, the statute itself. In that sense, it is authoritative text. This means that a majority of the legislature endorsed the statement of purpose or intention contained in the preamble. We need not worry about whether the preamble really reflects the intentions of the legislature as a whole because the legislature affirmatively voted to enact it into law. The problem of collective intent is also minimized because we can assume that a majority of the legislators who voted for the statute intended to accomplish whatever purpose or intent is stated in the preamble. Moreover, any cost and difficulty of finding evidence of legislative intent disappears. If you can find the statute, you can find the preamble or statement of purpose.[6] And the endless storage capacity of computers means that it would cost almost nothing to add a substantial preamble to every statute.

I would go a step beyond the traditional preamble, however, in order to solve some other problems caused by the language and textual conventions of the profession. Legal texts, as we all know, can be dense, lengthy, convoluted, and full of language that is troublesome for ordinary citizens. In fact, they are often hard for lawyers themselves to understand, especially for those unfamiliar with the subject matter.[7] Moreover, the length and complexity of certain statutes also undermine confidence in whether a legislature can legitimately be viewed as the author of its legislation. A major function of committee reports is to summarize for members of Congress, in plain and ordinary English, the purpose and effect of proposed legislation. In fact, the issuance of committee reports is essentially a concession that the average legislator is not expected to actually read or understand statutes.

My proposal is that we combine the functions of the traditional preamble and the modern committee report into an official summary, written in ordinary English, that would be enacted along with the statute to which it relates. This summary would be the official statement of legislative intent regarding the statute. It would not cover all the details of the legislation, of course, so there would still be room for traditional statutory construction, such as clarifying ambiguities and filling gaps. But any judicial interpretation should be consistent with the spirit and purpose of the law, as stated in the summary.

Such a summary would be more than an aid to construction. It would have the added benefit of informing interested members of the public about the purpose and effect of the new law. Newspapers might publish it verbatim, or reporters could consult the summary and more accurately report on its likely effects. The summaries could be posted on the Internet. Official summaries would therefore also improve public access to, and understanding of, the law.

By authoritatively placing evidence of the intent and purpose of legislation into the text itself, we can be textualists and intentionalists at the same time. That, it seems to me, is exactly what we should strive to achieve. As mentioned earlier in this chapter, certain types of statutory text demand that judges give relatively more deference to the text and the words contained in it. In other cases they should pay more attention to what the speaker meant by those words. But in either case, text and intent should both get their due.

## Notes

1. Mikva and Lane, *Introduction to Statutory Interpretation*, 138; http://www.archives.gov/legislative/.

2. Bernard S. Jackson, *Making Sense in Law* 57 (1995).

3. See www.wikipedia.org.

4. See, for example, the Legislative Intent Service (http://www.legintent.com) or the Legislative History Clearinghouse (http://www.lhclearinghouse.com/).

5. Scalia, Matter of Interpretation, 36.

6. Sometimes statements of legislative purpose or findings are not codified, which means they are part of the statutory law but are not bound with the operative parts of the statute. In that case the preamble or statement will not be quite as accessible, but will still be much easier to locate than a committee report.

7. See Tiersma, *Legal Language* (1999).

## 31

# The Textualization of Precedent*

Peter M. Tiersma

> The municipal law of England ... may with sufficient propriety
> be divided into two kinds; the *lex non scripta*, the unwritten or
> common law; and the *lex scripta*, the written, or statute law.
>
> —Sir William Blackstone[1]

In the English-speaking world, there are traditionally two major sources of
law: statutes and judicial opinions. The former consist of written texts that
have been carefully drafted in advance and which have been scrutinized
and formally enacted by a legislature. Determining the meaning of statutes
generally involves close textual analysis. Legislation thus came to be called
*lex scripta* ("written law"). In contrast, judicial opinions were traditionally
pronounced orally from the bench, and were thus known as *lex non scripta*
("unwritten law"). Figuring out what an opinion meant—determining the
*ratio decidendi*, or holding of a case—required engaging in the process of
legal reasoning. This unwritten law made by judges has long been touted by
the legal profession, especially in England, as being in many ways superior to
the written enactments of the legislature.

Given the massive numbers of judicial opinions or judgments that have
been preserved in writing since the thirteenth century, the notion that the
common law is unwritten seems like a quaint myth, or at least an anachro-
nism. Yet there is a surprising amount of truth to the notion that the common
law resided in the memories of judges and the select group of barristers who
practiced before them. In fact, a remarkable amount of orality has survived
in the English common law. Even today, English judicial opinions need not
necessarily be written down by the judge or by a reporter to have precedential force. And traditional legal reasoning remains a critical skill for English
lawyers.

* Excerpt from Peter M. Tiersma, The Textualization of Precedent, *Notre Dame Law Review*
82: 1187, 1187–89, 1257–62 (2007).

In the United States, however, the common law is embarking on a path toward becoming increasingly textual, just as statutes have been for hundreds of years. It is no exaggeration to say that in this country, the common law consists of what judges *write* in their opinions. What they *think* or what they *say* during the proceedings before them is almost entirely irrelevant. As a result, it is less and less necessary to search for the holding, or *ratio decidendi*, of a case; the judge writing for the majority will often specify exactly what the holding is in carefully crafted text that is meant to fetter the discretion of lower courts in the same way that a statute does. As a consequence, legal reasoning is gradually being supplanted by close reading.

More than two decades ago, Guido Calabresi wrote of the growing "statutorification" of American law.[2] Much of what was traditionally the domain of common law is now governed by statute. Oftentimes these statutes become obsolete. Calabresi's proposed remedy was to allow courts to update antiquated statutes. In essence, courts would treat legislation as though it were part of the common law.[3] But what Calabresi anticipated has not come to pass. Rather than treating statutes as common law, courts are beginning to treat the common law as legislation.

Minds will differ on whether this transformation is good or bad. There are many consequences that flow from writing down the law in an authoritative way, something that I call *textualization*. One of the most significant consequences is that the law becomes more transparent and less susceptible to subtle manipulation. The other side of the coin, of course, is that it becomes more rigid. Rules that reside in memory tend to be more conceptual. They can evolve—consciously or not—as circumstances change. Textualized law, on the other hand, places greater interpretive constraints on those who apply it, and it can usually be changed only by formal amendment or overruling, which can be a slow and cumbersome process.

Complicating the picture is that as the common law becomes ever more textual, the very notion of written text is undergoing dramatic and largely unpredictable changes. Paper is being replaced by pixels. Even though a computer display can mimic a text on paper, there are significant differences between them. Accessing a large corpus of written or printed information traditionally requires an index or digest of some sort, which means that a human being must categorize the content in some way. Accessing electronic text, on the other hand, typically involves requesting a machine to locate sequences of text that exactly match a search term. Moreover, publication, once an important emblem of the authority of a judicial opinion, is undergoing profound transformations in a culture where anyone can publish whatever he wants on the Internet. It seems likely that these developments, especially the massive increase in available cases and the ease with which they can be accessed online, will only intensify the shift from legal reasoning to close reading.

I should emphasize that this Article is more prophecy than empirical observation. To be more exact, it is prophecy based upon observation. There is no doubt that the common law and the nature of precedent have undergone dramatic changes during the past century or two, especially in the United States. What will ultimately result from these developments remains to be seen. It is clear, however, that American judicial opinions are far more textual than opinions or judgments made in the past. It seems inevitable that this trend will have important implications for the concept of precedent and the nature of common law adjudication.

## Quoting the Holding

How judges write their opinions and establish precedents is just one side of the coin. The other side is how those who are bound by a precedent read the opinion that establishes it. In other words, if it is true that judges are expressing their opinions in a more textual way these days, does it follow that those reading the opinions are interpreting them more textually, and less conceptually?

One way to approach the issue is by examining whether and how judges quote precedential opinions. It is instructive to compare American opinions with those produced by English judges. I have already suggested that the English notion of precedent is more conceptual, while the modern American notion is more textual. It turns out that both English and American judges quote extensively from the language of precedential cases. Yet the style of quotation is radically different.

Any American lawyer who reads a few English appellate opinions will immediately be struck by the lengthy quotations they contain, often set apart in indented paragraphs that sometimes extend over several pages. Recall the case from the English Court of Appeal, in which Judge Aldous refers to a nineteenth-century precedent decided by the multi-judge Court of Exchequer Chamber. Aldous first quotes a paragraph of around eighteen lines of text by Judge Erle. Later he quotes another fifteen lines from Erle's opinion. Aldous then recites twenty-five lines of text from the judgment of Judge Vaughan Williams. It is followed by excerpts of text consisting of seven lines twenty-one lines, and another twenty-one lines from the opinions of three other judges.[4] The point, of course, is to try to determine the *ratio decidendi* of the case, which can only be done by reading lengthy portions of text from the opinions of a number of judges who agreed on the outcome, but for somewhat divergent reasons. This is admittedly a rather extreme case, but it is still common practice for English judges to quote lengthy excerpts from the opinions of two or three judges in trying to ascertain the holding.

In fact, extensive quotations are the norm in England even when a single opinion seems to capture the essence of the case. Consider a judgment of the Court of Appeal discussing *Regina v. Gough*,[5] a 1993 decision by the House of Lords. "The gist of that decision, according to the Court of Appeal, was contained in "two brief extracts from the leading speech of Lord Goff.""[6] It then quoted twelve lines of text (129 words) from Lord Goff's opinion. It was followed by a second quotation from Lord Goff on the same point, consisting of twenty-three lines (276 words).[7]

Compare the English approach to an American case, *Chambers v. Nasco, Inc.*,[8] where the US Supreme Court discussed its own precedents regarding recovery of attorney's fees:

> As we explained in *Alyeska*, these exceptions [to the American rule against fee shifting] fall into three categories. The first . . . allows a court to award attorney's fees to a party whose litigation efforts directly benefit others. *Alyeska*, 421 U.S. at 257–258. Second, a court may assess attorney's fees as a sanction for the "willful disobedience of a court order." *Id.*, at 258 (quoting *Fleischmann Distilling Corp. v. Maier Brewing Co.*, 386 U.S. 714, 718, (1967)) . . .
>
> Third, and most relevant here, a court may assess attorney's fees when a party has "acted in bad faith, vexatiously, wantonly, or for oppressive reasons." *Alyeska, supra*, at 258–259 (quoting *F. D. Rich Co. v. United States ex rel. Industrial Lumber Co.*, 417 U.S. 116, 129 (1974)) . . . In this regard, if a court finds "that fraud has been practiced upon it, or that the very temple of justice has been defiled," it may assess attorney's fees against the responsible party, Universal Oil, supra, at 580, as it may when a party "shows bad faith by delaying or disrupting the litigation or by hampering enforcement of a court order," Hutto, 437 U.S. at 689, n. 14. The imposition of sanctions in this instance transcends a court's equitable power concerning relations between the parties and reaches a court's inherent power to police itself, thus serving the dual purpose of "vindicat[ing] judicial authority without resort to the more drastic sanctions available for contempt of court and mak[ing] the prevailing party whole for expenses caused by his opponent's obstinacy." Ibid.[9]

This excerpt not only contains quotations within quotations, but the quoted segments all consist of brief snippets of text, ranging from six to twenty-eight words.

Short quotations from precedential cases appear to be the rule in American opinions. A survey of ten modern United States Supreme Court opinions revealed that the average quotation from other (precedential) cases was around nineteen words long.[10] In contrast, the average quotation from precedential cases in ten House of Lords opinions from the same time period contained around seventy-seven words, about four times as many. Moreover, in the American sample, only one quotation was over 100 words. In the English sample there were sixteen quotations consisting of more than 100 words, along with several over 300 words, and one quotation containing more than 400 words.

It might be argued that the quotation practices of English and American judges should be considered mainly a matter of style. If so, it is a stylistic distinction that reveals underlying differences in how the judges view precedent. The American custom of quoting snippets of text from the holding of a previous case suggests that the courts are approaching precedential cases as a type of authoritative text. American judges seem to be looking for "sound bites" that encapsulate some or all of the holding of a case.

Judges writing the precedents seem increasingly happy to provide those judicial sound bites. As noted above, they conveniently mark the textual holding with the prefatory phrase "we hold." The ease with which a holding can be found is illustrated by a California appellate case, where the court described a precedential case as follows:

> The Supreme Court held: "In sum, we hold that the instant complaint, seeking the recovery of property seized and wrongfully withheld by defendants, does not involve a claim for 'money or damages' within the meaning of section 905, and thus would not fall within the presentation requirements of sections 911.2 and 945.4."[11]

Judges do not always signal their holdings so clearly, of course, but there seems to be a strong tendency to codify the rule of the case in a sentence or two, making it that much easier for lawyers and lower courts to find. Thus, in *Brady v. Maryland*,[12] the Supreme Court stated its holding as follows: "We now hold that the suppression by the prosecution of evidence favorable to an accused upon request violates due process where the evidence is material either to guilt or to punishment, irrespective of the good faith or bad faith of the prosecution."[13] Headnote number three in West's Supreme Court reporter repeated this language virtually verbatim, minus a few definite articles: "Suppression by prosecution of evidence favorable to an accused upon request violates due process where evidence is material either to guilt or to punishment, irrespective of good faith or bad faith of prosecution."[14] In many cases, all the headnote editors have to do is to find the appropriate sentence stating the holding, a task that is vastly simplified when the court prefaces it with the "we hold" phraseology, as it did here. Subsequent courts can use the same strategy to determine what the holding is, as did the Ninth Circuit in a case entitled *Anderson v. Calderon*[15]: "In *Brady v. Maryland*, the Supreme Court held 'that the suppression by the prosecution of evidence favorable to an accused upon request violates due process where the evidence is material either to guilt or to punishment, irrespective of the good faith or bad faith of the prosecution.'"[16] As opposed to the headnote editor, the Ninth Circuit left in the definite articles.

A final indication of how the holding of cases is being textualized is that the rules or standards or tests developed by American courts are now often named for very brief snippets of authoritative text. In other words, the test has been named for the text. Consider the "grievous wrong" standard,[17] the "outcome determinative" test,[18] or the "clear and present danger" rule articulated by Justice Oliver Wendell Holmes in *Schenck v. United States*.[19] Another celebrated Supreme Court case, *United States v. Carotene Products Co.*,[20] contained a textual standard, "discrete and insular minorities," in a footnote,[21] but its obscure location did not hinder it from being quoted and followed in literally hundreds of cases.[22]

Even if not intended to do so, textual standards of this sort—often consisting of no more than two or three words—tend to be interpreted in a more textual and less conceptual way, as indicated and encouraged by their enclosure within quotation marks in subsequent cases. As Michael Sinclair has observed, referring specifically to the footnote in *Carolene Products*, "[l]egal actors in lower decision-making roles take the reasons and verbal formula of higher courts as governing … following authoritative words, rather than rational analysis."[23]

Obviously, the point that I am making can be overstated; there are many modern cases where American courts do not expressly textualize their holdings. It would be foolhardy for law schools to stop teaching traditional legal reasoning. But it is true that, in general, English lawyers and judges concentrate on the concepts and reasoning contained in precedents, struggling to figure out what the judges meant and why they decided the cases as they did. To do so, you need as much evidence as possible, hence the lengthy quotations. Modern American judges are looking more closely at the exact words that the judge wrote in the precedential opinion. They therefore concentrate on extracting critical excerpts of text that they regard as authoritative. More and more, American judges are reading cases in a way that resembles how they read and interpret statutes.

## Notes

1. WILLIAM BLACKSTONE, 1 COMMENTARIES *63.
2. GUIDO CALABRESI, A COMMON LAW FOR THE AGE OF STATUTES 1 (1982).
3. *Id.* at 2.
4. Ord v. Upton, [2000] 1 All E.R. 193, 200–03 (C.A.).
5. [1993] 1 A.C. 646 (H.L.).
6. Locabail (UK) Ltd. v. Bayfield Prop. Ltd., [2000] 1 All E.R. 65, 73 (C.A.).
7. *Id.* at 73–74.
8. 501 U.S. 32 (1991).
9. *Id.* at 45–46 (footnotes and parallel citations omitted).

10. Oklahoma v. New Mexico, 501 U.S. 221 (1991); Litton Fin. Printing Div. v. NLRB, 501 U.S. 190 (1991); McNeil v. Wisconsin, 501 U.S. 171 (1991); Toibb v. Radloff, 501 U.S. 157 (1991); Burns v. United States, 501 U.S. 129 (1991); Gollust v. Mendell, 501 U.S. 115 (1991); Astoria Fed. Sav. & Loan Ass'n v. Solimino, 501 U.S. 104 (1991); Melkonyan v. Sullivan, 501 U.S. 89 (1991); Chambers v. Nasco, Inc., 501 U.S. 32 (1991); Connecticut v. Doehr, 501 U.S. 1 (1991); Deposit Prop. Bd. v. Dalia, [1994] 2 A.C. 367; Hunt v. Severs, [1994] 2 A.C. 350; Rhone v. Stephens, [1994] 2 A.C. 310; Cambridge Water Co. Ltd. v. E. Countries Leather plc, [1994] 2 A.C. 264; Attorney Gen. v. Associated Newspapers Ltd., [1994] 2 A.C. 238; Roebuck v. Mungovin, [1994] 2 A.C. 212; Regina v. Preston, [1994] 2 A.C. 130; Racz v. Home Office, [1994] 2 A.C. 45; Ackman v. Policyholders Prot. Bd., [1993] 3 All E.R. 384. The research was done in 1995. It is based on the first ten cases by the House of Lords in the then most recent bound volume of the Law Reports, Appeal Cases, which was 1994, Volume 2. I did the same for the U.S. Supreme Court, choosing the first ten cases in what was then the most recent bound volume of the United States Reports, Volume 501 (October Term, 1990).

11. TrafficSchoolOnline, Inc. v. Clarke, 5 Cal. Rptr. 3d 408, 412 (Ct. App. 2003) (quoting Minsky v. City of Los Angeles, 520 P.2d 726, 734 (1974)).

12. 373 U.S. 83 (1963).

13. *Id.* at 87.

14. 83 S. Ct. 1194, 1194 (1963).

15. 232 F.3d 1053 (9th Cir. 2000).

16. *Id.* at 1062 (quoting Brady v. Maryland, 373 U.S. 83, 87 (1963)).

17. Ruffo v. Inmates of Suffolk County Jail, 502 U.S. 367, 393 (1992).

18. Guaranty Trust Co. v. York, 326 U.S. 99, 109 (1945). The test is referred to as such by *Hanna v. Plumer*, 380 U.S. 460, 475 (1965).

19. 249 U.S. 47, 52 (1919).

20. 304 U.S. 144 (1938).

21. *Id.* at 152 n.4 (1938). Note that the use of footnotes is itself an indication of a literate mode of thinking. With their more oral tradition, English judges virtually never use them.

22. A Westlaw search conducted on December 19, 2006, on the "All Cases" database (ALLCASES) using the search terms "discrete and insular minority" resulted in 417 cases.

23. Michael B. W. Sinclair, *Anastasoff versus Hart: The Constitutionality and Wisdom of Denying Precedential Authority to Circuit Court Decisions*, 64 U. Pitt. L. Rev. 695, 738–39 (2003).

# 32

# Talk about Text as Text

Lawrence M. Solan

In his important article, *Textualizing Precedent*, Peter Tiersma (2006) writes about the phenomenon of American judges not only adhering to precedent (old news), but also writing opinions that resemble statutory pronouncements and later engaging in a textual exegesis of the language of their earlier opinions. The traditional distinction between holding and dicta has flown out the window.

Tiersma brings to light the surprising frequency with which judges quote themselves and then parse their own words. Classic common law reasoning, the kind of reasoning that US law students are taught to master, involves determining how well the facts of a current case fit the various precedents that have already been decided and then arguing whether the law should develop in favor of extending the precedent to the present case or deviating from it. Consider Edward Levi's (1949, 2013) characterization of the common law. Speaking of judges, Levi wrote:

> In arriving at his result he will ignore what the past thought important; he will emphasize facts which prior judges would have thought made no difference. It is not alone that he could not see the law through the eyes of another, for he could at least try to do so. It is rather that the doctrine of dictum forces him to make his own decision. (p. 7).

In traditional common law reasoning, some combination of factual analysis, characterization of an implied rule coming from the earlier decisions, and value-laden policy are adduced in an appropriately weighted package to argue for the position that best suits one's client. If Tiersma is right, then things have changed since the mid-twentieth century. My sense is that the law has indeed changed and that Tiersma has captured a profound historical development in the nature of judging.

Much of Tiersma's discussion is of judges textualizing the common law, making it more code-like in nature. Judges, however, not only make law, but also construe statutes, regulations, and the Constitution when there is disagreement about the application of such authoritative documents to the facts of a particular case. Expanding on Tiersma's work, it appears that judges not only have textualized the common law, but they have also textualized their own analyses of authoritative legal texts, substituting analysis of their earlier opinions for analysis of the statute, regulation, or constitutional provision whose application is in dispute (see Schauer 1986) for discussion of constitutional cases).

In the constitutional realm, consider the *Lemon* test, named after *Lemon v. Kurtzman*,[1] a 1971 Supreme Court decision prohibiting the use of taxpayer funds to support parochial schools. The establishment clause of the First Amendment of the US Constitution says: "Congress shall make no law respecting an establishment of religion." Distilling prior court opinions, the *Lemon* court held:

> Three such tests may be gleaned from our cases. First, the statute must have a secular legislative purpose; second, its principal or primary effect must be one that neither advances nor inhibits religion; finally, the statute must not foster "an excessive government entanglement with religion." (*Lemon*, 612–13, citations omitted).

Lemon has proven to be controversial over the years. Nonetheless, the test and its elements have become textualized, that is, subject to analysis as the law itself. Below in Table 32.1 are references made to the test and to the specific language of its third prong. The court's earlier words are now seen as legal text.

Whatever position one takes concerning the importance of the language used by the Constitution's framers, there is a great deal of analysis being conducted concerning the language used by judges who have interpreted the Constitution.

Cases dealing with statutes have also been textualized. The canons of construction are judge-made and are quoted verbatim routinely. But the

TABLE 32.1

**Federal Court Cases Making Reference to "Lemon Test" and "Lemon" within Five Words of "Excessive Government Entanglement," January 1971–January 2014**

| Courth | "Lemon test"" | "Lemon" within five words of "excessive government entanglement" |
|---|---|---|
| Supreme Court | 32 | 11 |
| US Court of Appeals | 284 | 99 |
| US District Courts | 514 | 167 |

textualization of precedent in statutory cases goes well beyond that. When a court defines a statutory term, and later courts parse the court's earlier words, leaving the legislature's original language as of secondary importance, the court has literally legislated. For example, the Lanham Act, the federal trademark statute, says little about the relative strength of a mark. However, in 1976, appellate court judge Henry Friendly created a hierarchy of distinctiveness—from generic at one end of the spectrum to fanciful at the other—which is still widely cited today.[2] The case is not merely cited for its reasoning. A Lexis search reveals that the words "arbitrary" and/or "fanciful" have been cited in the context of this case more than 275 times as of the end of 2013, showing that the Friendly hierarchy has not only been influential, it has been textualized. Linguists testifying as experts in trademark cases use the hierarchy routinely in their analyses (see Shuy 2002).

Thus, courts substitute the Friendly hierarchy of distinctiveness for the statutory language, which contains no such analysis.[3] For the most part, this substitution is benign. Apart from trial-level courts (district courts) within the jurisdiction of Judge Friendly's court (the Second Circuit, which includes New York and several other northeastern states), there is no obligation to follow his hierarchy. The best explanation for why judges do so is that it is a very intelligent and useful way to organize trademark law. If this is correct, then the textualization of statutory analysis is like the textualization of common law reasoning: later courts take the pronouncements of earlier courts as rules in their own right when they believe it is the right thing to do. In the case of statutory interpretation, the rules are rules about rules.

Not all textualization of precedent dealing with statutes is so benign, however. When courts define statutory words and later substitute an earlier court's definition for the legislative language itself, they necessarily distort meaning. In the philosophy of language, this is known as "the pet fish problem" (see Fodor and Lepore 1996). The prototypical pet is a dog, perhaps a setter. The prototypical fish is a trout or salmon. But the prototypical pet fish is a goldfish. This happens because we perform linguistic operations to combine smaller concepts into larger ones before we perform prototype analysis. Since law relies on prototypes—or on the ordinary meaning of a statute's terms, as the legal literature puts it—the textualization of precedent leads to a great deal of judicial input into statutory law.

Consider the federal anti-racketeering statute—RICO. A RICO violation requires proof that the defendant has engaged in a "pattern of racketeering activity." Other than to require at least two such activities within a given time period, the statute does not define the word "pattern." But the Supreme Court did define it in a 1989 case,[4] holding that a pattern consists of a combination of "relatedness" and "continuity." Since then, courts reduced their analysis of the word "pattern" in RICO cases and have increased their analysis of "relatedness" and "continuity." The Supreme Court has not revisited the issue. As of the end of 2014, however, the courts of appeals have cited the case and spoken of relatedness and ambiguity 94 times, and the district courts 499 times. It is very difficult to match the courts' results with one that would regard the facts of the case to constitute a pattern. As the pet fish problem tells us, a prototypical pattern is not equal to a prototypical case of relatedness plus a prototypical case of continuity, even assuming that the Supreme Court's definition is a good one.

What all of this tells us is that Tiersma's textualization of precedent appears to transcend the common law, and is a reflection of how courts view themselves, even in contexts where judges concede that they should be taking a backseat to other institutions, such as the constitutional framers and the legislature. While they deny it at every turn, it is hard to escape the conclusion that judges act as much as lawgivers as the law interpreters they profess to be.

## Notes

1. 403 U.S. 602 (1971).
2. Abercrombie & Fitch Co. v. Hunting World, Incl., 537 F.2d 4 (2d Cir. 1976).
3. See Section 2 of the Lanham Act, 15 U.S.C. § 1052.
4. H. J., Inc. v. Northwestern Bell Telephone Company, 492 U.S. 229 (1989).

## References

Fodor, Jerry and Ernest LePore (1996). The Red Herring and the Pet Fish: Why Concepts Still Can't Be Prototypes. *Cognition* 58: 253–270.

Levi, Edward H. (1949, 2013). *An Introduction to Legal Reasoning.* Chicago: University of Chicago Press.

Schauer, Frederick (1995). Opinions as Rules. *University of Chicago Law Review* 53: 682–689.

Shuy, Roger (2002). *Linguistic Battles in Trademark Disputes.* New York: Palgrave Macmillan.

Tiersma, Peter (2006). The Textualization of Precedent. *Notre Dame Law Review* 82: 1187–1278.

# 33

# Textualization, Textualism, and Purpose-Stating Preambles

Jeffrey P. Kaplan

As law becomes ever more textual—what Peter Tiersma calls textualization—statutory construction becomes ever more textualist (Tiersma 2010). The same holds for the "construction" of judicial opinions (Tiersma 2007). I will comment here only on the former trend, with focus on Tiersma's proposal that legislatures "textualize their intentions" by passing an official summary statement of purpose along with a bill (Tiersma 2010: 174–176). Such a move might facilitate statutory construction that is both textualist and intentionalist, without any of the problems usually associated with intentionalism. (More bluntly, it might make statutory construction much more textualist.)

Intentionalism suffers from the familiar problems of multiple intent and murky evidence (legislative history can be too complex, contradictory, and data-rich for reliable conclusions about legislative intent, and can even be doctored by participants to affect future court analysis) (Tiersma 2010: 174; Scalia 1997: 34). Tiersma observes that the evidence problem is one reason for Justice Scalia's commitment to textualism (Tiersma 2010: 174). Scalia is also motivated by what might be called the speech act problem—statutes, not the intentions behind them, are what are enacted into law:

> It is the *law* that governs, not the intent of the lawgiver.... Men may intend what they will; but it is only the laws that they enact which bind us. (Scalia 1997: 17)
>
> Do I have to defer to John Paul Stevens because he's the author? ... "Oh, John, you wrote *Chevron*. You must know what it means." Of course not! John doesn't know what it means! Once you let loose the judicial opinion, John, it has a life of its own, and it means what it says. Now, why should legislation be any different? ... Once Congress floats that text out

there, it has a life of its own. It means what it means. It means what it says. (Liptak 2009, quoting Scalia)

Enacted statements of purpose might solve all three problems (multiple intents, murky evidence, and the speech act problem): First, a purpose statement would be voted on and passed by the legislature, creating an official, authoritative statement of legislative purpose, thereby solving the multiple intent problem. Second, including such a statement might eliminate, or at least reduce, the relevance of legislative history, thereby solving the evidence problem. Third, because they would be enacted, purpose statements might solve the speech act problem.

Tiersma takes a middle ground between textualism and intentionalism: "By authoritatively placing evidence of the intent and purpose of legislation into the text itself, we can be textualists and intentionalists at the same time. That, it seems to me, is exactly what we should strive to achieve" (Tiersma 2010: 176). Because statutory construction is imperfect (Tiersma 1995: 1101), if text always trumps legislative history, textual analysis had better be done well. An interesting but challenging question is what "well" entails here.

One element, I believe, is taking the "interpretation"/"construction" distinction seriously. Tiersma (1995) revives, and changes slightly, this distinction as originally drawn by Lieber (1880). For Lieber, interpretation was "finding out the true sense of any form of words, that is, the sense which their author sought to convey," and construction was "drawing of conclusions ... that lie beyond the direct expression of the text, from elements known from and given in the text—conclusions which are in the spirit, though not within the letter of the text" (Lieber 1880: 23, cited by Tiersma 1995: 1097). Tiersma uses speech act theory to define the two somewhat differently: interpretation as a cognitive act of understanding language, construction as an illocutionary act, specifically a declaration, under Searle's (1976) taxonomy. Declarations are a class of illocutionary act that change the world by declaring that the world is—now—in such-and-such a state. A baseball umpire's calling a runner out is a familiar example. A court's holding that the legal meaning of a statute is such-and-such works in the same way. Every court's holding about statutory meaning is a construction. Just as an umpire's call can be wrong but will still stand, a court's construction can depart from interpretation. A difference is that such a departure will not necessarily be deemed wrong.

Tiersma notes that in a perfect legal world, construction would be trivial: a court could simply, directly, translate a cognitive act (interpretation) into a speech act (construction). Of course it's almost never so simple. Appellate cases are almost necessarily hard. If they were easy, they would never get to that level. A central insight in Solan 1993 was that judges often conceal construction by asserting that the language of some statute means (only) such-and-such, that is, calling what is actually construction, interpretation. Solan observes that judges do this to make their opinions persuasive, by making the case that the statutory language renders the decision inevitable. Of course the effort at concealing how tough the linguistic or legal questions are doesn't always succeed. Applying the distinction between interpretation and construction should clarify judges' articulation of their reasoning about statutory meaning. Under the plain meaning rule, interpretation should precede and limit construction (Tiersma 1995: 1100). Even Hart and Sacks's (1994: 1958) "legal process" theory, which defined statutory construction as deciding what "meaning ought to be given" to a statute by determining legislative purpose, barred giving "the words . . . a meaning they will not bear" (Eskridge, Frickey, and Garrett 2007: 718). Taking the distinction seriously, and recognizing that interpretation should precede construction, could push construers into better efforts to understand the statutory language. Or it could induce them to include more frank statements in their opinions of what the statutory language means, after which other considerations could be invoked—unless the construer is a strict textualist—to justify a different construction. A well-known model is *Rector of Holy Trinity Church v. U.S.*,[1] where the court admitted that the statutory language in question had a certain meaning and then proceeded to construe the statute in a dramatically different way. Contrast *D.C. v. Heller*,[2] about which I have argued that Justice Scalia's majority opinion badly blurred the distinction between interpretation and construction (Kaplan 2012) in connection with the Second Amendment ("A well-regulated militia being necessary to the security of a free state, the right of the people to keep and bear arms shall not be infringed").

Judges' records of understanding (or articulating their understanding of) statutory language accurately vary considerably. Well-known older cases like *U.S. v. X-Citement Video*[3] and *Smith v. U.S.*[4] illustrate this fact, but its reality can be seen in recent cases as well.[5] In *X-Citement Video*, Justice Rehnquist, writing for the majority, construed a statute differently from its syntactically mandated interpretation, which he identified as only "the most natural grammatical reading."[6] This formulation evoked scorn from Scalia in dissent: "To say, as the Court does that [the only grammatically possible interpretation] is . . . 'the most natural grammatical reading' is . . . rather like saying that the ordinarily preferred total for 2 plus 2 is 4."[7] In *Smith*, the majority interpreted the expression "use a gun" in a drug crime so broadly that it denoted trading a gun for drugs. Again Scalia disagreed, arguing that to "use an instrumentality ordinarily means to use it for its intended purpose," giving examples of "uses" of a firearm that were within the dictionary definition—scratching one's head, and selling it—but obviously not uses for its intended purpose, that is, as a weapon.[8]

So what about Tiersma's suggestion? Would enacted purpose summaries improve statutory construction by reducing it as much as possible to interpretation? Only maybe. Already some modern statutes contain purpose-stating preambles, as they did in earlier times. In *Heller*, Scalia asserts that the only function of preambles is to disambiguate[9]—a semantic function—but supports the claim not with linguistic argumentation and evidence[10] but with nineteenth-century treatises on statutory construction, that is, by appeal to (legal) authorities[11]—a clear case of obscuring the distinction between interpretation and construction. Volokh (1998) argues that preambles are mere "justification clauses" bearing only a weak semantic relation to operative language—to disambiguate, a claim echoed by Scalia in *Heller*—and are included for rhetorical or political reasons. Longo 2013 provides examples of Illinois appellate courts denying the relevance of preambles.[12] Justice Scalia and his co-author Bryan A. Garner summarize this tradition thusly: "[T]he function of a statute ... is to establish rights and duties, not to set forth facts or to announce purposes ... The prologue ... is ... not part of the congressionally legislated ... sets of rights and duties. It is an aside" (Scalia and Garner 2012: 217).

Should courts take more heed of purposive preambles? I believe in some cases they should. I do not believe there should be a blanket prohibition against treating them as integral, operative, parts of an enacted statute. For one thing, they are part of what is voted on and thereby enacted. By what principle should courts then disregard them? Sometimes, with semantic vision occluded by ignoring the interpretation/construction distinction—by looking first for legal meaning rather than language meaning—courts find a false distinction between a statute's supposed operative part and its supposed preamble, and conclude that only what is seen as the operative part is ... um ... operative. This is a mistake when the preamble conditions the operative language. Returning to the Second Amendment, semantically, there can be no question that the absolute phrase conditions the main clause, and if the proposition encoded in the absolute is false (as it demonstrably is), the main clause loses its grammatically encoded semantic conditioning and becomes—semantically—moot. The *Heller* decision would have been more persuasive had this been recognized, even if the Court had construed the Amendment as it did (to protect gun ownership without any militia connection). I am not sure that faith in courts would be strengthened if courts were consistently upfront about decisions to ignore statutory language in favor of legal construction, but there would be a considerable gain in intellectual honesty. And if Tiersma's implicit confidence is justified that courts would use enacted purpose statements "textualistically" (*contra* the tradition against counting preambles as operative), even if only to find legislative intent, so much the better.

## Notes

1. 143 U.S. 457 (1892).
2. 508 U.S. 223 (1993).
3. 513 U.S. 64 (1994).
4. 508 U.S. 223 (1993).
5. Fowler v. United States, 563 U.S. ___ (2011), 131 S.Ct. 2045 (2011).
6. 513 U.S. 64, 68 (1994)
7. Id. at 81.
8. 508 U.S. 223, 242 (1993).
9. 554 U.S. 570, 577–8 (2008).
10. Notable because Scalia does sometimes argue like a linguist, empirically and based on linguistic examples. See Kaplan 2012 for examples of Scalia's linguist-like argumentation in *Heller*.
11. 554 U.S. 570, 578 (2008).
12. Though not always. Longo includes an example of the Illinois Supreme Court citing a fetus-protecting preamble to an abortion law to justify a decision against claims made on behalf of genetically defective children for relief for "wrongful life."

## References

Eskridge, William, Philip Frickey, and Elizabeth Garrett (2007) *Cases and Materials on Legislation, Statutes and the Creation of Public Policy* (4th ed.). St. Paul, Minn.: West Publishing.

Hart, H. and A. Sacks (1994 (1958)) The Legal Process: Basic Problems in the Making and Application of Laws. Westbury, NY: Foundation Press.

Kaplan, Jeffrey P. (2012) Unfaithful to Textualism. *Georgetown Journal of Law & Public Policy* 10: 385–428.

Lieber, Francis (1880/2002) *Legal and Political Hermeneutics*. Clark, NJ: The Lawbook Exchange.

Liptak, Adam (2009) On the Bench and Off, the Eminently Quotable Justice Scalia, *New York Times*, May 11, 2009, available at http://www.nytimes.com/2009/05/12/us/12bar.html.

Longo, Anthony J. (2013) Beware: Preambles Not Always Reliable. *Chicago Daily Law Bulletin*, Volume 159, No. 98 (May 17, 2013).

Scalia, Antonin (1997) *A Matter of Interpretation*. Princeton, NJ: Princeton University Press.

Scalia, Antonin and Bryan Garner (2012) *Reading Law: The Interpretation of Legal Texts*. St. Paul, Minn.: Thomson/West.

Searle, J. (1976) A Classification of Illocutionary Acts. *Language in Society* 5: 1–23.

Solan, Lawrence M. (1993) *The Language of Judges*. Chicago: University of Chicago Press.

Tiersma, Peter M. (1995) The Ambiguity of Interpretation: Distinguishing Interpretation from Construction. *Washington University Law Quarterly* 73: 1095–1101.

Tiersma, Peter M. (2007) The Textualization of Precedent. *Notre Dame Law Review* 82: 1187–1278.

Tiersma, Peter M. (2010) *Parchment, Paper, Pixels.* Chicago: University of Chicago Press.

Volokh, Eugene (1998) The Commonplace Second Amendment. *NYU Law Review* 73: 793–810.

**Cases**

Rector of Holy Trinity Church v. U.S., 143 U.S. 457 (1892).

D.C. v. Heller, 508 U.S. 223 (1993).

U.S. v. X-Citement Video, 513 U.S. 64 (1994).

Smith v. U.S., 508 U.S. 223 (1993).

Fowler v. United States, 563 U.S. ___ (2011), 131 S.Ct. 2045 (2011).

# Between Paper and Pixels—How the Form of Modern Laws Changed Their Function

Dru Stevenson

In *Parchment, Paper, and Pixels*, Peter Tiersma deftly traces the evolution of law from oral traditions and decrees to written texts and finally to digital files (Tiersma 2010). Tiersma observes that the shift from oral laws to text allowed editing by the original writers, and that writing gave the laws a greater sense of permanence and further reach across space and time. For a long period, he notes, the legal texts were subordinate, in terms of authority, to the oral laws or decrees that they memorialized. Eventually, as populations became more literate and procedural rules safeguarded (or at least symbolized) governmental legitimacy, the written laws took primacy. Even today, however, courts routinely look to the legislative history of statutes, including the transcripts of oral debates, in construing the meaning of statutory provisions; the oral component of laws has not disappeared completely. After discussing the advent of modern statutes and modern technology, Tiersma moves on to speculating about how the Internet and computer word processing software could allow for judicial editing of statutes or easier public referenda.

Drawing on Tiersma's historical vision, here I will add to the discussion by filling in some history that occurred between the "paper" and "pixels" eras, when codification replaced the publication of statutes sequentially. This shift raises an important issue: How the format of the body of statutory law, its arrangement in compilations, can affect the legal system overall. During the Victorian Era, the shift from chronologically published enactments to topically arranged, continuously updated codes brought major systemic changes, a point that Tiersma describes thoughtfully in his article, *The Textualization of Precedent* (Tiersma 2007: 1234). The change to the legal landscape, in fact, was nearly as great as when law leapt from the spoken to the written word in the Medieval period. Along with other factors such as immigration, urbanization, population growth, and new technologies, the wave of codification (Cook 1991; Lieberman 1989: 181–85, 239–55) contributed to the explosion of legislation and regulations in the United States during the twentieth century.

Between the Civil War and the Second World War, both federal and state governments changed their approach to the compilation of legislation (Clarke 1898: 33–43, 263–341). The new approach partially adopted the ideals of the codification movement—statutes published with systematic-topical arrangement, indexing, and hierarchically numbered sections and subsections. Prior to the Civil War, legislatures published enactments in chronological order by date of passage. The traditional arrangement made it very difficult for lawyers, judges, or even legislatures to determine whether the legislature had previously addressed a subject in an obscure part of an enactment (Cook 1991). In theory, one would have to read all the enactments of a legislature, from the beginning, to find what enactments had mentioned a legal issue and whether there were subsequent repeals, amendments, or revisions. Legislatures could pass a new law, in fact, without realizing that a prior law existed on the same subject. With no computers, statutory research was nearly as cumbersome as case research—looking for a needle in a haystack. Topical summaries of laws—called digests—were invaluable (Lieberman 1989), but were major undertakings; someone had to do the work of reading everything, sorting it, summarizing it, and publishing it. Previously, private bills, by which the legislature granted benefits such as land grants to named individuals, often exceeded the number of public laws, but these personalized legislative edicts became quite rare after codification (Davidson 2013).

The adoption of codified statutory systems in the United States did not happen in a vacuum; it coincided, unsurprisingly, with other cultural trends that bear conceptual overlap, such as the introduction and rapid adoption of hierarchical library classification systems by Cutter and Dewey (Wright 2007: 165–182). The topical sorting, hierarchical logic structure, and numbering systems were a method of information management that suddenly had a burst of popularity in the society.

The newer codes—whether they use that moniker (as in the United States Code) or not (as in Texas Revised Statutes)—dramatically change the accessibility of the law for all users, for better or worse. Penal statutes from all years appear together, as do laws pertaining to land use, taxation, elections, schools, and so on. Sequential numbering of sections, and subordinate numbering or lettering of subsections, allowed a uniform system of citation, cross-referencing, and indexing (Keyes 2004; Del Duca and DeLiberato 1999: 1313 n.15). For legislatures, the change lowers the transaction costs of legislating. Information costs are lower in the sense that a legislator can more easily find problematic sections or even gaps in the statutory coverage of an area, and can propose amendments, revisions, repeals, and other tweaks.

Once the gaps in legislative coverage are visible, they become inviting targets for new enactments (Easterbrook 1983: 550). Similar phenomena occur with bureaucracies promulgating ever-more-thorough regulations.

Lower information costs—in terms of gaps to fill and provisions already in place—also facilitate bargaining between legislators, reducing the transaction costs of achieving a legislative compromise for new enactments. When legislators from both political parties have a clear picture of the current statutory or regulatory framework and can see how various provisions of a proposed bill will modify sections across the existing code, it is easier to agree on tradeoffs, priorities, and precise verbiage. In addition, the proliferation of model acts, uniform codes, and restatements of the law gave legislatures readily available legislation drafted by respected legal authorities to add to their codes. This assisted harmonization of law across jurisdictions, but it also caused the volume of statutes to bulk up quickly.

Codification was certainly not the sole cause of statutory proliferation. The scale, complexity, and diversity of modern society necessitated an expansion in the legal system. Lawmaking would have accelerated in any event. Yet the new form or packaging of laws in topical, systematic arrangement, with indexing and hierarchical numbering, reduced the costs of enactment so that the societal pressures for legal reforms could push forward with greater speed and less friction (Rosenthal and Forth 1978). Social changes provided pressure for more laws and expanded government, but codification provided the necessary spigot for the proliferation of statutes (Duxbury 1993: 628).

This change in our legal formulations also affected the courts' interpretive role. Tiersma links the advent of printed statutes with judicial emphasis on the plain meaning of the text in the nineteenth century, to be eventually abandoned in the early twentieth century in favor of an emphasis on legislative intent. The shift toward searching for legislative intent is a logical consequence of this change in the form of statutes in their codification. Codified statutes tend to include definitional sections, suggesting to the judiciary that each word in the law had resulted from deliberation and consensus in the legislature (Vermeule 2001). Small amendments and tweaks in wording are easier, and thus more frequent, once statutes take a codified form, so courts more often confronted statutes in which the legislature altered one critical word or phrase. Courts usually assume the legislature intended the change to expand the scope of the rules, rather than narrow it (Solan 2010: 67). Because codification facilitates more statutory amendments, courts have tended to apply the laws more expansively, searching further for the intended meaning of individual words. Similarly, courts increasingly assumed that statutory silence was also a matter of deliberation and achieved consensus on the part of the legislature, and thus drew meaningful inferences from such gaps. Legislative history thus took on much more importance as documentation of legislative deliberation, decision, and consensus.

It is difficult to measure how much codification alone contributed to the modern proliferation of statutes, as there is no easy way to isolate it from other societal factors pushing toward expanded government regulation. However, to the extent codification reduces the costs of enactment, whether through lowering information costs, legislative bargaining costs, or drafting costs through borrowing from other codes, it contributed to increasing the quantity of enactments. That steep increase in the volume of laws necessarily raises information costs for the end-users, that is, the citizenry. At some point, sheer quantity outweighs efficiency gains of logical organization and indexing, making law less accessible. If law becomes inaccessible to the citizenry, this has important implications for the role of courts and the legal profession, and for the functioning of democracy.

## References

Clarke, R. Floyd (1898) *The Science of Law and Lawmaking.* London: Macmillan.

Cook, Charles M. (1981) *The American Codification Movement: A Study of Antebellum Legal Reform.* Westport, Conn.: Greenwood Press.

Davidson, Roger H. (2013) The Presidency and Congressional Time, in *Rivals for Power: Presidential-Congressional Relations* 87–112 (James A. Thurber, ed.). Plymouth, UK: Rowman & Littlefield.

Del Duca, Louis F. and Louis F. De Liberato (1999) Simplification in Drafting—The Uniform Commercial Code Article 9 Experience, *Chicago.-Kent L. Review* 74: 1309–1337.

Duxbury, Neil (1993) Faith in Reason: The Process Tradition in American Jurisprudence, *Cardozo Law Review* 15: 601–705.

Easterbrook, Frank H. (1983) Statutes' Domains, *University of Chicago Law Review* 50: 533–552.

Keyes, John Mark (2004) Incorporation by Reference in Legislation, *Statute Law Review* 25: 180–195.

Lieberman, David (1989) *The Province of Legislation Determined.* Cambridge: Cambridge University Press.

Rosenthal, Alan and Rod Forth (1978). The Assembly Line: Law Production in the American States, *Legislative Studies Quarterly* 3: 265–291.

Solan, Lawrence M. (2010) *The Language of Statutes: Laws and their Interpretation.* Chicago: University of Chicago Press.

Tiersma, Peter (2010) *Parchment, Paper, and Pixels.* Chicago: University of Chicago Press.

Tiersma, Peter (2007) The Textualization of Precedent, *Notre Dame Law Review* 82: 1187–1278.

Wright, Alex (2007) *Glut: Mastering Information Through the Ages.* Ithaca, NY: Cornell University Press.

PART V

# Language and Criminal Justice

# Crimes of Language

35

# The Language of Perjury
## SPEAKING FALSELY BY SAYING NOTHING*
## Peter M. Tiersma

The question presented by *Bronston v. United States*[1] was "whether a witness may be convicted of perjury for an answer, under oath, that is literally true but not responsive to the question asked and arguably misleading by negative implication."[2] The defendant, Samual Bronston, was the president of Samual Bronston Productions, Inc., a movie production company. He had personal as well as company bank accounts in various European countries. The company petitioned for bankruptcy. At a bankruptcy examination, the following exchange occurred between the lawyer for a creditor and Mr. Bronston:

Q. Do you have any bank accounts in Swiss banks, Mr. Bronston?
A. No, sir.
Q. Have you ever?
A. The company had an account there for about six months, in Zurich.[3]

The "truth" was that Bronston once had a large personal bank account in Switzerland for five years, where he had deposited and drawn checks in an amount over $ 180,000.

Mr. Bronston was tried for perjury. The prosecution's theory at trial was that Bronston answered the second question with literal truthfulness, but unresponsively addressed his answer to the *company*'s assets, thereby implying that he had never had a *personal* Swiss bank account. The trial court essentially agreed that Bronston's answer could form the basis of a perjury charge, instructing the jury that Bronston could be convicted if he gave an answer "not literally false but when considered in the context in which it was

---

* Excerpts from Peter Meijes Tiersma, The Language of Perjury: "Literal Truth," Ambiguity and the False Statement Requirement, *Southern California Law Review* 63: 373, 378, 409–14 (1990). **217**

given, nevertheless constitute[d] a false statement."[4] Bronston was convicted and the court of appeals affirmed.

The Supreme Court unanimously reversed.

Perhaps the main argument for the Supreme Court's decision in *Bronston* was that the outcome was mandated by the federal perjury statute, codified as 18 U.S.C. Section 1621. Section 1621 provides in pertinent part that the offense of perjury obtains when the witness "willfully . . . states . . . any material matter which he does not believe to be true."

The Court emphasized the use of the verb "state" and continued that "the statute does not make it a criminal act for a witness to willfully state any material matter *that implies* any material matter that he does not believe to be true."[5] The Court suggested that to hold that Bronston had made a false statement would "go beyond the precise words of the statute" and that there was no compelling reason to do so.[6] Although not directly addressing the issue, the *Bronston* Court suggested that it not only construed the verb "state" to exclude indirect statements and inferences drawn from words but might also limit the concept "statement" to words in spoken or written form.

Silence will not often constitute a false statement, but under the communicative approach, a person may well communicate something false by means of silence. At the outset, it should be stressed that communication by silence must not be confused with drawing inferences from silence. The jury can and will draw certain inferences from the fact that in a murder trial a crucial witness hemmed and hawed instead of providing a direct answer regarding the defendant's guilt, or that a defense witness who could potentially provide an alibi did not testify. But those witnesses hardly intend to send the jury messages to that effect, so the silence is not linguistically communicative.

A true example of perjury by silence is provided by the California case *People v. Meza*.[7] Mr. Meza was a prospective juror in a burglary trial. Before *voir dire* the court clerk administered an oath to all the potential jurors. The court then introduced the defendant and asked whether any of the potential jurors knew him. One raised his hand and another spoke verbally. The court inquired if there was anyone else. Meza remained silent and did not raise his hand. The court then asked a further series of questions, specifically directing jurors to raise their hands to indicate an affirmative response. One of the questions was whether there was any reason a juror could not be fair and impartial. Once again, Meza did not speak or raise his hand. Later it was discovered that Meza was, in fact, the defendant's brother-in-law and that there was bad blood between them.

Meza was tried for perjury. The trial court set aside the information on the ground that failure to respond to questions could not constitute perjury.

The court of appeal reversed. The court rejected the suggestion of an older California opinion that silence could not constitute perjury.[8] It noted that the California perjury statute, like its federal counterpart, refers to what a witness "states."[9] The California Evidence Code defines a "statement" as "(a) oral or written verbal expression or (b) nonverbal conduct of a person intended by him as a substitute for oral or written verbal expression."[10] Especially in the context of collective questioning of prospective jurors, the court of appeal held that silence or inaction could be taken as a response. The trial judge had specifically informed jurors to indicate an affirmative answer by raising their hands, in effect directing those who had a negative answer to so indicate by silence or inaction. The court concluded that the trier of fact should determine whether Meza intended his silence to mean "no."

In a recent federal case, *United States v. Mattox*,[11] the court came to a similar conclusion regarding a perjury defendant who left spaces blank on a form requiring him to report all employment during a specified period of time. The appellate court held that leaving a blank space in these circumstances was equivalent to answering "none" or a statement that there are no facts to be reported. "Silence may be falsity when it misleads ... [F]ailure to [fill in the blank] was equivalent to an answer, and a false one at that."[12]

These decisions comport with the law's general willingness to concede that people can communicate via silence and inaction. For example, the law of contracts has long recognized that acceptance of an offer (and its communication) can occur by silence or conduct.[13] Likewise, the Supreme Court has recognized that for the purposes of the first amendment, the term "speech" includes communicative conduct[14] as well as silence.[15] Even perjury cases have recognized that the term "statement" cannot be limited to what a witness literally "states."[16]

Although perjury convictions based on silence or conduct will be relatively rare, no good reason exists to systematically exclude such instances because of an overly narrow construction of the term "statement." Admittedly, people do not mean (intend to communicate) anything by silence or conduct in all but fairly unusual instances.[17] But in well-defined circumstances, as illustrated by the *Meza* case, it is quite possible to intentionally communicate a specific message through silence. Meza was told to speak or raise his hand if he wished to signal an affirmative answer to a question. His inaction was, therefore, reasonably understood to signal a negative response to the questions posed by the judge.

This conclusion will hold true unless the witness or potential juror is unwilling or unable to cooperate in the conversation. If unable to cooperate—the person cannot hear or understand the questions, for example—her silence would be meaningless. The same is true if she cannot speak or raise her hand. In the *Meza* case, such arguments were not made.

Somewhat more difficult issues are raised by the possibility that the declarant may be unwilling to cooperate and therefore says nothing. In that case, silence may also be meaningless.[18] This is roughly the equivalent of an evasive answer in spoken communication, where the witness also attempts to avoid answering the question. Giving an unresponsive reply or failing to answer a question does not, in itself, constitute perjury. In the case of refusal to answer, the court may compel a response, and the remedy for an unresponsive reply is for the questioner to lead the witness back to the mark. This is consistent with the communicative approach because there is here no intent to communicate by silence or an evasive response—in fact, the point is not to communicate at all.

Nonetheless, in cases such as those discussed in this section, it is fair to say that the defendants communicated something false. Note that, despite the adversarial nature of our legal process, jurors or witnesses are under an obligation to cooperate with the truth-finding process. Absent evidence to the contrary, their responses are legitimately interpreted in that light. In both *Meza* and *Mattox*, the defendants gave no indication that they were not participating in the "conversation." Furthermore, what people communicate is not a matter of what they secretly have convinced themselves the statement means, but rather how they intend or know that the hearer will take it.[19] A jury could quite reasonably conclude that the defendants in *Meza* and *Mattox* must have intended their silence or conduct to be taken as a negative response, or at least must have known that it would be understood as such.

If cases of this type are properly prosecuted as perjury, then the language of perjury statutes referring to what a witness "states" must be construed to include what a witness *communicates*, not just what a witness literally states by the use of spoken language. Not only are silence and conduct not spoken language, but they also have no literal meaning apart from the context or circumstances. Silence can never be literally true. Consequently, it is difficult to accept that Congress intended the reference in 18 U.S.C. Section 1621 to what a witness "states" to exclude what the witness communicates by means of words, actions, or silence.

### Notes

1. 409 U.S. 352 (1973).
2. *Id.* at 352-53.
3. *Id.* at 354.
4. *Id.* at 355.
5. *Id.* at 357–58 (1973).
6. *Id.* at 358. At least under Rule 801 of the Federal Rules of Evidence, a "statement" is more broadly defined and may include "nonverbal conduct."

7. 188 Cal. App. 3d 1631, 234 Cal. Rptr. 235 (1987).

8. People v. French, 134 Cal. App. 694, 26 P.2d 310 (1933). Also rejecting the *French* holding is People v. Hedgecock, 201 Cal. App. 3d 174, 240, 247 Cal. Rptr. 404, 446, *review granted on other grounds*, 758 P.2d 596, 250 Cal. Rptr. 268 (1988).

9. CAL. PENAL CODE § 118 (West 1988).

10. CAL. EVID. CODE § 225 (West 1966).

11. 689 F.2d 531 (5th Cir. 1982). The defendant challenged the sufficiency of evidence supporting his conviction of making a false statement under 18 U.S.C. §§ 1001, 1920.

12. *Mattox*, 689 F.2d at 533. Interestingly, the defendant certified only that the information was "true and correct," not that it was complete or the whole truth. *Id.* at 532. This supports the argument made above that the truth requires relatively complete responses, as indicated by Grice's maxim of quantity. Another case reaching this conclusion is People v. Hedgecock, 201 Cal. App. 3d 174, 247 Cal. Rptr. 404 *review granted on other grounds*, 758 P.2d 596, 250 Cal. Rptr. 268 (1988). *Hedgecock* involved the former mayor of San Diego, who was prosecuted for perjury for leaving blanks in a disclosure form where he should have provided information. The court held that he could be convicted of perjury, rejecting the *Bronston* literal truth defense. This was so even though the defendant had sworn only that the forms were "true and correct," not that they were complete. *Id.* at 237–41, 247 Cal. Rptr. at 444–47; *see also* United States v. Ryan, 828 F.2d 1010, 1017 (3d Cir. 1987) ("statement" for the purposes of 18 U.S.C. § 1014, which relates to making false statements to a federally insured bank, includes silence and assertive nonverbal conduct; in this case, putting a dash through a space requesting a Social Security Number could constitute a false statement).

13. *See generally* Peter Tiersma, Comment, *The Language of Offer and Acceptance*, 74 CALIF. L. REV. 189, 215–20 (1986) (presenting linguistic principles regarding the use of silence or conduct to communicate assent to an offer).

14. *See, e.g.*, Texas v. Johnson, 109 S. Ct. 2533 (1989) (burning of American flag protected by first amendment); Tinker v. Des Moines Indep. Community School Dist., 393 U.S. 503 (1969) (wearing black armbands in protest of Vietnam War protected by first amendment).

15. *See, e.g.*, Wooley v. Maynard, 430 U.S. 705 (1977) (first amendment includes right not to speak).

16. The court in United States v. Ryan, 828 F.2d 1010, 1017 (3d Cir. 1987) noted that "[c]ommon experience teaches that people often make 'statements' with the nod or shake of a head, or with a particular motion of the hand, or with a myriad of symbolic, non-verbal actions that, through a common cultural understanding, have communicative content. Thus, the fact that a word was not spoken or written, does not necessarily mean that a message was not sent and received." The court continued by pointing out that the Federal Rule of Evidence 801(a) defines "statement" as not only an oral or written assertion but also as "nonverbal conduct of a person" intended as an assertion. The court concluded by holding that nonverbal conduct could constitute a "false statement" under 18 U.S.C. § 1014. *Id.*

17. Of course, inferences are often drawn from silence or actions, but it is much less common for communication to take place by this means.

18. It might be possible to infer from silence that the witness does not wish to cooperate, but this is not a communication.

19. Some philosophers have justified lying by focusing on what the speaker secretly believes, rather than on the false sense in which the hearer will interpret the statement. This hidden belief has been termed a *mental reservation*. St. Augustine felt that all lies were sinful, a view that had a powerful influence throughout much of the Middle Ages in Europe. Certain thinkers, in order to avoid this absolute prohibition, stated that lying depended on what one had in one's heart. For example, if you were to ask me whether I have ever been to Mexico, I could truthfully answer "no" with the mental reservation "not in the past month," even though I had been there two months ago. *See* S. Bok, Lying: Moral Choice in Public and Private Life 34–39 (1978).

# 36

# Threats*

## Lawrence M. Solan and Peter M. Tiersma

I am going to get you, bitch!

Threatening people is generally considered bad form, but threats are usually not criminal in and of themselves. An employer has not committed a crime if she tells one of her workers, "If you make one more obscene gesture at a customer, you'll be fired." Threats become illegal, however, if they are made to accomplish certain goals, or if they are directed at certain people. It is illegal under federal law, for example, to threaten federal officials or the US president.[1]

Similarly, to ask a person on the street for money is usually nothing more than begging or panhandling; there may be restrictions on when and where a person can solicit money, but it is not normally a crime. But if the request or demand is accompanied by a threat that causes the victim to hand over property against her will, the action may constitute robbery. Threats are also an intimate part of the crimes of extortion and blackmail, where the victim consents to give money or property to the extortionist, but only because of his threat to do something bad to the victim in the future.[2] Likewise, using threats to cause another person to engage in sexual intercourse is generally considered rape.

Crimes like robbery, extortion, and rape often involve using physical force to overcome the will of the victim. Force typically involves actual violence. Threats provide a basis for criminal liability if they instill fear of violence as retribution for failing to comply with a demand. Obtaining money, property, or sex from someone is a crime if it is done against the will or without the consent of the giver, or if the giver consents only under duress. Whether such actions are accomplished by actual violence or the threat of violence is

---

* Excerpt from Lawrence M. Solan and Peter M. Tiersma, *Speaking of Crime: The Language of Criminal Justice* 198–204 (2005).

usually immaterial. In contrast, threats that do not instill fear are not likely to be considered crimes.

Thus, while threats are not essential in committing crimes like extortion, robbery, or rape, they are frequently used to accomplish them. Rather than dealing with each of these crimes separately, we here consider the nature of threats in general.

### What Constitutes a Threat?

Threats are similar to warnings and predictions in that all three concern events or states of affairs that are likely to happen in the future. Threats must therefore be carefully distinguished from these other speech acts. Linguist Bruce Fraser posits that to make a threat, a speaker must

1. express an intention to personally commit an act, or to be responsible for having an act occur;
2. believe that the act will lead to an unfavorable state of affairs to the addressee; and
3. intend to intimidate the addressee through the addressee's awareness of the speaker's intention.[3]

An additional requirement is that a threat, like most other speech acts, must be intended to be taken seriously.

The first of Fraser's requirements implies that threats deal with matters that will happen in the future. In this sense, they resemble *predictions.* Yet there is an important difference. When we predict that something will happen, we simply state that we believe that a certain state of affairs will come about in the future. When we make a threat, on the other hand, we express our intention to bring about or cause the state of affairs to happen. This distinction was important not long ago in a labor dispute. During an election by factory workers deciding whether to be represented by a union, plant officials stated that unionization would lead to increased costs of doing business and intimated that as a result it might become necessary to close the plant. Was this a threat to shut down operations (which would have been illegal under these circumstances) or merely a prediction? The answer depends on whether the employer was stating or suggesting that it intended to bring about this future state of affairs (a threat), or was simply saying that this state of affairs was likely to come about if the workers voted to unionize (a prediction). The court held that the statements did not constitute a threat to close the plant in case of a union victory.[4]

Just as requests and commands can be hard to distinguish from one another, threats can be hard to distinguish from predictions. Both types of verbal acts tend to use the future tense. Consider the plight of an impetuous youth who sent a letter to the White House during the presidency of Ronald Reagan. It read, "Ronnie, Listen Chump! Resign or You'll Get Your Brains Blown Out." Below these words was a drawing of a gun with a bullet emerging from it. The sender, David Hoffman, was convicted of threatening the life of the president and sentenced to four years in prison.[5] Was this merely a prediction, as the dissent argued on appeal, or a real threat, as decided by the majority? Hoffman used the future tense, which could signal either a threat or a prediction. The critical issue, as noted above, is whether he communicated his intent to bring about this state of affairs (that is, to kill Reagan or have him killed), or whether he was simply predicting that, given the mood of the country, someone else out there was likely to commit the deed. The jury concluded that he had done more than speculate about the future, and the appellate court affirmed. The dissent pointed out that Hoffman used the passive voice ("You'll Get Your Brains Blown Out"), which suggests that he did not plan to be personally responsible for the killing.[6] When combined with evidence that he had psychiatric problems, one wonders whether he was really making a credible threat.

In another case, a man made a potentially threatening statement about the future to a woman whom he had dated in high school. She had since married and started a family with someone else. At some point the man wrote her this letter:

> Your Husband, David Goldstein will have his health take a turn for the worse this Christmas Season and you will be widowed in 1990. I am truly sorry that this is the "Kay Ser Ra Ser Ra" scenario that has to take place. However you will always be the foci of my desires as I remember you to be the most exuisite [*sic*] creature that has ever taken me in. I'm always grateful that we have had the moments given to us and I will be there should you ever desire me again. I can say with all sincerity, I Love You.[7]

Does this letter contain merely a prediction that the husband will die? The trial court held this and similar communications to be so ambiguous that it granted the defendant a judgment of acquittal before the case went to the jury. The court of appeals, however, reversed the lower court's decision and sent the matter to trial. It pointed out that the defendant had a twenty-year history of stalking and harassing the woman and her family. Against this background, what might seem like a prediction (regarding a bad state of affairs that might happen in the future) could quite reasonably be viewed as a threat: a bad state of affairs that the speaker intended to bring about.[8]

A second requirement for a threat is that the speaker believe that the future state of affairs will be bad for the addressee. Someone usually does not threaten you by saying that he intends to *give* you a million dollars. It might be a threat, on the other hand, if someone tells you that he intends to *take* money from you.

In this respect threats resemble *warnings*, which also refer to a bad future state of affairs. Sometimes, in fact, threats are made in the guise of warnings, as when a known thug says, "Just a friendly little warning—if you date my girlfriend again, you're dead meat." But if a friend tells the amorous young man that he should stop dating the thug's girlfriend, it would be a warning. Warnings are typically aimed at protecting the addressee from a potential harm caused by natural forces or someone else.[9] We can warn someone against a harm that we cause ourselves, but in that case the injury would have to be unintended ("Get out of the way! My brakes are failing!").

A relevant incident occurred in the Santa Ynez Valley in California, which is an increasingly popular wine-producing area. Some local residents have become concerned about ancient oak trees being cut down and natural areas being plowed over to make way for more vineyards. An article in the magazine *Earth First!* declared that if vintner Kendall Jackson, which had cut down many oak trees to allow planting of vineyards, "doesn't remove their newly-planted grapevines and irrigation pipes in a prompt and orderly fashion, perhaps some brave midnight warriors will have to do it themselves, the old fashion way."[10] Is this a prediction, a warning, or a threat? Law enforcement officers took it as a threat, and promptly told area vintners to be on the lookout for midnight eco-warriors. The critical issue is whether this statement was aimed at alerting Kendall Jackson to a potential danger caused by others, or whether the article suggested that the magazine's supporters would do the act themselves, which would make it a threat. The phrase "will have to" certainly lends some weight to finding it a threat rather than a warning.

Similarly, people often use the word "promise" to issue what are actually threats. Like threats, promises express an intention to engage in an act or create a certain state of affairs in the future. Typically, however, a promise involves an act or future state of affairs that will benefit the addressee, while a threat portends something harmful. Thus, saying to someone, "Lay one hand on my car, and I promise you'll regret it" is a threat, whether or not it is also a promise.

The third of Fraser's criteria for a threat is that the speaker must intend to *intimidate* the addressee through the addressee's awareness of the speaker's intention. The intent to intimidate can be critical when prosecuting hate crimes. The government can generally prohibit threats of racial violence. Even though such threats are technically a type of "speech," the Supreme Court has repeatedly held that they are not protected by the Free Speech Clause of the First Amendment.[11]

Consequently, when someone burned a cross near an apartment building that was experiencing racial tensions, he could be prosecuted for violating a federal statute that prohibited threatening or intimidating people who are exercising rights guaranteed by the Constitution or federal law. Ultimately, whether he actually threatened residents would be up to the jury to decide, but the fact that the cross-burning took place near a specific apartment building would support the conclusion that it was meant to intimidate the occupants of the building, rather than merely making a political statement.[12] In contrast, burning a cross as part of a political rally at a remote location would be less likely to threaten any person in particular.[13] In light of American history, the message of hate conveyed by cross-burning is quite frightening to most people, but the context of a political rally would usually prevent it from being taken as expressing an intent to cause a specified harm to a particular person. Here, it seems correct to regard it as more of a political statement, not a threat.

The intent to intimidate was also an issue in the prosecution of a student named Baker who was accused of making a threatening communication through interstate commerce, which is a federal crime.[14] Using a computer in Ann Arbor, Michigan, Baker exchanged email messages with someone named Gonda in Ontario, Canada. The men exchanged messages describing some violent fantasies about sexual acts that they would like to commit on young girls, such as the following:

> I highly agree with the type of woman you like to hurt. You seem to have the same tastes I have. When you come down, this'll be fun! Also, I've been thinking. I want to do it to a really young girl first. 13 or 14. Their innocence makes them so much more fun—and they'll be easier to control. What do you think?[15]

This is certainly offensive, but probably not criminal. As the trial judge observed, describing fantasies or desires does not necessarily rise to the level of actually expressing an intent to commit those acts.

This was not the end of the matter, however. Before long the men seem to come much closer to expressing an intention to carry out their morbid fantasies, as the following exchange of emails reveals:

> BAKER: Just thinking about it anymore doesn't do the trick. . . . I need to do it.
> GONDA: My feelings exactly! We have to get together. . . . I will give you more details as soon as I find out my situation. . . .
> BAKER: Alrighty then. If not next week, or in January, then definitely sometime in the Summer. Pickings are better then too. Although it's more crowded.[16]

It sounds as though the men have moved from fantasizing to actually planning to carry out their fantasies. But did they intend to intimidate the addressee through the addressee's awareness of their intentions? Because this was private email correspondence between two individuals, the answer clearly is no. Baker obviously did not intend to intimidate Gonda, and no one else was aware of the messages. As the court of appeals observed, "Even if a reasonable person would take the communications between Baker and Gonda as serious expressions of an intention to inflict bodily harm, no reasonable person would perceive such communications as being conveyed to effect some change or achieve some goal through intimidation."[17] Repulsive as this young man's messages might be, they did not constitute real threats.[18] Of course, it would have been another matter entirely if Baker had sent his messages to a potential victim, or if he were being prosecuted for participating in a conspiracy.

A final requirement, common to many speech acts, is that a threat must appear to be *sincere* [just as] someone who makes what seems to be a promise, while secretly not intending to carry out the promised act, will be understood to have made a promise nonetheless. The same is true of threats. People often jokingly make statements that might be considered threats if taken literally, but that are evidently not meant to be taken as such. In one case a firefighter claimed that his superior threatened him by saying, "I should just shoot you." In light of the circumstances and the firefighter's own testimony that he did not take the comment seriously, the court held that the statement was merely intended as a joke.[19]

It is important to emphasize that to make a threat, the speaker does not *actually* have to be sincere, but need only *appear* sincere. To be more exact, the speaker must intend the hearer to believe that the speaker intends to carry out the threatened act.[20] If a robber approaches you in a dark alley, shows you a gun, and tells you that he will kill you unless you give him your wallet, it does not matter that the robber might have absolutely no intention of carrying out his threat. He has made a threat nonetheless, because his intention was to appear sincere and thereby intimidate you into handing over your money.

## Notes

1. 18 U.S.C. § 115 (threats to assault, kidnap, or murder, a US official); 18 U.S.C. § 871 (threats against president and successors to the presidency).

2. The crimes of robbery, extortion, and blackmail are obviously closely related. All seek to get money or other items of value from the victim. A robber usually threatens immediate harm; an extortionist threatens harm in the future; and the blackmailer threatens a particular type of future harm: exposing embarrassing secrets. See Steven Shavell, *An Economic Analysis of Threats and Their Illegality: Blackmail, Extortion, and Robbery*, 141 University of Pennsylvania Law Review 1877 (1993).

3. Bruce Fraser, *Threatening Revisited*, 5 Forensic Linguistics 159, 171 (1998).

4. Crown Cork & Seal Co. v. NLRB, 36 F.3d 1130 (D.C. Cir. 1994).

5. United States v. Hoffman, 806 F.2d 703 (7th Cir. 1986).

6. Id. at 720–21.

7. United States v. Taylor, 972 F.2d 1247, 1249 (11th Cir. 1992). The court's *"sic's"* have been omitted.

8. Id. at 1250–52.

9. See Peter M. Tiersma, *The Language and Law of Product Warnings*, in *Language in the Legal Process* 54 (Janet Cotterill ed., 2002).

10. Dawn Hobbs and Mark van de Kamp, *Vintners Alert after Sabotage Warning*, Santa Barbara News-Press, Feb. 25, 1999, A1.

11. Frederick Schauer, *Categories and the First Amendment: A Play in Three Acts*, 34 Vanderbilt Law Review 265, 270 (1981) (the First Amendment does not protect the right to "fix prices, breach contracts, make false warranties, place bets with bookies, threaten, [or] extort").

12. See United States v. Lee, 6 F.3d 1297 (8th Cir. 1993) (en banc), *cert. denied*, 511 U.S. 1035 (1994). What complicates the situation is that some threats are protected by the First Amendment. Hence, in this case the court of appeals reversed Lee's original conviction because the jury instructions did not make it clear that only certain types of threats could form the basis of a conviction (e.g., a threat "intended to cause residents of the Tamarack Apartments to reasonably fear the use of imminent force or violence"). The court remanded for a new trial with corrected jury instructions. Id. at 1304. The US Supreme Court has recently held that burning a cross with intent to intimidate is not protected by the First Amendment. Virginia v. Black, 538 U.S. 343 (2003).

13. See Brandenburg v. Ohio, 395 U.S. 444 (1969).

14. United States v. Baker, 890 F. Supp. 1375 (E.D. Mich. 1995), *aff'd sub nom.* United States v. Alkhabaz, 104 F.3d 1492 (6th Cir. 1997).

15. 890 F. Supp. at 1387.

16. 104 F.3d at 1501.

17. Id. at 1496.

18. This does not mean that what he did is not or should not be criminal. If the men actually intended to carry out the acts, they would arguably be guilty of conspiracy, and there may well be other crimes that might have been committed.

19. Cignetti v. Healy, 89 F. Supp. 2d 106,125 (D. Mass. 2000).

20. Because this is a very subjective inquiry, many courts do not look at the defendant's actual (subjective) intent, but instead focus on whether "a reasonable person would foresee that the listener will believe he will be subjected to physical violence upon his person." United States v. Orozco-Santillan, 903 F.2d 1262, 1265–66 (9th Cir. 1990).

37

# How We Play Games with Words in the Law
Janet Ainsworth

David Mellinkoff (1963: vii) began his germinal volume "The Language of the Law" with this observation: "The law is a profession of words." Perhaps it would be more accurate to say that the law is a profession in search of the meaning that inheres in words. Lawyers and judges—particularly those of the textualist persuasion—are inclined to look for literal word meaning by consulting authoritative sources such as dictionaries when meaning is at issue. Linguists—particularly those of the descriptive persuasion—are more inclined to agree with the philosopher Ludwig Wittgenstein that meaning is use. But it is that rare combination of perspectives in the lawyer-linguist like Peter Tiersma that can appreciate that meaning in law is to be found somewhere betwixt and between authority and practice. Law, both in its most mundane and particularized instances—the drafting of a contract, the testimony of a witness in court—and in its grandest and more generalized exemplifications—the framing of a constitution, the pronouncement of a high court opinion—is fundamentally constituted by the meaning of the language used in achieving its ends. As a result of his dual training and experience in linguistics and law, Tiersma is well situated to apply his understanding of the nature of language and communication to shed light on a wide spectrum of legal problems and practices.

One of his earliest explorations of language issues inherent in legal doctrines was Tiersma's 1990 article, "The Language of Perjury: 'Literal Truth,' Ambiguity, and the False Statement Requirement." In this article, Tiersma examines the linguistic issues entailed in the crime of perjury, the intentional making of a false material statement under oath. He considers the surprisingly limited scope of perjury laws, noting that many forms of communicative deception are entirely outside the reach of the law. In particular, Tiersma focuses on a 1973 Supreme Court case, *U.S. v. Bronson*, as an example of how the law's approach to deceptive answers in perjury doctrine is inconsistent with what linguists know about how people use non-literal language in their everyday communication.

The *Bronston* case arose out of a bankruptcy proceeding in which Bronston was asked on the stand about whether he had any Swiss bank accounts. He truthfully answered that he did not. The follow-up question, "Have you ever . . .?" was answered with, "The company had an account there for about six months." This was also true; however, Bronson himself had formerly had a Swiss bank account as well, which his answer did not disclose. The Supreme Court unanimously overturned Bronson's conviction for perjury, holding that his answer was literally true, even though non-responsive and evasive.

In analyzing this case, Tiersma (1990: 381–383) observes that the literal propositional content of our utterances seldom corresponds with what we are actually trying to communicate to others. H. P. Grice (1975) attempted to systematize the conversational rules of implicature that allow us to draw conclusions about intended meaning that transcend the literal meaning of the words we use. Gricean implicature is grounded in the over-arching Cooperative Principle—that interactions are cooperative situations in which parties' utterances should be construed as relevant to their context. For example, when a colleague comes by my office at 1:00 p.m. and asks "Have you eaten?" he is not likely to be asking whether I have ever, at any point in my life, consumed food. Nor is he likely to be making a disinterested inquiry into the state of my digestive system. Instead, the Cooperative Principle suggests that I should interpret this question as a speaking turn of current relevance both to my colleague and myself—in this situation, as an indirect invitation to lunch together. Of course, a different implicature might be reasonable if the person making the identical noontime inquiry "Have you eaten?" is the surgical nurse preparing me for an operation later that afternoon. There, the nurse is not likely suggesting that we dine together but more likely asking about whether my digestive tract is empty—a topic of high contextual relevance both to surgical nurses in their professional capacity and to me in my situational identity as a pre-operative patient.

Grice's implicature conventions grease the wheels of conversational interaction. Spelling out the attendant implicatures in one's communicative interactions, in contrast, would mark an individual as socially pathological. The fact that we frequently say things that, if literally parsed, would not be at all what we intend to convey is no problem in ordinary interactions. When cases of true ambiguity in implication arise and an addressee is unsure of how to interpret the intended meaning of an utterance, she can simply ask the speaker for clarification and eliminate the unintended implicature.

So, given the ubiquity of these interpretive conventions that all competent communicators fluently use in ordinary interactions, why does the law interpret language like that from the *Bronston* case in such a single-mindedly literal fashion? Anyone with even basic communicative competence would interpret the answer in the paired sequence "Have you ever had an X?" "The company had an X." as implicitly answering, "No, I didn't have an X, but the company had an X." Tiersma criticizes the *Bronston* opinion for ignoring the communicative conventions through which people actually make meaning in favor of a literalism that fails to identify deception by witnesses.

The Supreme Court's perplexing turn to literalism in this case is consistent with the law's paradoxical attitude toward perjury. Perjury is, on the one hand, seen as a grave threat to the legal system's ability to deliver just results. Commentators, judges, and scholars have long decried the frequency with which witnesses lie in court. For example, the eminent jurist and scholar Jerome Frank (1949: 85) wrote, "Scarcely a trial occurs in which some witness does not lie." Especially in criminal cases, perjury is believed to be endemic. It is thought that criminal defendants, with their incentive to avoid conviction, may often lie on the stand. As the Seventh Circuit Court of Appeals noted with disapproval in their 1999 opinion in *U.S. v. Stewart*, "Many defendants seem to be under the misapprehension that an oath to tell the truth means nothing."

Nor is the problem of perjury in criminal cases limited to the testimony of defendants. Commentators on the criminal justice system (e.g., Cloud 1995; Slobogin 1996; Capers 2008; Loevy 2010) have pointed out the frequency with which police officers lie in their testimony; the problem is apparently so pervasive that police themselves coined the special term "testilying" to refer to that particular form of perjury (Slobogin 1996: 1040). Yet for all the hand-wringing about the prevalence of perjured testimony, perjury prosecutions are exceptionally rare. Raymond McKoski (2012: 1613) cites the most recent statistics: out of over 90,000 felony prosecutions in federal court in 2010, only 52 were for perjury.

If perjury is so widespread, why is it so seldom charged? And might the reason be related to the Supreme Court's puzzling insistence that literally true but palpably misleading testimony cannot be punished as perjury? Perhaps the reluctance of the Supreme Court to find a statement to be perjurious even when a witness appears to be intentionally deceptive—as long as the answer is literally true—results from a tacit recognition that witness examination is not the kind of cooperative language game that Grice's maxims of interpretation best fit. Although witness examination is structured as a series of questions by the examining attorney and answers by the witness, this language game is no ordinary question-and-answer sequence. Typically people ask a question because they are looking for information from the addressee. However, the questioning lawyer is not truly seeking information from the witness; in fact, one of the fundamental axioms of cross-examination is that a cross-examiner should never ask a question to which the lawyer does not already know the answer. The cross-examining lawyer asks questions that are only nominally questions; they are often tag questions—assertions followed by a tag such as "isn't that true?" or "correct?" Sometimes the cross-examiner's question is not syntactically a question at all, but merely an assertion with a slight questioning intonation. Regardless of the particular form of the cross-examination question, it is the lawyer who chooses its specific wording, with all the nuances and connotations entailed by that wording. The response by the witness is merely to accept or deny the assertion entailed by the question. This power asymmetry between the communicative power wielded by the attorney-questioner and the exceptional lack of communicative options open to the witness-answerer means that the attorney is in effect playing with a stacked communicative deck.

Lawyers themselves fully understand that cross-examination is a language game in which they hold all the high cards. Manuals for lawyers on trial advocacy stress the importance for lawyers of holding fast the "tight rein of cross-examination." (Jeans 1993: 432). Steven Lubet (2009: 96) writes that, "The essential goal of cross-examination is witness control." Thomas Mauet (2007: 211) points out that controlling the witness "by asking precisely phrased leading questions never gives the witness an opportunity to hurt you." Michael Fontham (2009: 41) goes even further, acknowledging that in cross-examination, "The attorney—not the witness—generally states the facts that will become evidence." Given that the linguistic production that we call testimony is almost entirely controlled by the attorney rather than its nominal producer—the witness—it would be harsh to hold witnesses criminally accountable for the implicatures of that production. This is especially so in cases like *Bronston*, where the cross-examining lawyer could easily have asked follow-up questions to eliminate ambiguity in the witness's answer. Perhaps foregoing easy perjury prosecutions has come to seem to courts a reasonable trade-off for the maintenance of rigid control by lawyers over the production of evidence.

## References

Bronston v. U.S., 409 U.S. 352 (1973).

Capers, Bennett (2008). Crime, Legitimacy, and Testilying. *Indiana Law Journal* 83: 835–880.

Cloud, Morgan (1995). Judges, Testilying and the Constitution. *Southern California Law Review* 69: 1341–1388.

Fontham, Michael R. (2009). *Trial Technique and Evidence* (3rd ed.). Louisville, CO: National Institute for Trial Advocacy.

Frank, Jerome (1949). *Courts on Trial: Myth and Reality in American Justice*. Princeton, NJ: Princeton University Press.

Grice, H. P. (1975). Logic and Conversation. *Syntax and Semantics* 3: 41–58.

Jeans, James W. (1993). *Trial Advocacy* (2d ed.). St. Paul, MN: West Publishing.

Loevy, Jon (2010). Truth or Consequences: Police "Testilying." *Litigation* 36: 13–20.

Lubet, Steven (2009). *Modern Trial Advocacy* (4th ed.). Louisville, CO: National Institute for Trial Advocacy.

Mauet, Thomas A. (2007). *Trial Techniques* (7th ed.). New York, NY: Wolters Kluwer.

McKoski, Raymond J. (2012). Prospective Perjury by a Criminal Defendant: It's All about the Lawyer. *Arizona State Law Journal* 44: 1575–1646.

Mellinkoff, David (1963). *The Language of the Law*. Boston: Little Brown.

Slobogin, Christopher (1996). Testilying: Police Perjury and What to Do About It. *University of Colorado Law Review* 67: 1037–1060.

Tiersma, Peter Meijes (1990). The Language of Perjury, "Literal Truth," Ambiguity and False Statements. *Southern California Law Review* 63: 373–431.

U.S. v. Stewart, 198 F.3d 987 (7th Cir. 1999).

# 38

# Toward a Communicative Approach to Law- and Rule-Making

Philip Gaines

In "The Language of Perjury," Peter Tiersma (1990) argues for a *communicative approach* to determining what constitutes the truth or falsity of a witness's statement in court. Most interesting to Tiersma are those utterances that are "arguably true on one level but false on another" (1990: 374). The example he takes up is a statement made at a bankruptcy examination when Samuel Bronston, the president of a failed movie production company, was asked a pair of questions by the lawyer for one of the company's creditors:

> Q. Do you have any bank accounts in Swiss banks, Mr. Bronston?
> A. No, sir.
> Q. Have you ever?
> A. The company had an account there for about six months, in Zurich.
> (1990: 378)

As a result of his attempt to mislead the examination board with his second answer, implying that he had not had *personal* bank accounts in Switzerland, Bronston was tried and convicted of perjury—a conviction that was subsequently affirmed on appeal. When the US Supreme Court took the case, they agreed that Bronston's answer certainly implied that he had not had personal accounts in Swiss banks but that such an implication did not constitute a perjurious statement. Instead, the Court insisted that the key question was whether his actual statement—the second answer above—was "literally" true or false. Finding that it was true, the Court reversed the conviction.

According to California law, perjury occurs when a witness willfully "states as true any material matter which he knows to be false" (California Penal Code § 118 [1988]). In the federal code version, perjury is committed when a witness "willfully ... states ... any material matter which he does not believe to be true" (18 US Code § 1621 [1982]). Tiersma's claim is that for the Supreme Court to have focused exclusively on the literal truth or falsity of the defendant's actual words is misguided and ignores what the witness meant (Tiersma 1990: 375). For Tiersma, the crucial question is: "How does the speaker intend the hearer to understand the utterance?" Tiersma extensively recruits Speech Act Theory to show that uncovering the *meaning* of a statement involves much more than analyzing only the words stated. Thus, according to Tiersma, a proper perjury prosecution requires that "the language of perjury statutes referring to what a witness 'states' must be construed to include what a witness *communicates*, not just what a witness literally states by the use of spoken language" (Tiersma 1990: 413). The analysis should include a multifaceted, finely nuanced approach to the communicative intent of an utterance rather than a superficial treatment of the propositional content of a sentence. As Tiersma points out, however, such an approach risks being perceived as impressionistic and "unnecessarily fuzzy" (Tiersma 1990: 413) to those who find security in simply determining the truth conditions of an isolated statement. His point is that if we want to find out what a speaker intended for an utterance to communicate to a jury and whether that utterance was a means to mislead perjuriously, we have to immerse ourselves in the much more complicated milieu of the pragmatics of communication.

Such an insistence on a "thick" (a la Geertz 1973) description of communicative force can be applied to a range of situations in which false statements are prohibited. One concerns the verbal behavior of lawyers during legal proceedings. Rule 3.3 of the *Model Rules of Professional Conduct* states that "[a] lawyer shall not knowingly make a false statement of fact or law to a tribunal." The comment to that rule notes that the obligation of zealous advocacy for a client is "qualified by the advocate's duty of candor to the tribunal." This obligation means that "the lawyer must not allow the tribunal to be misled by false statements of law or fact or evidence that the lawyer knows to be false." On Tiersma's account, to "knowingly make a false statement of fact ... to a tribunal" must be construed to include what the lawyer intends to *communicate* by means of a statement.

Aside from trial statements made in opening and closing—most likely the discursive contexts targeted by the false statement injunction—lawyers also communicate to juries through the cross-examination of witnesses, using questions and their answers to imply to the jury things that are not overtly stated, and to judges in legal argument. Cross-examination, a staple of trial lawyers, often recruits *impeachment evidence* to cast doubt on the veracity of a witness's testimony. Even though the affirmative or negative utterance—often simply "yes" or "no"—is spoken by the witness, both the propositional content and its intended implicature are controlled by the lawyer in the wording of the question; the "literal" statement, then, is the impeachment evidence, co-constructed by the questioning lawyer and answering witness; the implicature is what might be called the *meta-statement* intended by the lawyer. Through an extension of Tiersma's model, the lawyer can be said to be communicating to the jury through the meta-statement that the witness's testimony may not be trustworthy.

Sometimes, however, a hostile witness is telling the truth ... and the cross-examining lawyer knows it. The matter of impeaching a truthful witness has been a nagging ethical question since the early days of the Anglo-American adversarial trial. The extreme case of endorsing such a technique was famously articulated by Monroe Freedman when he argued that impeaching a truthful witness was not only allowable but a necessary duty of the advocate (Freedman 1966). As recently as 2012, the essence of this ethical dilemma was explored again—this time in a Canadian context, with the author arguing for what he calls a "contextual approach" to dealing with the question of when it is proper to impeach a truthful witness and when it is not (Tatum 2012). I will argue, however, that on Tiersma's account it is never proper to impeach a truthful witness, since to do so violates the *Model Rules*.

If a lawyer knows that the witness is telling the truth, then communicating to the jury by means of an impeachment evidence statement and its accompanying implicative meta-statement that the witness's testimony may not be trustworthy, is communicating something that she/he knows to be false. Understanding the meaning of "false statement" as Tiersma has construed it, it is clearly arguable that the lawyer has violated the *Model* rule that "[a] lawyer shall not knowingly make a false statement of fact ... to a tribunal." Further, this communication violates the spirit of the comment to the rule that "the lawyer must not allow the tribunal to be misled by false statements ... of fact or evidence that the lawyer knows to be false." It might be a "literally" true statement, for example, that a truthful witness had been arrested for drug possession, but the meta-statement that, for this reason, the witness's testimony should be called into question is false.

Even Freedman admits that sometimes when impeaching a truthful witness—and thus "misleading the finder of fact"—"under the euphemism of 'testing the truth of the prosecution's case,' the lawyer communicates, to the jury and to the community, the most vicious of lies" (Freedman 1975: 45). But eliciting impeachment evidence, even from a truthful witness, is allowed, and does not run afoul of the *Model Rules* on an interpretation that limits the understanding of a false statement to the literal meaning of the words of an utterance. From this perspective, for a lawyer to communicate to a jury through implications derived from the elicitation of impeachment evidence that the witness is not to be trusted when the lawyer knows that the witness *is* to be trusted passes as ethical conduct. Understanding the notion of a false statement in light of Tiersma's communicative approach can lead to a very different conclusion.

Both Tiersma's analysis from the *Bronston* case and the one undertaken here illustrate the disconnect between the intent of a statute prohibiting false statements and the ways in which the communicative implications of a literally true but misleading statement can subvert that intent. If the goal of perjury law is to deter a witness from misleading a tribunal which has been charged with fact-finding in a legal dispute, this purpose is undermined when courts apply an interpretation of "false statement" that emerges from an impoverished, superficial view of meaning as nothing more than literal surface meaning. So also with the *Model Rules'* prohibition on false statements by lawyers—if the intent of the *Model Rules* is to prevent jurors from being misled by lawyers as they deliberate on matters of sometimes great consequence. The fact that in the *Bronston* case the first appeals court and the Supreme Court came to opposite conclusions suggests that the minimalist wording of laws and rules, limiting itself to the conventional notion of a "false statement," allows for a problematically wide range of interpretive possibilities. This, in turn, gives judges with conflicting perspectives on the policies that underlie the perjury law the opportunity to construe the law according to their own values. If the point of the law or the *Model Rules* injunction is to prevent juries from being misled, then one solution would be for these texts to be written from a *communicative* perspective that identifies the various and multilayered ways in which such misleading can occur. This need not result in impressionistic and "unnecessarily fuzzy" interpretations. But it would require a very different way of thinking about how language constructs meaning in legal contexts—and would benefit greatly from the expert opinions of linguists who are trained to isolate and identify the illocutionary and perlocutionary force of utterances that lay people naturally intuit.

### References

*ABA Model Rules of Professional Conduct*, 2010 edition, American Bar Association.

Freedman, M. (1966) Professional Responsibility of the Criminal Defense Lawyer: The Three Hardest Questions. *Michigan Law Review* 64:1469ff.

Freedman, M. (1975) *Lawyers' Ethics in an Adversary System*. New York: Bobbs-Merrill.

Geertz, Clifford (1973) Thick Description: Toward an Interpretative Theory of Culture. In *The Interpretation of Cultures*. New York: Basic Books.

Tatum, J. (2012) Navigating the Fine Line of Criminal Advocacy: Using Truthful Evidence to Discredit Truthful Testimony. *Western Journal of Legal Studies* 2/2:1ff.

Tiersma, Peter Meijes (1990) The Language of Perjury. *Southern California Law Review* 63:373ff.

39

# Threats

A PRAGMALINGUISTIC APPROACH TO THE ANALYSIS OF A
SPEECH CRIME

## Susan Berk-Seligson

Of Peter Tiersma's numerous contributions to the field of Language and the Law, his work in the area of pragmatics, and speech act theory in particular, is especially important. By demonstrating to legal practitioners that speech acts such as orders, requests, and threats can be made both directly and indirectly, and that carrying out these verbal acts indirectly can entail the use of such ambiguous language that the illocutionary force of the act can later be plausibly denied, Tiersma has shown the non-linguist that the interpretation of an indirect speech act often turns on the social power of the hearer. His work with Solan in *Speaking of Crime* (2005) has demonstrated that appellate courts resolve ambiguity in the interpretation of speech acts in favor of authorities like the police rather than in favor of defendants. This essay focuses on one speech act: threats.

Threats are not merely speech acts; they can be language crimes. In their essay on threats, Solan and Tiersma (2005: chapter 10) show that threats share features with other speech acts, such as warnings and predictions. However, contextual factors accompanying a speech act can eliminate much of the ambiguity in it, and the recipients of a threat will clearly understand its illocutionary force.

It is not easy to gather direct evidence of a threat. The most convincing evidence would be an audio recording of an oral threat or a written form of communication making such a threat. But this kind of evidence is often not available. Juries and judges often have nothing more to go on than the report of a threat by alleged victims or other witnesses.

I conducted a study of threats commonly made by members of gangs and drug cartels based in Central America. In this part of the world, threats are being made on a daily basis, and the recipients of those threats talk about them, sometimes quoting the source of the threat, at other times using indirect speech. Between 2011 and 2013, 465 community "stakeholders" (school teachers, police officers, community leaders, clergy, members of municipal crime prevention councils) were interviewed in Guatemala (N = 146) and El Salvador (N = 319).[1] Many reported that they, their family members, or neighbors had been targets of threats, mainly of extortion, but also of murder. The police interviewed reported that threats of extortion—particularly of merchants—were among their most common crimes. Interestingly, many of these threats were made by gang members using cell phones from prison cells. Because some police are in league with the gangs, many people in El Salvador and Guatemala do not trust the police and are afraid to report gang crimes.

What follows below are two narratives involving threats. Both were communicated in Spanish (translated here by the author) by the former president of a Salvadoran community development association (ADESCO); she is a woman in her late forties. The first narrative is in response to the interviewer's question as to how she feels about the police and whether she is afraid or mistrustful of them.

### Excerpt 1

[Ex-president, ADESCO: Fear and mistrust, both things, both of them.]
[Interviewer: Why?]

[Ex-president, ADESCO: Because look, I'm going to explain something to you, but I'm going to explain it, I'm going to talk about last year. Umm, I, I was being extorted badly; they even said that they were going to kill me on the street and all that, when the police inspector of (name of municipality) suddenly shows up. I told him certain things and afterwards, they call me again and they tell me that I had talked to these people. So you tell me what to think, 'cause they're the same people, the same people. I'm, I am, I'm mistrustful. Fear I don't have because I'm a daughter of God and I know that He, if He allows it, something bad will happen to me, and if He doesn't permit it, nothing is going to happen to me. As I said to those individuals, "If you people," he told me that he knew where I lived, that he knew where I was in the habit of walking. "Good God, you already know that; but I am a daughter of a powerful king, of a living God, not of a dead God, and if you are my God then you will, will kill me, and if he allows it, and if he doesn't allow it you aren't going to do anything to me because God won't give you permission to," I said, and, and, that is, from that moment on I have been mistrustful of, let's say, the police. So, and I don't have any desire to meet with them again because of what happened, what happened to me, a leader, not let's say to a poor person. And I've always been trust-, very certain about God, about God, despite the fact that we have our weaknesses, weaknesses, but I, that's why I don't trust the police any more.]

The thrust of her narrative is that the police are deeply involved in the extortion racket and that they are members of the same group. The same community leader, speaking later on in the interview, when asked if she had been the victim of a crime in the past twelve months, describes how the extortionist threatened to kill her grown son if she didn't pay him the $2,500 that he was trying to get from her.

### Excerpt 2

[Yes, yes, I will never forget it, it was a (date, month), it was the last, the last, how can I explain it to you, umm, the last bitter moment I spent in my life, because if I didn't hand over $2,500 he was going to kill my son, and they wanted me to leave it at a certain place. And I spoke tough to that good-for-nothing guy, and I told him not to kill my son but to kill me instead, because whether he killed my son or killed me, I wasn't going to give him even a nickel, and what he was going to get was a war, because my husband was a war veteran, who spent (X) years in the army, I told him.]

Both of these reported threats are embedded in larger units of discourse. Given the speech situation of the interview, however, in which a Salvadoran college-educated young man was lending the interviewee a sympathetic ear and allowing her to narrate freely, it is not surprising that the woman was so forthcoming, even going so far as to reveal her husband's role in the country's protracted civil war. While the victim used both quoted and reported speech in her narratives, the utterances that she reproduced word-for-word were her own, and not those of the man who had threatened her. Rather than to quote him, what she did was to express her strongly felt emotions on being threatened. Given the findings of scholars who have analyzed the effectiveness of different types of narrative styles in informal judicial contexts such as restraining order application interviews (Trinch and Berk-Seligson 2002) and small claims courts (Conley and O'Barr 1990), one has to wonder if this Salvadoran leader's approach to narrating her experiences with death threats would be an effective discourse strategy in a formal court of law.

## Note

1. These interviews were gathered under a three-year impact-evaluation study funded by the US Agency for International Development in four Central American countries. The study involved determining whether a violence and crime prevention program aimed at youth was effective or not.

## References

Conley, John. M. and William M. O'Barr (1990) *Rules Versus Relationships: The Ethnography of Legal Discourse*. Chicago: University of Chicago Press.

Solan, Lawrence M. and Peter M. Tiersma (2005) *Speaking of Crime: The Language of Criminal Justice*. Chicago: University of Chicago Press.

Trinch, Shonna L. and Susan Berk-Seligson (2002) Narrating in Protective Order Interviews: A Source of Interactional Trouble. *Language in Society* 31: 383–418.

# Criminal Justice and
# Everyday Speech

# 40

# The Judge as Linguist*

## Peter M. Tiersma

In *Rhode Island v. Innis*,[1] a defendant was suspected of killing a taxicab driver with a shotgun. Once arrested, the police read him the customary *Miranda* warning.[2] The defendant consequently asked to speak to an attorney.[3] The police then placed the defendant in a vehicle to be taken to the police station.[4] Under the *Miranda* decision, once a suspect in custody asks to speak with a lawyer, all interrogation must cease until a lawyer is present.[5] Thus, the officers in *Innis* could not question the defendant during the drive to the station.[6] Importantly, the police had not yet found the murder weapon, which would doubtless provide important evidence against the accused.[7] While en route to the station, one of the accompanying officers mentioned that there were a lot of disabled children in the area, and said, "God forbid one of them might find a weapon with shells and they might hurt themselves."[8] The defendant, expressing concern about the children, then showed the officers where the gun was located.[9]

The issue before the Supreme Court in *Innis* was whether the officers had engaged in "interrogation" or "questioning." It would have been easy enough for the Court to dispose of the case by observing that the officers asked no questions of the defendant, but merely stated that they were worried about the schoolchildren. Instead, the Court concluded that *Miranda*'s prohibition against further "questioning" extends not only to literal questioning, but also to its "functional equivalent."[10] The Court ultimately held that the officers did not, under this definition, engage in questioning.[11]

The Court correctly recognized that speech acts are often accomplished by indirect means, although one might dispute its ultimate conclusion. Consider the following sentence, said by a burglar with a gun to the

---

* Excerpt from Peter Meijes Tiersma, The Judge as Linguist, *Loyola of Los Angeles Law Review* 27: 269, 279–83 (1993).

occupant of a house: "I will kill your child unless you tell me where your money is." Obviously, this is not just a statement about what may happen in the future. Implicit in the threat is a command to provide information ("Tell me where the money is") or at least a question ("Where is the money?").

Now compare this with what the police in *Innis* essentially told the suspect: "A disabled child may die unless you tell us where the shotgun is." While not a threat to the defendant, the sentence conveyed that something very bad might happen unless he provided the information. It clearly functioned as a request for information, and was therefore the "functional equivalent" of a question.[12]

## Consensual Searches

Another instance in which the Supreme Court analyzed the language of the police occurred in *Schneckloth v. Bustamonte*.[13] There, the defendant challenged the constitutionality of a search of a car trunk in which police found incriminating evidence of the crime of possessing a check with intent to defraud.[14] The police had stopped the car in which the defendant was riding because of minor vehicle code violations.[15] Since the officers had neither a warrant nor other grounds to search the car, a search would have been constitutional only if the defendant or another occupant had voluntarily consented to it.[16] After rummaging through the car itself, the officer asked the occupants: "Does the trunk open?"[17] One of the occupants said "yes," got the keys, and opened the trunk.[18]

Literally, the officer simply inquired whether the trunk was capable of being opened. The occupant's response—to actually open the trunk—indicates that he understood the officer's question as more of a request or command to open the trunk. This comports with linguistic research on indirect requests or demands. For example, asking a fellow diner, "Can you pass the salt?" is not merely a question regarding the diner's capability to pass the salt, but a request or command to do so.[19] If the addressee says "yes" but does nothing, she has acted inappropriately, or at best made a joke by playing on the literal meaning of the words. A similar historical example is the words attributed to King Henry II regarding his enemy, Thomas Becket. King Henry said to his knights: "Will no one rid me of this turbulent priest?" Not long later, four of Henry's knights assassinated Becket.[20] "Does the trunk open?" is therefore not simply a question about the capabilities of the trunk, but is at least a request to open the trunk, or a command to do so.

Whether the utterance is a request or is instead a command is critical to the voluntariness of the consent, and thus to the constitutionality of the search. Where a uniformed police officer commands someone to open a car trunk, any "consent" can hardly be termed voluntary because the person who consents will assume that the officer has the authority to ensure compliance and there is no choice in the matter.[21] Following the orders of a uniformed and armed officer ("Pull over" or "Place your hands on the car") is never truly voluntary.

Whether a question like "Does the trunk open?" or "May I look in the trunk?" is merely a request that can be refused or a command that must be obeyed depends not so much on the language used, but on the power relationship between the speaker and addressee. If an ordinary citizen, taking a tour of the White House, asks a guard standing in front of the door to the Oval Office, "May I enter this room?" it is simply a request. If the president asks, he is ordering the guard to step aside.[22] Likewise, suppose that a police officer pulls over a car and asks the driver, "May I see your license?" "No" is simply not an appropriate response. We know that the officer has the right to see our license, has the power to enforce this right, and that refusing to show our license would only get us into worse trouble, or at least greatly inconvenience us. The officer's polite request is really nothing less than a command.[23]

We now return to the plight of Mr. Bustamonte. While the facts do not directly say so, it seems a reasonable assumption that he and his friends, all apparently Chicano and driving a borrowed car,[24] were not particularly high on the socioeconomic ladder, nor particularly well educated. Most likely, they were not particularly aware of their constitutional right to be free of unreasonable searches. Would someone engaged in activities of questionable legality consent to any type of police search?

In any event, with three armed police officers on the scene, the lights on their squad cars flashing, Bustamonte and his friends may well have concluded that even if they might have had the right to refuse access to the car trunk, it would have been unwise to do so. Like the speeder who says nothing but simply hands the officer his driver's license when the officer asks if he or she "may see" it, Mr. Bustamonte and his friends simply opened the trunk when the officer requested to look inside.

When someone in a position of power and authority makes what is literally a request to a subordinate, and the person in power has the right to command the other, the request will be interpreted as a command. It is phrased in the language of requesting permission in order to express politeness, by giving a superficial choice to the addressee. In fact the power relationships dictate that when the police make a "request," and they could apparently compel the suspect to carry out the request, the suspect will view the request as a command.

Applying this principle to the *Bustamonte* case, only if Mr. Bustamonte and his friends were aware that the police had no authority to order them to open the trunk could the "request" to look inside be interpreted as an actual request that could be refused with no negative consequences. The Supreme

Court explicitly rejected requiring such awareness in *Bustamonte*, suggesting that although knowledge of the right to refuse consent was a factor to consider in deciding whether consent was voluntary, it was not determinative.[25] Requiring proof that the suspects knew their right to refuse would allow them to frustrate the use of the evidence at trial by failing to testify that they were aware of this right.[26]

The Court also rejected the obvious solution to the problem—having police advise suspects of their right to refuse.[27] The Court declined this solution because "it would be thoroughly impractical to impose on the normal consent search the detailed requirements of an effective warning."[28] In actuality, simply adding "You have the right to say no" to any search request would be quite effective in advising suspects of their rights, and does not seem particularly burdensome.

As a linguistic matter, the notion that Mr. Bustamonte and his friends freely consented to the search is highly questionable. The real animus behind the decision becomes apparent in the Court's observation that "[c]onsent searches are part of the standard investigatory techniques of law enforcement agencies"[29] and its acknowledgement of the "legitimate need for such searches."[30] Thus, the Court's concern seems to be that advising suspects of their constitutional right to refuse will encourage them to exercise that right, thus leading to fewer criminals being apprehended.[31] While apprehending criminals is certainly a laudable goal, one wonders whether it might not be attainable without manipulating the meaning of voluntary consent.

### Conclusion

Judges often engage in various types of linguistic analysis. The United States Supreme Court, for example, has exhibited both surprising linguistic acumen and, on the other hand, woeful disregard for how language operates in real-life situations. Of course, there is not always a single correct linguistic analysis of legislative texts or conspiratorial conversations. Additionally, factors other than language are often relevant in determining the meaning of legal language; these factors are particularly relevant when the text is incomplete or ambiguous. But when interpreting a text, be it statutory or conversational, a careful linguistic analysis should always be the point of departure.

### Notes

1. 446 U.S. 291 (1980).
2. *Id.* at 294.

3. *Id.*

4. *Id.*

5. Miranda v. Arizona, 384 U.S. 436, 474 (1966).

6. *Innis*, 446 U.S. at 294.

7. *Id.*

8. *Id.* at 294–95 (internal quotation marks omitted).

9. *Id.* at 295.

10. *Id.* at 300–01. The court defined the functional equivalent of questioning as "any words or actions on the part of the police (other than those normally attendant to arrest and custody) that the police should know are reasonably likely to elicit an incriminating response from the suspect." *Id.* at 301 (citation omitted).

11. *Id.* at 302.

12. Should there be any remaining doubt, consider the following. A mad scientist has developed a small but lethal bomb that can only be deactivated with a secret code. He plans to test it in an isolated barn, and places it there. Unfortunately, a small child becomes trapped in the barn. If the child plays with the bomb, there is a danger that it may explode. People now come to the scientist and say: "The child may die unless you tell us what the secret code is." Surely they are asking for the secret code!

13. 412 U.S. 218 (1973).

14. *Id.* at 219–20.

15. *Id.* at 220.

16. *Id.* at 219.

17. *Id.* at 220 (internal quotation marks omitted).

18. *Id.*

19. *See* John R. Searle, *Indirect Speech Acts*, in PRAGMATICS: A READER 265, 265 (Steven Davis ed., 1991).

20. THE MACMILLAN DICTIONARY OF QUOTATIONS 34 (1989).

21. *See* Bumper v. North Carolina, 391 U.S. 543, 548–49 (1968) (holding that consent was not voluntary where officers appeared at defendant's residence and falsely claimed to have warrant).

22. John Searle provides a similar example. "If the general asks the private to clean up the room, that is in all likelihood a command or an order. If the private asks the general to clean up the room, that is likely to be a suggestion or proposal or request but not an order or command." John R. Searle, *A Classification of Illocutionary Acts*, 5 LANGUAGE SOC'Y 1, 5 (1976).

23. Consider some other types of indirect commands (at least in the right context). None of these are literally imperatives, although all could be phrased as such: "You are standing on my foot" (Get off my foot!); "I would like you to go now" (Go now!); "Officers will henceforth wear ties at dinner" (Officers, wear ties at dinner!); "Would you mind not making so much noise?" (Be quiet!); "How many times have I told you not to eat with your fingers?" (Don't eat with your fingers!). These examples are from Searle, *supra* note 19, at 268–69.

24. *Bustamonte*, 412 U.S. at 220.

25. *Id.* at 226.

26. *Id.* at 230.

27. *Id.* at 231.

28. *Id.*

29. *Id.* at 231–32.

30. *Id.* at 227–28.

31. Note, incidentally, that while liberal judges have often been accused of engaging in "result-oriented" jurisprudence, this analysis reveals that moderate and conservative judges are likewise capable of doing so.

# 41

# Applied (Forensic) Linguistics in Autochthonic and Allochthonic Use

Hannes Kniffka

Peter Tiersma's "The Judge as Linguist" (1993) concerns the question(s) of what judges should know about linguistics and could learn from linguists doing their job and vice versa. His hypothesis is that "knowing that" and "knowing how" about linguistics will help and improve judges' work. To be sure, for someone trying to apply linguistics to various areas of law, the hypothesis is plausible. One of the main facts underlying this is that judges' work presupposes and "implies" linguistic knowledge and analysis. Yet this self-evident, central, and "natural" (Solan and Tiersma 2012) status, referring to the formula "language and law" as a whole, deserves an in-depth theoretical and empirical testing. This is what Tiersma does and what I would like to comment on very briefly.

It is to Tiersma's credit to have introduced the phrase "Language and Law" as a systematic classificatory grid and the most general common denominator that includes all kinds and branches of forensic linguistic work across the globe. We owe mainly to him that Language and Law has become something like a modern magical *Zwillingsformel*, a trademark of an area of true interdisciplinary research. There is no better term for "language and law" to this date. It is mainly due to Tiersma's decade-long study and academic mission as indicated by his work for ILLA (International Language and Law Association). Yet all these impressive facts don't explain the full impact of his work—and this paper. What is unique and new in his scholarly work is the *depth* and *breadth* of its intellectual approach. This is also part of what makes Peter Tiersma's scientific work so appealing. He is one of the precious few (in the United States and even more so in Europe) who are academically at home equally well in both disciplines (linguistics and law), and who are able to move back and forth with ease in both areas. When he talks about shortcomings and lack of sensitivity of judges' linguistic analysis in subfields such as pragmatics and semantics, it makes sense immediately to all recipients. It is also to Tiersma's credit that this 1993 paper at the same time provided linguists with a reservoir of fascinating examples from the field of law.

Let me point out some facts about the history of linguistics in Europe. As a student of General Linguistics in a German university in the early 1960s, I and my fellow students were taught that a linguistic analysis should *start* with the "clear facts" of the data, say what you can hear on a tape and what you read "black on white" on paper (with no additional caveats). Our teachers were historicalIndo-European linguists, linguistic typologists and mostly German taxonomic structuralists, who had been studying in the United States. The groups of scholars had, at least, one conviction *in common*: Do the "safe," "solid" analysis of linguistic *form* first, and thereafter proceed to the "less safe," less accessible, analysis of *meaning*. For a "forensic linguist" this seemed to pay off.

While agreeing entirely with Tiersma's criticism of the insensitivity and "lack of linguistic sophistication" of parts of the judiciary (274 and passim), I also want to side with judges' shortcomings about their knowledge of linguistics. It was difficult for linguists to understand that there are various classes, areas, levels, layers, and reservoirs of data that are as solid, safe, and accessible as those mentioned above that had not yet been accounted for. Before the early development of sociolinguistic research by Bright, Labov, Ferguson, Hymes, Shuy, Gumperz, and many others some 50 years ago, and before the early pragmatics work of Austin, Searle, Grice, and many others, linguists were possibly as shortsighted and insensitive about linguistic data as some judges are today. There may be a generational factor here: older judges may have had little or no exposure to more recent developments in sociolinguistics and pragmatics in their training. They were unlikely to know about the matters discussed by Tiersma's important 1993 paper. The list of research fields mentioned by Tiersma in this paper (270–283) deals almost exclusively with the field of *pragmatics* (performative utterances, meaning analysis—what words can mean and cannot mean), rules governing interpretation of texts, ambiguity (structural and lexical), metaphor and metonymy, non-verbal communication, natural vs. non-natural signs from which to draw inferences, indirect speech acts, and context (situational and linguistic).

The most fascinating example in Tiersma's paper is "Does the trunk open?," uttered by a police officer searching a car, which functions identically with "Can you pass the salt?" Together with the famous entry in a ship's logbook "Captain Smith not drunk" (and no other information), these are examples that can convince even the hardest skeptic of pragmatic evidence. What is in-between the lines and who is talking to whom, when, where, why, and how may contain data even harder than those represented black and white on paper.

What does "apply science x to science y" exactly mean? Which empirical predicates can be stated for either? What does science y "applies" and "uses" methods and concepts to science x realistically amount to as a device to achieve "descriptive adequacy" or even "explanatory adequacy"? Tiersma's aphoristic expression "The Judge as Linguist" can be understood on a more critical note also as: How can academically trained members of a profession x *act as* or *do the job of* academically trained members of a profession y? Is this at all possible? And justified? To what extent is the aphoristic *The Judge as Linguist* reversible as *The Linguist as Judge*?

The point I want to make here is to advocate a specification and revision of some theoretical concepts and terminological distinctions used for describing the application of one science (linguistics) to another (jurisprudence). If we say we work in "Applied Linguistics" dealing with questions and matters from a forensic context, this does not reveal much of the content of what we are actually doing. It does not really fit as a bottom line of a definition of what we do. I think that the notions of "application," "applied," and others need further differentiation, thorough revision and rethinking—including *unconventional* modifications and alterations. The term "applied" does not yield insights into its substance, intension, and extension. In German the term "Angewandte Linguistik" (not matching "Applied Linguistics") frequently distinguishes *to which field* the application is made. In particular, it refers to whether it is an application to another science or applied science (say Aphasiology to Medicine, Homiletics to Theology, Forensic Linguistics to Criminology), or whether the application is addressed to a "Praxisfeld" (field of practice in real life): Speech training of aphasic patients, practical exercise in a theological seminary, training of police officers to account for linguistic data at the site of a crime.

I would suggest yet another distinction. In a (cautious) analogy to the use of two terms in opposition in the earth sciences, the environmental sciences, and also the social sciences, I would distinguish the *autochthonic* use of a linguistic term used in an area where it was formed (used in linguistics proper), versus an *allochthonic* use of a linguistic term (used in an area other than the one in which it was formed). *Idiolectal behavior* could be called an example for autochthonic use if employed in linguistics, allochthonic use if employed in law texts and juridical nomenclature. *Miranda Warnings* could be called an allochthonic use if occurring in linguistics, an autochthonic use if occurring in law texts, verdicts, court orders, and so on. This distinction may be helpful and necessary in some scientific contexts. The terms themselves do not matter, but the perspectives gained. Tiersma's paper provides an almost unlimited reservoir for that.

## References

Tiersma, Peter Meijes (1993). The Judge as Linguist, *Loyola L.A. Law Review* 27: 269–284.

Solan, Lawrence M. & Peter M. Tiersma (2012). The Language of Crime. In: Peter M. Tiersma and Lawrence M. Solan (eds.) *The Oxford Handbook of Language and Law*. Oxford: Oxford University Press.

42

# The Sound of Silence

MIRANDA WAIVERS, SELECTIVE LITERALISM,
AND SOCIAL CONTEXT

Richard A. Leo

In 2010 the United States Supreme Court ruled in *Berghuis v. Thompkins* that a waiver of a suspect's Miranda right to counsel can be implied through silence. At the beginning of what would be a three-hour interrogation, police presented Mr. Thompkins with a standard Miranda form that notified him of his rights to silence and appointed counsel as well as of the possible in-court consequences of making a statement to police. In addition to these standard Miranda warnings, the investigator added a fifth warning to the form, which he had Mr. Thompkins read out loud: "You have the right to decide at any time before or during questioning to use your right to remain silent and your right to talk with a lawyer while you are being questioned." (*Berghuis v. Thompkins*, 2010: 2256). The detective subsequently requested that Mr. Thompkins sign the Miranda waiver form, but Mr. Thompkins declined to do so. Although Mr. Thompkins never stated that he wished to remain silent, he did remain "largely" silent during the subsequent interrogation. Approximately two hours and 45 minutes into accusatory questioning, the detective asked Mr. Thompkins whether he prays "to God to forgive you for shooting that boy down?" and Mr. Thompkins "answered yes and looked away." (*Berghuis v. Thompkins*, 2010: 2257).

This incriminating statement was ultimately treated as a confession and used to convict Mr. Thompkins, who argued on appeal that by persisting in silence for almost three hours, he had communicated that he did not wish to speak to the police and thus had invoked his Miranda right to silence. His incriminating statement, elicited in violation of Miranda, therefore should have been excluded from evidence at trial and because it was not, his conviction should be reversed. The Supreme Court rejected his argument, holding that "a suspect who has received and understood the Miranda warnings, and has not invoked his Miranda rights, waives the right to remain silent by making an uncoerced statement to police." (*Berghuis v. Thompkins*, 2010: 2264).

*Thompkins* is widely regarded as one of the most significant Miranda cases yet decided (Weisselberg, 2010; Thomas and Leo, 2012). This is because the Miranda decision in 1966 made clear that police detectives could not interrogate a custodial suspect prior to obtaining an explicit waiver to both the rights to silence and counsel, and that the state bears a heavy burden to demonstrate the waiver was both knowing and voluntary. *Thompkins* seems to defy one of the founding premises of Miranda, namely that Miranda warnings can only mitigate the inherent compulsion of police interrogation when waivers are freely and voluntarily given. As Justice Sotomayor complained in dissent in *Thompkins*, "Today's decision turns Miranda upside down. Criminal suspects must now unambiguously invoke their right to remain silent—which, counterintuitively, requires them to speak. At the same time, suspects will be legally presumed to have waived their rights even if they have given no clear expression of their intent to do so." (*Berghuis v. Thompkins*, 2010: 2278). Charles Weisselberg adds: "the Court [in *Berghuis v. Thompkins*] has transformed Miranda from a rule aimed at protecting suspects to one that protects police … So long as officers give warnings, their interrogation practices will be largely immune from any legal challenge." (Weisselberg, 2010: 1).

Did the majority in *Berghuis v. Thompkins* get it right? To find the answer we must divide the question into two: First, as an empirical matter, did Thompkins invoke his right to silence by remaining silent? And second, as a normative matter, should the court have allowed him to invoke his right to silence by remaining silent?

I believe the work of Peter Tiersma and Lawrence Solan on the interactions (spoken and unspoken) between police and suspects helps us better frame, understand, and answer these questions. As Tiersma and Solan (2004) have shown, the court tends to selectively require literal speech when interpreting the utterances of criminal suspects seeking to assert their rights but not when a suspect's utterances arguably forego asserting their rights. So, for example, the court requires a hyper-literal assertion of the right to counsel when a suspect seeks to invoke it to cut off police interrogation, but at the same time recognizes indirect statements or acts of consent by suspects when they are foregoing constitutional rights. Likewise, the court interprets indirect language by police in asking for suspect consent to search as though it were a direct request. Put differently, the Supreme Court, along with most appellate courts, expects the speech style of criminal suspects to be direct and assertive, while it allows the speech style of police to be indirect or implied. As a result, courts maintain assert that criminal defendants are held to a higher linguistic standard than police, thereby using selective linguistic modes of interpretation that always favor the state over the accused.

Courts' selective literalism fails to take pragmatic information and social context into account when interpreting the speech acts of custodial suspects. Because of implicit social norms as well as asymmetrical power relations, most people tend to make requests and commands—such as assertions of constitutional rights—to police indirectly in order not to seem confrontational. This tendency is even more pronounced during custodial interrogation where police exercise more control than usual over the encounter. And, as Ainsworth (1993) has shown, women and members of lower socioeconomic classes tend to use more indirect language and a greater instance <amount?? of hedging phrases, thus speaking in a less direct and more polite way than men and members of higher socioeconomic classes. Yet as Tiersma and Solan (2004: 256) note, courts are less likely to interpret these indirect modes of speech as qualifying as assertions of constitutional rights, whereas when police engage in indirect modes of speech and interpretation, courts do interpret vague and ambiguous utterances as commands and requests.

We return to the questions posed by *Berghuis v. Thompkins*. In light of the linguistic research by Tiersma, Solan, Ainsworth, and others (e.g., Lakoff, 1990), it is clear that the court did not have an accurate understanding of how people actually use language to express themselves—suspects will tend to express themselves indirectly because of the social, pragmatic, and conversational norms inherent in police interrogation encounters, not because they do not intend to exercise their rights. Mr. Thompkins lacked knowledge of the legally required language needed to invoke his right to silence and instead expressed his intent to exercise his right to remain silent by declining to sign the Miranda waiver form and by remaining almost entirely silent for two hours and 45 minutes of accusatory interrogation. The court should not have selectively demanded that Mr. Thompkins literally assert his right to remain silent by saying something akin to "I hereby wish to invoke my right to remain silent," because custodial suspects almost never talk this way. Instead, the court should have interpreted Mr. Thompkins's actions in its proper social and pragmatic context. Mr. Thompkins was signaling to his interrogator that he wished to remain silent by remaining silent and refusing to sign the Miranda waiver form. Had the trial court properly interpreted Mr. Thompkins's communicative intent, it would have suppressed Mr. Thompkins's subsequent incriminating statement as the product of an inherently compelling interrogation to which Mr. Thompkins did not voluntarily and freely consent. Instead, the trial court allowed Mr. Thompkins's statement to come in, and the Supreme Court upheld his conviction, making this case yet another example of the court's selective literalism in a long line of cases watering down the original Miranda decision (Leo and Koenig, 2010).

As Tiersma and others have pointed out in the related context of ambiguous invocations of the right to counsel, the Supreme Court should have, at the very least, required the interrogator in Thompkins to ask him to clarify why he refused to sign the Miranda waiver at the onset of interrogation and whether he wished to voluntarily participate in the interrogation given his almost complete silence in response to the detective's accusatory questions. More generally, as Tiersma has argued in a related context (Tiersma, 1990), courts should look to the *communicative intent* of the suspect when interpreting whether *through words or actions* he or she wishes to invoke the right to silence during police interrogation rather than relying on selective court-created fictions about what constitutes a freely and voluntarily chosen Miranda waiver.

## References

Ainsworth, Janet E. (1993) In a Different Register: The Pragmatics of Powerlessness in Police Interrogation. *Yale Law Journal* 103: 259–322.

Berghuis v. Thompkins, 130 S.Ct. 2250 (2010).

Lakoff, Robin (1990) *Talking Power: The Politics of Language.* New York: Basic Books.

Leo, Richard A. and Alexa Koenig (2010) The Gatehouse and Mansions: Fifty Years Later. *The Annual Review of Law and Social Science* 6: 323–339.

Miranda v. Arizona, 384 U.S. 436 (1966).

Solan, Lawrence M. and Peter M. Tiersma (2005) *Speaking of Crime: The Language of Criminal Justice.* Chicago: University of Chicago Press.

Thomas, George C. III and Richard A. Leo (2012) *Confessions of Guilt: From Torture to Miranda and Beyond.* New York: Oxford University Press.

Tiersma, Peter Meijes (1990) The Language of Perjury: Literal Truth, Ambiguity, and the False Statement Requirement. *Southern California Law Review* 63: 373–431.

Tiersma, Peter M. and Lawrence M. Solan (2004) Cops and Robbers: Selective Literalism in American Criminal Law. *Law & Society Review* 38: 229–266.

Weisselberg, Charles (2010). Elena Kagan and the Death of Miranda. *Huffington Post*, (June 1, 2010) 1.

# 43

# Words Alone

Laurie L. Levenson

Words matter. That is the profound lesson of Peter Tiersma's work on language and criminal justice. Sometimes, those of us in the criminal justice field get lost in the physical world of blood and guts. We naively think that what really makes a difference in a case are the murder weapons or fraudulent documents. While physical evidence is important, the most important evidence in most criminal cases is the testimony from witnesses. Witnesses provide the real DNA of criminal trials. Most criminal cases do not feature scientific evidence proving a defendant's guilt beyond a reasonable doubt. Rather, jurors must rely on the collective recollection of the testimony of witnesses. It is those words that tell the story of the crime and it is in those words where reasonable doubt most often lies. Words, even with their ambiguities, provide the real corpus of a criminal case.

My brilliant colleague, Peter Tiersma, has written three compelling works regarding language and criminal law. His first, *The Language of Perjury* (Tiersma 1990), examined the dilemma of determining when a witness's statements can be considered legally false. Poetically, Peter starts with the age-old question: "What is truth?" He focused on the challenges raised in the seminal case of *Bronston v. United States*,[1] but today's reader cannot help but think of the perjury accusations against President William J. Clinton during his impeachment hearings. The impeachment trials boiled down to determining what the word "is" meant when Clinton stated in his 1998 grand jury that "there's nothing going on between" him and Monica Lewinsky at the time he was questioned. Tiersma's genius was in giving us tools to make a determination that would be based upon something more than raw politics. While words might be "literally true," the focus in perjury cases must be on how the witness intends the utterance to be understood. If perjury is a crime because it obstructs and misleads the decision maker, a person should be punished if he has the intent to cause such harm. This fundamental lesson continues to guide courts in the most high-profile of cases. In 2013 famed baseball giant Barry Bonds had his convictions for obstruction of justice affirmed because what he told the grand jury, although perhaps literally true, was still intended to mislead.[2] Words have power and the intention of the speaker tells us whether that power is being used for good or wrong.

In 2005 Tiersma and his co-author, Lawrence M. Solan, continued this theme in their chapter on "Threats" in *Speaking of Crime: The Language of Criminal Justice* (Solan and Tiersma 2005). When are words alone enough to be a crime outside of the perjury arena? The answer? All the time. Crimes like robbery, extortion, and rape are frequently based upon threatening words, not just threatening actions. Again, Peter gets to the heart of why we choose to punish a person who uses threats of future harm to obtain money or sex. The critical issue is whether the defendant intended more than a prediction. If a suspect yells, "If you move, I'll blow your brains out!" the intent is not just to predict future behavior, but to communicate the defendant's intent to bring about this state of affairs unless the victim complies. Words are being intentionally used as a coercive force to intimidate. Words are being used as a weapon. Punishment is justified just as much as if the suspect held a gun or knife and used it as a means of securing the victim's compliance.

Judges generally consider themselves to be masters of words. As Justice Charles Evans Hughes noted, "We are under a Constitution, but a Constitution is what we say it is."[3] Nonetheless, Tiersma (1993) has addressed the need for judges to consider the use of linguistic experts in criminal cases. The most important words that govern both our country and criminal trials only mean what the judges say they mean. Yet, in all my time as a federal prosecutor, I never once heard a judge admit the testimony of a linguistics expert to explain the meaning of English words.

Tiersma's observations are simple, but brilliant. We should take words in the courtroom much more seriously than we do. Given the problems with wrongful convictions by eyewitness testimony,[4] we should press to understand exactly what a witness means when she tells an officer that the defendant "looks like" or "is similar to" or "resembles" the defendant. The legal system should not add to the problem of misidentification. A significant problem with identification testimony is that jurors may misunderstand a witness's intended meaning when the witness gives a vague report of what he or she purportedly saw. A person's liberty lies in clarifying any ambiguities.

Yet as important as words' meanings are, I wish to suggest that the manner in which words are said (or not said) may also be pivotal in the courtroom. Jurors may quickly forget the exact words used by a witness; what they tend not to forget is the overall message of the witness and whether the witness's demeanor was credible. People are not machines that spout out words. Even if every syllable a witness pronounces is 100-percent unambiguous, jurors might be right in interpreting the witness's statements differently from their literal meaning. We speak not just with our words, but with our mannerisms, inflection, and expressions. We expect people to read between the lines as we communicate, just as when we construe the words of others. This is why what Tiersma calls "indirect threats" can be so effective. When a member of an organized crime syndicate tells the prosecution's leading witness, "I hope your children are healthy," the witness has good reason to worry.

What kind of training, what kind of expertise, can be offered to jurors to interpret the manner in which words are conveyed? To what extent do cultural differences in communication affect testimony more than even the words said? The linguist has an important role in guiding us, but not just in interpreting words. How well do we interpret people?

Finally, whereas Tiersma has focused on legitimate sources of communication in the courtroom (i.e., words uttered by witnesses and judges), we might also want to think about how communications or conduct by those otherwise designated as the passive players in a trial affect the jury's verdicts (see Levenson, 2008). The defendant at counsel's table is not under oath and not testifying, but an overheard whisper to counsel or an expression in reaction to a witness's testimony can also impact a jury.

Peter Tiersma is the great communicator. His greatest gift to those of us who work in the criminal justice arena is to create an awareness of the power and limitations of words. In the criminal justice system, people are not just punished because of their acts. They are punished because of their intentions. Words, together with those actions, reveal those intentions. Yet, because people are complex, and because they have the ability to distort, so may their words. Peter's work is invaluable because it reminds us that criminal justice is an extraordinarily human endeavor. No machine has been created that can pierce the intention of words like a judge or jury. People need to determine what other people mean, and that takes a lot more than accepting their words at face value.

## Notes

1. Bronston v. United States, 409 U.S. 352 (1973).

2. United States v. Bonds, 730 F.3d 890 (9th Cir. 2013).

3. Of the 340 exonerations in the United States from 1989 to 2003, 64 percent, or 219, involved eyewitness misidentification. Gross et al. (2005: 524); Vallas (2011: 101) (citing Eyewitness Misidentification, Innocence Project, http://www.innocenceproject.org/understand/Eyewitness-Misidentification.php, visited February 6, 2012) ("According to the Innocence Project, eyewitness testimony played a role in a surprising 75% of the convictions that have been overturned as a result of DNA evidence. In 50% of those cases, eyewitness testimony was the central cause of conviction.").

4. See Thompson (2008: 1522) ("Wrongful convictions have put greater focus on the integrity of investigations viewed in their entirety, but the area of eyewitness identifications raises the most pressing concerns."); McMurtrie (2005: 1275–79) (discussing mistaken eyewitness identification "as a leading cause of wrongful convictions").

## References

Gross et al., Samuel R. (2005) Exonerations in the United States 1989 Through 2003, *Journal of Criminal Law & Criminology* 95:523–560.

Levenson, Laurie L. (2008) Courtroom Demeanor: The Theater of the Courtroom, *Minnesota Law Review* 92:573–633.

McMurtrie, Jacqueline (2005) The Role of the Social Sciences in Preventing Wrongful Convictions, *American Criminal Law Review* 42:1271–1286.

Solan, Lawrence M. and Peter M. Tiersma (2005) *Speaking of Crime: The Language of Criminal Justice.* Chicago: University of Chicago Press.

Thompson, Sandra Guerra (2008) Beyond a Reasonable Doubt? Reconsidering Uncorroborated Eyewitness Identification Testimony, *University of California Davis Law Review* 41:1487–1545.

Tiersma, Peter Meijes (1990) The Language of Perjury: "Literal Truth," Ambiguity and the False Statement Requirement, *Southern California Law Review* 63:373–431.

Tiersma, Peter M. (1993) The Judge as Linguist, *Loyola of Los Angeles Law Review* 27:269–284.

Vallas, George (2011) A Survey of Federal and State Standards for the Admission of Expert Testimony on the Reliability of Eyewitnesses, *American Journal of Criminal Law* 39:97–146.

44

# Sizzling Irons

SPEAKING OF CRIMINAL JUSTICE

Frances Rock

In his 1990 paper "The Language of Perjury," Peter Tiersma revisits the story of Tristan and Isolde. He notes that the medieval practice of trial by ordeal (specifically the ordeal of grasping burning irons), on which the story hinges, has been replaced over time by trial using legal decision making. This decision making he suggests, whilst not as haphazard as the sizzling irons, could be improved through recourse to linguistics. This light-hearted parallel between ancient torment and contemporary linguistics, so typical of Tiersma's engaging writing, has informed my title, for it is in considering language study as a means to improve the administration of justice that Tiersma's work has added particular fire to further scholarship and legal change. The second half of the title, adapting one of his recent co-authored book titles, *Speaking of Crime*, cues up my focus in this piece further by recognising concentration not on crimes, and the language through which they are committed and tried, but on criminal justice, and the language through which investigations are administered and understood. The subtitle additionally flags that in publications such as chapter 10 of *Speaking of Crime*, Tiersma investigates how the law construes utterances from the lay world. Elsewhere he focuses on the reverse of this process, examining how laypeople make sense of legal texts (e.g., 2001) or legally regulated texts (e.g., 2002). This is the direction examined here—the construal of the legal world by laypeople.

I have chosen to respond to several excerpts from Tiersma's work that all analyse delicate relationships among intentions, actions, and outcomes expressed through language. Tiersma's scholarship explores how normal conversational processes, such as those entailed by Grice's maxims or those encapsulated by Searle's writings on indirectness, take on particular significance in relation to law. He shows how this happens either because these conversational processes have particular meaning when they occur within legal settings (1990; 1993) or because they are taken in particular ways when legally assessed, potentially defining criminal offences (2005). Below, we see what happens when laypeople enter arenas where conversational norms are suspended.

Tiersma repeatedly reminds us that establishing a particular speech act's meaning can be fraught with uncertainty. He notes that a question may easily be taken for a request or even a command (1993: 281) and that "threats are similar to warnings and predictions" (2005: 199), for example. A speech act whose function has received extensive scrutiny is that performed by a Miranda Warning or police caution. Do these wordings truly convey the sense of warning or cautioning that their names suggest or are they merely informing or even threatening or instructing (see, e.g., Kurzon 1996)? Tiersma's work has prompted me to push this debate in a new direction by considering previously unpublished data that shows not what scholars, academics, or police officers make of these issues, but instead indicates perspectives of the laypeople who attempt to untangle them. The trigger for this was Tiersma's observation that Miranda warnings are often accompanied by additional non-Miranda language and this talk can influence how the warnings themselves are understood (1993: 279). He illustrates by citing the case of *Innis*, in which a suspect was told that a weapon that the crime's perpetrator had perhaps abandoned near the crime scene could get into the hands of children. This prompted the suspect to take the officers to the weapon, thus placing himself very much in the frame. The persuasive potential of co-text and context bears further examination, then.

In research interviews with suspects, an awareness that the meaning of the caution could be shaped by accompanying talk and actions is evident. One suspect noted, for example, *I know lads who've been intimidated by the police*, through talk alongside cautioning and even through strategic manipulation of circumstances. He specified, *I know a couple of people who touch heroin and that (.) you know (.) and they [the police] will wait (.) they turkey them and then they'll like go in and they'll say "give us some information like we'll let you go".* Yet as well as strategically exploiting the caution's co-text to encourage talk, the reverse also occurs. Let me introduce an excerpt in which a suspect (name anoymised) recounts his conversation with a police officer when he was arrested:

---

1    he was pretty good (.) he read me my rights and told me I was arrested and what
2    have you and . . . I said to him myself "I'm taking this to eat and ur well not taking it
3    pinched to eat" is what it was and ur he turned round he said
4    "Errol" he said "there's no need to say anything yet" (.) he said "don't say anything
5    to me at the moment"
6    he said (.) ur "decide whether you want to see a solicitor and speak to a solicitor first
7    before you say anything at all to me"
8    he said "I don't want to know so I'll just get you back (.) get you booked in" he said
9    "we'll (.) sort everything out from there"
10   he said "you're no good telling me now" he said because he- "it's just not fair on
11   you" he said cos- so you know he is pretty good like that

---

This suspect points to an officer's efforts to draw out a pragmatic force of the caution, which is very definitely not concerned with requesting talk. The suspect has, upon being arrested and cautioned, begun to blurt out a confession to stealing food (lines 2–3). The police officer immediately intervenes. The officer's objections, as recalled by the suspect, are thoroughly grounded in the suspect's rights on arrest. He specifically mentions the right to silence (lines 4–5) and the right to legal advice (lines 6–7). The rest of the reported turns concern the caution's practical implications for the participants' subsequent activities (lines 8–9) and its legal upshots in terms of a dichotomous just/unjust distinction (lines 10–11). Tiersma recalls Fraser's assertion that for a speech act to function as a threat, it should indicate intention to act and specifically to intimidate and must describe a negative outcome (2005: 199). In doing so, he joins many scholars who have explored the defining characteristics of particular speech acts as they relate to legal settings (e.g., Shuy 1993; Svennevig 2012). This suspect's colourful description speaks to such speech act characterisations in that he presents the officer turning up the caution's potential to warn the suspect against speaking. This necessitates him dialing down the caution's potential to warn him about the potential for withholding information to damage one's defence, which is also part of the English and Welsh caution. The officer's talk, as reported, draws on reformulation in lines 4–5, where *there's no need to say anything* is upgraded to *don't say anything* and in lines lines 6–7 (do x *before you say anything*); 8 (*I don't want to know*) and 10 (*you're no good telling me now*). This calls to mind Tiersma's concern with the blurring of the boundary between various speech acts (1993: 281; 2005: 199), as the officer can be seen to have gone beyond warning into instructing or even ordering. In this case silence is the object, rather than talk as in the earlier examples.

Tiersma (1990) recounts cases in which a person's perceived failure to give particular information, by omitting to speak, gesture, or write, creates implicatures that might or might not be taken up within the legal process. Whether implicatures are taken up depends, in his examples, on legal rules rather than conversational norms. In the situations that Tiersma discusses, courts are able to consider in detail, and over a protracted period, the pragmatic issues entailed. In the policing settings from which my own data typically come, decisions about how to respond to indirectness and speech act ambiguities are often made immediately, as is the case in the excerpt above. The suspect's evaluation of the officer as being *pretty good*, which bookends his account, suggests that the suspect positively evaluated the interpretative guidance in this fast-moving environment.

Emotions run high around arrest and custody, so such indications of pragmatic intention might be very influential. Tiersma describes a roadside search in which consent was at issue. In that case the consenters might not have realised that they had an option not to consent. Tiersma notes that with "three armed police officers on the scene, the lights on their squad car flashing," even if those apprehended had realised that consent was optional, it would have seemed "unwise to refuse" a search (1993: 282). Again, a suspect offers a perspective on this in considering his right to silence:

> I always find it best to shut my mouth and wait (.) you know (.) until you get a solicitor but sometimes you don't (.) because you're angry and you know (2) then you can get yourself in a lot of trouble

For this suspect, a reminder of the caution's pragmatic force would have been useful. These excerpts in combination indicate the complexity of pragmatic and para-pragmatic issues in legal settings but also the value of studying them, as has been stressed by Tiersma in both his writing and his academic practice.

The editors of this book suggested that contributors "use Tiersma's work as a springboard" to discuss law and language. Tiersma's work serves our field as a catalyst to a huge variety of areas of intellectual engagement through his gentle yet insightful writing and the way that he makes the complex simple with illuminating use of examples. This generosity of spirit in his writing is also reflected in his collegiality. When I was a doctoral candidate, I recall how grateful I was to find a padded envelope he had dispatched to me, full of off-prints of his work to help with my research. His willingness to engage with all, irrespective of their background or position in the academic hierarchy, was itself a springboard.

Transcription key

(.) Indicates a short pause of less than a second

(2) Indicates a pause of 1 second or more with the duration of the pause indicated by the number inside the bracket

". . ." Indicates reported speech within the flow of talk

## References

Kurzon, Dennis (1996) "To Speak or Not to Speak": The Comprehensibility of the Revised Police Caution, *International Journal for the Semiotics of Law* 9(25): 3–16.

Shuy, Roger W. (1993) *Language Crimes: The Use and Abuse of Language Evidence in the Courtroom.* Oxford: Blackwell Publishers.

Solan, Lawrence M. and Peter M. Tiersma (2005) *Speaking of Crime: The Language of Criminal Justice.* Chicago: University of Chicago Press.

Svennevig, Jan (2012) On Being Heard in Emergency Calls: The Development of Hostility in a Fatal Emergency Call, *Journal of Pragmatics* 44(11): 1393–1412.

Tiersma, Peter (1990) The Language of Perjury: "Literal Truth," Ambiguity, and the False Statement Requirement, *So. Cal. Law Review* 63: 373–431.

Tiersma, Peter (1993) The Judge as Linguist, *Loyola of Los Angeles Law Review* 27: 269–284.

Tiersma, Peter (2001) The Rocky Road to Legal Reform, *Brooklyn Law Review* 66(4): 1081–1119.

Tiersma, Peter (2002) The Language and Law of Product Warnings, in Cotterill, Janet (ed.) Language in the Legal Process. Basingstoke: Palgrave 54–71.

# PART VI

# Jury Instructions

45

# The History of Jury Instructions*

Peter M. Tiersma

Originally, there was a rule in England that judges were not supposed to instruct jurors at all; they could only answer questions.[1] Even then, the answers to jury questions were not always very helpful. In the 1314 case of *Abbot of Tewkesbury v. Calewe*, a jury was asked to decide whether certain land was "free alms" or "lay fee."[2] They pointed out to the judge, "We are not men of law," implicitly requesting his assistance.[3] The judge replied, "Say what you feel."[4] This is the problem, of course. If a judge does not explain to the jury what it is supposed to do, the jury will do what it feels is best. This is precisely the sort of arbitrary decision making that the rule of law seeks to prevent.

Eventually, judges in England did begin to instruct jurors on the law. But even today, English jury instructions (part of the judge's "summation") remain oral and relatively informal. The judge summarizes the facts and possible inferences to be drawn from them and then tells jurors in his own words what the relevant law is.

As in England, American judges originally did not instruct jurors on the law. Jurors were expected to use their common sense. Common sense may have worked well enough when the country was largely rural. But as the country industrialized, legal disputes became more complex and the need for consistently applied rules of law became more pressing. Eventually, jurors lost the right to decide questions of law. Additionally, toward the end of the nineteenth century, many states took away the power of the judge to charge juries on the facts. Thus arose the modern division of labor in which the judge decides the law and the jury is entrusted with the facts. Inevitably, jurisdictions began to require the judge to instruct the jury on the relevant law.

---

* Excerpt from Peter Tiersma, The Rocky Road to Legal Reform: Improving the Language of Jury Instructions, *Brooklyn Law Review* 66: 1081, 1082–88 (2001).

The legal profession soon came to realize that instructing the jury could involve a lot of work and duplication of effort. With every trial, judges and attorneys would spend time drafting the instructions. Another problem was that instructions were often inconsistent from judge to judge. And judges were often reversed for instructional error.

In 1935 Judge William J. Palmer of the Superior Court of Los Angeles, California, addressed some of these issues in an article recommending that a committee be formed to compile approved instructions for civil cases.[5] The presiding judge of the court was impressed by the idea and appointed a committee of lawyers and judges to accomplish this goal. The committee published a book of instructions a few years later. The descendant of this book of instructions is still used in California, where it is known as the *Book of Approved Jury Instructions* ("BAJI"). A similar book of criminal instructions, *California Jury Instructions: Criminal* ("CALJIC"), soon followed.[6] The venture was a tremendous success and has since been imitated by many other states.[7]

Tellingly, the name of the original collection of civil jury instructions in California, and especially the reference to "approved" jury instructions, lays bare both the strengths and weaknesses of the approach that was generally taken by the committee of judges and lawyers in California and in many other American jurisdictions. The philosophy of much of the original pattern jury instruction movement was to search for language to which a court or legislature had given its stamp of approval. This approved language was found, for the most part, in judicial opinions and in statutes. The approach had a very powerful advantage. Copying verbatim the language of statutes—and, to a somewhat lesser extent, judicial opinions—was a virtually foolproof method of insulating the instructions from legal attack on appeal. After the Constitution, legislation is supreme in our legal system. Who could fault a judge for reading to the jurors from a statute when the statute, by definition, is an accurate statement of the law?

Yet there were and are some significant downsides to copying approved language. Many of the cases and statutes that contain the rules of law were drafted quite a while ago. The words in one version of the reasonable doubt instruction, still used today, were taken verbatim from a Massachusetts case decided in 1850.[8] Moreover, cases and statutes are written primarily for an audience of lawyers and, thus, have never been intended to be read and understood by the lay public. Consequently, using approved language and publishing the results did save time and probably resulted in fewer reversals for instructional error. But it did not increase jurors' understanding of the law. In fact, it may have had the *opposite* effect.

Research confirms that jury instructions are hard for the average juror to understand. The seminal study by Robert and Veda Charrow analyzed some of California's BAJI (civil) instructions. The Charrows found that their research subjects understood roughly one-half of the instructions. They then rewrote the instructions in a way that maintained the meaning but avoided some of the linguistic problems in the originals, producing better—albeit not perfect—comprehension scores.[9] A substantial number of studies of instructions in other jurisdictions have produced similar results.[10] The message is that it is possible to reform the language of jury instructions and thereby achieve greater comprehension. Jurors may never fully understand the law, but we *can* do better.

Assuming that communication with juries can and should be improved, how do we achieve that goal? The most common formal mechanisms for changing the law are legislation and judicial decisions. Although there are statutes requiring that jurors be instructed on certain matters, and sometimes even in specified language, for the most part legislatures have not particularly concerned themselves with the language of jury instructions. They have little expertise in the area, and appear content to leave the matter to the legal profession. This means that reform is most likely to occur through the courts, or—as discussed below—through the work of the committees of lawyers and judges who draft the instructions.

## The Reaction of the Courts

For the most part, the courts have not been especially effective as a mechanism for reforming the language of jury instructions. One reason is that litigants seldom seem to raise the issue when the instructions are being selected. Perhaps understandably, lawyers are much more interested in the question of which instructions are given, and in possibly slanting those instructions in their favor, than they are in how the instructions are expressed. Initially, this may seem logical enough, but on reflection it is somewhat surprising. One would think that in a fair number of trials one side would have an interest in jurors following the law, while the other side might prefer to ignore or minimize the legal rules. The former would presumably fight for clear instructions, while the latter would prefer the existing obscurity. As far as I know, however, lawyers seldom use this strategy, at least as far as jury instructions are concerned. As a result, lawyers tend not to object to the language of jury instructions until perhaps raising it on appeal, after they have lost the case. At this point, of course, appellate judges are likely to reply that it is too late; they should have objected at trial.

Even when lawyers are aware of the comprehensibility issue, many states with pattern or standardized instructions either require or strongly recommend that they be used when available.[11] Add to this the suspicion of judges that the instructions offered by the parties are almost always slanted in some way and it should be evident that it will be difficult, perhaps impossible, for individual parties to propose modifying the language of existing pattern instructions.

Judges also tend to be unhelpful when during deliberations the jurors ask a question about the meaning of an instruction. In several jurisdictions it has been held inadequate to respond to jury questions or confusion by simply referring back to the instructions that were already given.[12] Nonetheless, it is all too common for judges to simply reread the original instructions, or to refer jurors back to them. Unfortunately, this inadequate practice is frequently upheld on appeal.[13] Consider the recent New York case of *People v. Redd*,[14] in which jurors wrote a note to the judge seeking in vain a "laymen's" explanation of the concept of reasonable doubt. Although the appellate court ducked the issue on procedural grounds, it suggested that the trial court correctly relied on its original instruction. In fact, it advised lower courts to adhere to the language of New York's pattern instruction.[15]

Consider what would happen if a law school instructor answered student questions by simply rereading her notes verbatim. She would quickly be looking for a different line of work. Yet this is exactly what many judges do. Unfortunately, there is a rational reason for judges to react so cautiously: the fear of reversal. It is a rare judge who has been reversed for responding to questions by repeating an instruction word for word. Judges who bravely try to explain a concept in their own words, on the other hand, risk having the verdict overturned. This is especially true with important—and conceptually very difficult—standards like reasonable doubt.[16]

Sometimes there is evidence after trial that a particular jury was actually confused by an instruction. One might think that when this happens, courts would realize that their instructional efforts were inadequate. Yet evidence of actual confusion has had very little impact because of the rule that juries are not allowed to impeach their own verdicts.[17] This procedural barrier means that even when interviews with jurors show that they did not understand, for example, the difference between aggravation and mitigation in a death penalty case,[18] there is no way to present such evidence to a court.

The rule against a jury impeaching its verdict is reinforced on appeal by a presumption that jurors understood their instructions.[19] In practice, this presumption is nearly impossible to rebut. As noted, interviews with jurors after the verdict are generally inadmissible for this purpose. Moreover, although the questions that juries ask would seem to indicate uncertainty on that point, appellate courts seem to assume that rereading the instruction will solve the problem. Hence, jury questions on the meaning of an instruction, even though they are strong evidence of confusion, and are often unanswered, also will not rebut the presumption.

Finally, it would be unrealistic to ignore political considerations. Because jury instructions are standardized, judges are very reluctant to declare that a particular instruction was poorly drafted, especially in criminal cases, because there might be dozens or hundreds of prisoners in the jurisdiction who were convicted on the same instruction. Judges understandably fear opening the floodgates to massive amounts of litigation. If the case involves the death penalty, the stakes are even higher, and the political pressure to let sleeping dogs lie is even more intense.

## Notes

1. William W. Schwarzer, *Communicating With Juries: Problems and Remedies*, 69 Cal. L. Rev. 731, 732–37 (1981).

2. J. H. Baker, An Introduction to English Legal History 95 (3d ed. 1990) (citing Abbot of Tewkesbury v. Calewe, (1314) 39 SS 158, 161).

3. *Id.*

4. *Id.* at 95 n.40.

5. Robert G. Nieland, Pattern Jury Instructions: A Critical Look at a Modern Movement to Improve the Jury System 6 (1979).

6. The most recent edition is Cal. Superior Court (L.A. County), Comm. on Standard Jury Instructions, California Jury Instructions: Criminal (6th ed. 1996) [hereinafter CALJIC].

7. *See generally* Nieland, *supra* note 5.

8. Commonwealth v. Webster, 59 Mass. 295, 320 (1850).

9. Robert Charrow & Veda Charrow, *Making Legal Language Understandable: A Psycholinguistic Study of Jury Instructions*, 79 Colum. L. Rev. 1306 (1979).

10. *See, e.g.*, Amiram Elwork et al., Making Jury Instructions Understandable (1982); Phoebe C. Ellsworth, *Are Twelve Heads Better Than One?*, 52 Law & Contemp. Probs. 205 (1989); Geoffrey P. Kramer & Dorean M. Koenig, *Do Jurors Understand Criminal Jury Instructions? Analyzing the Results of the Michigan Juror Comprehension Project*, 23 U. Mich. J. L. Reform 401 (1990); Bradley Saxton, *How Well Do Jurors Understand Jury Instructions? A Field Test Using Real Juries and Real Trials in Wyoming*, 33 Land & Water L. Rev. 59 (1998); Laurence J. Severance & Elizabeth F. Loftus, *Improving the Ability of Jurors to Comprehend and Apply Criminal Jury Instructions*, 17 Law & Soc'y Rev. 153 (1982); David U. Strawn & Raymond W. Buchanan, *Jury Confusion: A Threat to Justice*, 59 Judicature 478 (1976).

11. Illinois is one example. *See* Shari Seidman Diamond, *Instructing on Death: Psychologists, Juries and Judges*, 49 Am. Psychol. 425 (1993).

12. Bollenbach v. United States, 326 U.S. 607, 612–13 (1946); McDowell v. Calderon, 130 F.3d 833, 838–39 (9th Cir. 1997) (en banc); United States v. Bolden, 514 F.2d 1301, 1308–09 (D.C. Cir. 1975); United States v. Petersen, 513 F.2d 1133, 1136 (9th Cir. 1975); Powell v. United States, 347 F.2d 156, 157–58 (9th Cir. 1965); Seattle v. Gellein, 768 P.2d 470, 471–72 (Wash. 1989); Leonardo v. People, 728 P.2d 1252, 1254–55 (Colo. 1986); Commonwealth v. Smith, 70 A. 850, 850–51 (Pa. 1908).

13. *See, e.g.*, Weeks v. Angelone, 528 U.S. 225, 234 (2000); Waterford v. Halloway, 491 N.E.2d 1199, 1207 (Ill. App. Ct. 1986); People v. Gonzalez, 77 A.D.2d 654, 654, 430 N.Y.S.2d 655, 655 (2d Dep't 1980) (holding it is not error to reread the original instructions after the jury came back and asked for additional instructions "in layman's terms"); Biegler v. Kirby, 574 P.2d 1127, 1129 (Or. 1978).

14. 266 A.D.2d 12, 698 N.Y.S.2d 214 (1st Dep't 1999).

15. *Id.* at 215.

16. *See, e.g.*, People v. Ruge, 35 Cal. Rptr. 2d 830 (Cal. Ct. App. 1994) (reversing trial court for trying to explain reasonable doubt in laymen's terms); People v. Garcia, 126 Cal. Rptr. 275 (Cal. Ct. App. 1976) ("Well intentioned efforts to 'clarify' and 'explain' [reasonable doubt] criteria have had the result of creating confusion and uncertainty, and have repeatedly been struck down by the courts of review.").

17. *See* Wingate v. Lester E. Cox Med. Center, 853 S.W.2d 912, 915 (Mo. 1993) (stating that an affidavit or testimony of a juror is inadmissible in evidence for the purpose of impeaching the verdict of a jury); Watson v. Navistar Int'l Transp. Corp., 827 P.2d 656, 662 (Idaho 1992) (stating that juror affidavits cannot normally be used to impeach verdict); Murphy v. County of Lake, 234 P.2d 712, 715 (Cal. Ct. App. 1951) ("The rule is well established in this state that affidavits or other oral evidence of either concurring or dissenting jurors which tend to contradict, impeach or defeat their verdict, are inadmissible.").

18. *See* Ursula Bentele, *How Jurors Decide on Death: Guilt is Overwhelming; Aggravation Requires Death; and Mitigation is No Excuse*, 66 BROOK. L. REV. 1011 (2001); *see also* LORELEI SONTAG, DECIDING DEATH, A LEGAL AND EMPIRICAL ANALYSIS OF PENALTY PHASE JURY INSTRUCTIONS AND CAPITAL DECISION-MAKING (1990) [dissertation: Univ. Microfilms].

19. *See, e.g.*, Richardson v. Marsh, 481 U.S. 200, 211 (1987) ("A jury is presumed to follow its instructions."); Parker v. Randolph, 442 U.S. 62, 73 (1979) (plurality opinion) ("A critical assumption underlying [the] system [of trial by jury] is that juries will follow the instructions given them by the trial judge."); Jackson v. Denno, 378 U.S. 368, 382 n.10 (1964); Opper v. United States, 348 U.S. 84, 95 (1954); *see also* ROGER J. TRAYNOR, THE RIDDLE OF HARMLESS ERROR 73–74 (1970) ("In the absence of definitive studies to the contrary, we must assume that juries for the most part understand and faithfully follow instructions.").

# 46

# Capital Instructions

COMPREHENSION AS A MATTER OF LIFE OR DEATH*

## Peter M. Tiersma

The importance of reform is most starkly evident when comprehension is truly a life-or-death matter. We need not delve into the details of death penalty jurisprudence here. Suffice it to say that in most American jurisdictions with capital punishment, it is the jury that decides the defendant's fate. Yet the jury's power of life and death is limited; the United States Supreme Court has made it clear that its discretion "must be suitably directed and limited so as to minimize the risk of wholly arbitrary and capricious action."[1]

Obviously, the only way to suitably guide the discretion of the jury is by having the judge properly instruct them. If that guidance is to be at all meaningful, the jury will have to understand the judge's instructions. Incomprehensible guidance is an oxymoron.

Yet incomprehensible—or at least, convoluted—guidance is exactly what many death penalty juries receive. Under the typical American death penalty statute, the jury must first decide that the defendant has murdered someone under circumstances that make it a possible capital case; this limits the death penalty to only the most serious crimes. The jury must then consider both the **aggravating** and the **mitigating** circumstances. Typical aggravating factors are that the defendant tortured the victim before killing him or has a long history of committing violent crimes. Mitigating factors could be his unhappy childhood, his remorse, mental problems, or his mother testifying that he was a good boy who fell in with the wrong crowd. If the jurors decide that the aggravation outweighs any mitigation, they should vote for death. Otherwise, they should vote for imprisonment (often without the possibility of parole).[2]

---

* Excerpt from Peter M. Tiersma, *Legal Language* 233-40 (1999).

While this scheme does indeed give the jury some guidance on how to decide the defendant's fate, it has a serious flaw: its reliance on the technical terms *aggravation* and *mitigation*. Most courts blithely assume that jurors understand these words in their legal sense. The Supreme Court of Georgia has asserted—with no supporting evidence—that *mitigation* "is a word of common meaning and usage."[3] California's high court apparently agrees, having held that these words do not have to be defined for the jury.[4]

The reality is that even in its ordinary sense, *mitigate* is a formal word that many ordinary jurors will not understand very well.[5] As former Justice Thurgood Marshall observed, in its technical legal usage, *mitigating* is "a term of art, with a constitutional meaning that is unlikely to be apparent to a lay jury."[6] This is confirmed by a study of California's capital jury instructions by Lorelei Sontag, who discovered that even relatively well-educated college students poorly understood the word.[7]

In contrast, *aggravate* is a fairly common word. But familiarity can be deceptive. In fact, it is a legal homonym. As linguist Robin Lakoff has written: "*Mitigation* is an uncommon word, bad enough, but *aggravation* is worse—its meaning here (*worsening*) is far from its normal colloquial sense (*annoying*)."[8] This ordinary meaning of *aggravate*, to which the entire judiciary of the United States seems oblivious, is not exactly a recent innovation. Well over a hundred years ago, John Stuart Mill wrote:

> The use of "aggravating" for "provoking," in my boyhood a vulgarism of the nursery, has crept into almost all newspapers and into many books; and when writers on criminal law speak of aggravating and extenuating circumstances, their meaning, it is probable, is already misunderstood.[9]

In fact, Otto Jespersen noted that this meaning can be traced back at least as far as 1611.[10] *Aggravate* therefore ordinarily means "annoy" or "irritate." But surely jurors should not vote to put someone to death merely because the defendant, or his crime, *aggravates* them!

Virtually irrefutable evidence that jurors fail to fully grasp the meaning of these terms comes from several reported cases where capital jurors—after they have been "instructed"—come back to ask the judge to define or clarify what these terms mean, or request a dictionary to look them up. In one California case, the jury sent a note to the judge requesting "a definition of aggravation and mitigation." The judge replied that the words should be given their "commonly accepted and ordinary meaning." The jury responded: "Being unfamiliar with the term of mitigation we would like the dictionary meaning of both mitigation and aggravation, please."[11]

In response to such questions, judges tend to just reread the original instructions. Other judges, trying to be more helpful, read a definition like the following from a legal encyclopedia or dictionary, obviously not written for laymen:

> *Aggravation.* Any circumstance attending the commission of a crime which increases its guilt or enormity or adds to its injurious consequences, but which is above and beyond the essential constituents of the crime itself. I will next define "mitigating." Circumstances such as do not constitute a justification or excuse of the offense in question, but which, in fairness and mercy, may be considered as extenuating or reducing the degree of moral culpability.[12]

Ironically, the judge who read these definitions did so in response to a jury's request for "additional definitions of these words in *layman's* terms."[13]

In the published American opinions alone, there are at least ten capital cases during the past decade or two in which the jury is reported to have requested a definition or clarification of *mitigating* and/or *aggravating*.[14] No doubt these represent merely the tip of the iceberg. Sontag's study of capital juries in California presents further evidence that the problem is endemic.[15] She interviewed jurors who had participated in ten capital cases, half of which reached death verdicts.[16] Of the thirty jurors with whom she spoke, only thirteen showed adequate understanding of *aggravating* and *mitigating*.[17] No less than half of the juries asked their trial judges for definitions of these critical terms.[18] One juror reported:

> The first thing we asked for after the instructions was, could the judge define mitigating and aggravating circumstances ... I said, "I don't know that I exactly understand what it means." And then everybody else said, "No, neither do I," or "I can't give you a definition." So we decided we should ask the judge. Well, the judge wrote back and said, "You have to glean it from the instructions."[19]

Another member of the jury broke down in tears, confessing "I still don't understand the difference between aggravating and mitigating."[20]

This evidence strongly suggests that there have probably been dozens of people who have been condemned to die by juries who poorly understood the legal principles that were supposed to guide their decision. Ironically, the problem is one of the most basic errors in communicating with the public: throwing technical terminology at a lay audience. Every lawyer realizes, during questioning of witnesses, that technical terms must be explained in ordinary language. Yet once the instruction ritual begins, they seem to have forgotten.

Just as legal language consists of more than technical terminology, the problem with jury instructions transcends vocabulary. The late Professor Hans Zeisel, an expert on the American jury, surveyed potential jurors in Cook County, Illinois, to determine how well they understood the instructions that were typically given in a death penalty case in Illinois. Interestingly, the subjects comprehended several concepts relatively well. For instance, most of them correctly understood that if any individual juror decides that some factor (like the defendant's age) is a mitigating factor, the juror can consider that mitigating circumstance in the weighing process. This point is somewhat counterintuitive, because virtually all other jury determinations must be made unanimously.[21]

Yet other points were more problematic. Consider the following instruction on the nature of mitigating evidence:

> Mitigating factors include but are not limited to the following circumstances,
>
> One, the Defendant has no significant history of prior criminal activity.
>
> Two, the murder was committed while the Defendant was under the influence of extreme mental or emotional disturbance, although not such as to constitute a defense to prosecution.
>
> If, from your consideration of the evidence, you find that any of the above mitigating factors are present in this case, or that any other mitigating factors are present in this case, then you should consider such factors in light of any existing aggravating factors in determining whether the death sentence shall be imposed.[22]

Observe that jurors are told to consider any *mitigation*, which is a broad or flexible term, and which is then amplified by a list of two specific examples. In other words, jurors are to consider any X, *including but not limited to, a and b.* There is virtually always some tension between the general and the specific. Here, the law requires maximum flexibility: jurors must be allowed to consider any mitigation whatsoever, no matter how trivial it might seem to others. Yet the existence of a specific list plainly suggests that any mitigation ought to resemble those items on the list. Not surprisingly, Zeisel's survey suggests that this is exactly how many jurors interpreted the instruction. For example, most of Zeisel's subjects concluded that more moderate mental disturbance did not count as mitigation.[23]

As opposed to empirical studies that languish in scholarly journals, the Zeisel survey came to the attention of lawyers who represented James Free, a convicted murderer on the Illinois death row. Free's appeal in state courts had failed.[24] As is quite common in such cases, he then petitioned the federal courts for a writ of habeas corpus, requesting the federal judiciary to overturn his sentence because of an alleged violation of his federal constitutional rights. Specifically, Free asserted that Illinois' death penalty instructions did not properly guide the discretion of the jury that sentenced him to death.

Free's lawyers presented Zeisel's research to a federal district court. After examining the evidence, the judge agreed that in a number of areas, Free's jury most likely did not understand the law correctly. The judge issued a writ of habeas corpus vacating Free's death sentence, but stayed the order pending an appeal.[25] As one of the first cases where a judge seriously examined how well juries actually understand instructions, it was a significant decision.

While vacating Free's death sentence may sound extreme, his conviction would have remained valid. The order would most likely have led to another "penalty phase," in which a properly instructed jury would again balance the aggravating versus mitigating factors to decide whether the penalty should be death or imprisonment. Unfortunately, many—perhaps all—of the prisoners on Illinois' death row had been condemned by juries instructed in very similar language. From the point of view of the legal system, the *Free* decision was not a bold step to reform legal language, but offered a straw to dozens and perhaps hundreds of cold-blooded killers, who could grasp it to avoid—or at least, delay—their executions. And grasp it they did.

One of the first to do so was none other than the infamous John Wayne Gacy, a serial killer who had murdered thirty-three young men and disposed of their bodies under his house. Gacy has been described as the "undisputed champion among American serial killers."[26] Riding on Free's coattails, he made a last desperate attempt to stave off his impending execution. Gacy petitioned the federal courts for a writ of habeas corpus, arguing that his jury instructions were similar to Free's, that Zeisel's survey proved that the jury had not properly understood them, and that his sentence of death should likewise be vacated. A different judge rejected his contentions.[27]

Gacy appealed to the Seventh Circuit Court of Appeals. For various procedural reasons, Gacy's appeal was decided before that of Free. The panel of judges deciding Gacy's appeal admitted that "[p]olysyllabic mystification reduces the quality of justice."[28] Yet it rejected the appeal. The court's primary rationale was that the instructions were complex not just because of language, but because of their complicated content, making them hard to master on first exposure, and perhaps too difficult for jurors to understand at all.[29] This is a common objection to improving jury instructions, and, indeed, to legal use of plain language in general. How can amateurs learn a complicated body of law in a matter of minutes or hours when law students have to study it for three years in law school, followed by extensive training in practice? Of course, if ordinary people cannot understand the law, they should not be forced to decide who should be imprisoned and who should be sentenced to death. Poorly instructed jurors will render poor decisions. In addition, they will leave the process frustrated at being compelled to do something that they are not equipped to handle.

The Gacy panel also raised a more formidable obstacle to his appeal: the presumption that jurors understand their instructions:

> Instead of inquiring what juries actually understood, and how they really reasoned, courts invoke a "presumption" that jurors understand and

> follow their instructions ... [T]his is not a bursting bubble, applicable only in the absence of better evidence. It is a rule of law—a description of the premises underlying the jury system, rather than a proposition about jurors' abilities and states of mind.[30]

This truly converts the jury into the proverbial "black box," with evidence and instructions as input, and an unassailable verdict as output. With such a presumption, what happens inside the box is legally irrelevant.

The presumption that jurors understand the law, and that they follow it, does have the advantage that it lends a finality to verdicts that they would otherwise lack, and it lessens the prospect of the losing party harassing the jurors after their decision has been made. Yet as illustrated above, this presumption flies in the face of all available evidence.

After Gacy's failed appeal, Free's case itself came before the Seventh Circuit Court of Appeals. A different panel of judges reached the same conclusion as had Gacy's, but emphasizing different objections to Zeisel's research. The opinion, authored by well-known Judge Richard Posner, complained that Zeisel had not rewritten the instructions and tried them out on a control group. It was therefore impossible to say that revised instructions would have had any influence on the outcome, according to the court.[31]

Of course, as one judge noted in dissent, the solution to this problem would have been to send the case back to the district court, which could then have allowed Free's academic defenders to conduct another survey with a control group.[32] In fact, a subsequent study did exactly what Judge Posner suggested. It found that rewritten instructions did indeed lead to greater comprehension than the original ones.[33] The study also addressed the issue of deliberation. It is often suggested that lack of comprehension because of poorly worded jury instructions is not really a problem because jurors can deliberate before reaching a verdict. Consistent with earlier studies, the researchers found that deliberation increased comprehension only when a substantial number of subjects already had a correct understanding in the first place.[34] If most jurors did not understand the instruction properly to begin with, deliberation just created further confusion as jurors propounded contrasting interpretations of what the judge meant.

A final point is that we may not be able to attain perfection in our quest to create legal language that the ordinary public can understand, Even revising instructions in the *Free* case led only to around 60-percent comprehension. This is consistent with other studies. The team of Elwork, Sales, and Alfini, who also conducted a study comparing standard instructions with more intelligible equivalents, aimed for a comprehension rate under which two-thirds of all jurors on a panel understood a given point of law, and they hoped to achieve that goal with eight out of ten panels. Of 86 questions testing various points of law, only 16 percent met this level of comprehension using the original (standard) instructions. Using revised instructions led to a great improvement, but even then, just over half of the questions met the desired comprehension level.[35]

Results such as these confirm that the law is indeed quite complex. There are limits to how well even the best instructions in plain language can convey complicated concepts to an untrained lay audience in a short period of time. This should not be unexpected; even after years of rigorous education in law school, a substantial number of students fail the bar examination in New York or California. To expect that we will ever achieve 100-percent comprehension of jury instructions—or other legal documents—may be unrealistic.

Yet there is no excuse for not doing better. Jurors who understand their task will have far more confidence in the system than those who do not. And even though the jury will remain something of a "black box," we will receive a more trustworthy output as we raise the quality of the input.

Unfortunately, the legal profession has many goals and interests that may override efforts to communicate clearly with the jury. Free's lawyers adopted the Zeisel survey not so much because they were proponents of better jury instructions, but because they were desperate for a legally sufficient reason to overturn his sentence. When the law is on their side, lawyers will generally try to convey it as intelligibly as possible to the jury. When the law is against them, they tend to favor obscurity.

Judges have their own agenda. Faced in the *Free* case with the prospect of flinging open the doors of the Illinois death row, and the political fracas that it would evoke, they chose to ignore strong evidence that jurors did not understand their task. The possibility of reversals, especially on a large scale, strikes fear in the hearts of most judges, who will have to spend a great deal of time retrying the cases, or face popular and political pressure because they released convicted criminals. Many prefer to hide behind the presumption that jurors understand their instructions.

We will never know whether Gacy and Free would have received a death sentence if their juries had better understood the law. Gacy's crime was heinous enough that the niceties of the law would have had very little impact. It might have, however, made a difference in Free's case. In any event, it is a moot question: the State of Illinois has executed them both.

## Notes

1. Gregg v. Georgia, 428 U.S. 153, 189 (1976).

2. For further details on the legal standards, see Peter Meijes Tiersma, *Dictionaries and Death: Do Capital Jurors Understand Mitigation?* 1995 Utah L. Rev. 1.

3. Cape v. State, 272 S.E.2d 487, 493 (Ga. 1980).

4. People v. Lang, 782 P.2d 627 (Cal. 1989).

5. See Tiersma, *Dictionaries and Death*, at 14.

6. Watkins v. Murray, 493 U.S. 907,910 (1989) (Marshall, J., dissenting from denial of certiorari).

7. Lorelei Sontag, *Deciding Death: A Legal and Empirical Analysis of Penalty Phase Jury Instructions and Capital Decision-Making* 76 & (1990) (available from University Microfilms International in Ann Arbor, Michigan; order number 9033148).

8. Robin Lakoff, *Life-or-Death Confusion in the Law: State Supreme Court Realized Issue Wasn't Only Semantics*, L.A. Times, Jan. 3, 1986, at 5.

9. Stuart Mill, *A System of Logic* 451 (People's ed., 1886), *cited in* Otto Jespersen, *Growth and Structure of the English Language* 111 (10th ed. 1982).

10. Jespersen, *Growth and Stucture*, at 111–12.

11. People v. McLain, 757 P.2d 569, 580 (Cal. 1988).

12. People v, Hamilton, 756 P.2d 1348, 1362 (Cal. 1988).

13. Emphasis added. The definitions came from *Black's Law Dictionary*. Id. at 1362.

14. Tiersma, *Dictionaries and Death*, at 15–18.

15. See generally Sontag, *Deciding Death*.

16. Id., at 89–90.

17. Id., at 115. See also Craig Haney and Mona Lynch, *Comprehending Life and Death Matters: A Preliminary Study of California Death Penalty Instructions*, 18 Law & Hum. Behavior 411, 420–21 (1994) (fewer than half of the subjects could provide even a partially correct definition of mitigation).

18. Two judges told the jurors to derive the meaning from the instructions as a whole. One gave them definitions out of *Black's Law Dictionary*. Another jury got definitions, but the source was unclear. And as to the fifth, the juror who was interviewed recalled only that the judge's response was very obscure. Sontag, *Dedding Death*, at 121.

19. Id., at 111.

20. Another juror also reported that her jury did not understand "aggravating" and "mitigating" on the verdict forms. Id., at 124–25.

21. Tiersma, *Dictionaries and Death*, at 20–21.

22. Id., at 27.

23. Id., at 26–28.

24. People v. Free, 447 N.E.2d 218 (Ill. 1983); 492 N.E.2d 1269 (Ill. 1986) (denying postconviction relief); 522 N.E.2d 1184 (Ill. 1988) (affirming dismissal of second postconviction petition).

25. United States ex rei. Free v. Peters, 806 F. Supp. 705 (N.D. Ill. 1992).

26. *The Tortuous Tale of a Serial Killer*, Newsweek, April 25, 1994, at 30.

27. United States ex rel. Gacy v. Welborn, 1992 WL 211018 (N.D. Ill.), *motion to suspend judgment denied,* 1992 WL 358851.

28. Gacy v. Welborn, 994 F.2d 305, 314 (7th Cir. 1993).

29. Id., at 311.

30. Id., at 313 (citations omitted).

31. Free v. Peters, 12 F.3d 700 (7th Cir. 1993).

32. Id., at 709.

33. Shari Seidman Diamond and Judith N. Levi, *Improving Decisions on Death by Revising and Testing Jury Instructions*, 79 Judicature 224, 230 (1996).

34. Id.

35. Elwork, Sales, and Alfini, *Making Jury Instructions Understandable*, at 54–55.

47

# Navigating the Rocky Road
Bethany K. Dumas

When I think of Peter Tiersma, two words come to mind immediately: *steadfastness* and *success*, hallmarks of his professional life as a legal scholar. When I think of Peter Tiersma and *jury instructions*, the expressions that come to mind are *comprehensibility* and legal *adequacy*.

While Tiersma has been as steadfast in his work on jury instructions as on the other topics he has addressed, he would probably say that he has not achieved complete success in that arena. As Tiersma has acknowledged more than once, there is still a need for improving the comprehensibility and usability of jury instructions in most jurisdictions. Objectively speaking, however, Tiersma has been quite successful in explaining (1) exactly why jury instructions are often incomprehensible to lay jurors, (2) the challenging nature of the requirement that jury instructions be legally accurate, and (3) the need for instructions to consider context fully in order to explain jurors' responsibilities clearly and unambiguously so that instructions do not undermine crucial legal rules such as evidentiary presumptions and burdens of proof. In addition, in his writings and in his active role in jury instruction drafting bodies, he has shown how improvements can be made by the combined efforts of informed and involved drafting committees as well as by trial and appellate judges, trial lawyers, and linguists.

Tiersma's work on improving jury instruction is grounded in his earlier scholarship on the nature of legal language, work such as his 1999 book *Legal Language*, which he has continued to develop and update through his website. In that work, he addresses the use of so-called "plain language" in the law and also the related matter of the comprehensibility of jury instructions.

In 2001 he published "The Rocky Road to Legal Reform: Improving the Language of Jury Instructions," an article based on feedback and discussion of his ideas that had occurred in presentations in previous symposia. In the article, he summarized the history of jury instructions and the roles of courts and jury instruction committees in their construction and potential improvement. The article describes in some detail typical problems involving vocabulary items, syntax, inadvertently slanted presentations of legal issues, and the awkward templates often used in pattern jury instructions. Drawing upon the early research of Charrow and Charrow (1979) and others examining the adequacy of jury instructions, he pointed out that this earlier research on California's civil instructions demonstrated that mock jurors understood only about one-half of their instructions, but that rewriting the instructions for greater clarity produced much better results. His conclusion, based on this mock jury research and on his own experience and analysis, was that "it is possible to reform the language of jury instructions and thereby achieve greater comprehension" (2001: 1085). Tiersma later summarized his analysis in a useful guide for judges, lawyers, and drafting committees to revise instructions so as to meet both comprehensibility and legal adequacy requirements (Tiersma 2006).

As I began my own research into the comprehensibility of jury instructions, I learned a great deal from Tiersma and other law professors concerned with the issue of comprehensibility and also from social scientists and two judges, both of whom taught me a great deal about the need for clearer instructions and the dangers that lie in the path. Publications by Judge B. Michael Dann of Arizona (Dann and Logan 1986, Dann 1993) and opinions by and conversation with Chief US Magistrate Judge Dennis H. Inman, Eastern District of Tennessee (whom I met when he was still on a state bench), also taught me a great deal.

My own work on jury instructions has involved jury surveys (often in trial context), continuing legal education presentations, and work as a member of the Tennessee Bar Association Jury Reform Commission and the Tennessee Judicial Conference Committee on Pattern Jury Instructions (Civil). I could not have done this research without the guidance of legal professionals, particularly Tiersma and Lawrence Solan, who have often collaborated. I am very grateful for the care with which they have instructed others of us about the need not only for clarity of language but also for the need for full legal adequacy. That involves a full consideration of context and thus includes not only satisfying all jurisdictional requirements (statutory and case law), but also acknowledging (explicitly or otherwise) the relationship between law and fact and stating jurors' responsibilities clearly and unambiguously in such a way that instructions do not undermine crucial presumptions/burdens.

In recent years, drawing upon both my work with jury instructions and my work with regional and social dialects of American English, I have proposed classroom teaching methods for students who speak a nonstandard dialect of our language. In one law school presentation, "Teaching Students Who Are Native Speakers of Stigmatized Regional/Social Dialects of American

English" (Dumas 2012), I addressed the issue by pointing out that few US students speak or understand legalese, then suggesting that legalese is really a domain-specific social dialect, one that must either be acquired intentionally (in law school) or avoided. Similarly, for some speakers of American English, standard English is very much a domain-specific social dialect. Methods of acquisition vary, but classroom activities will facilitate acquisition if classroom instructors understand that speakers of stigmatized regional/social dialects are not breaking rules; they are following different rules.

Several sets of rules are often in use in US courtrooms. Not all players speak all the social dialects in use, and not all players make use of the same discourse patterns in reporting narrative incidents. As early as 1978, researchers were pointing out some of the courtroom implications of the fact that the speaking styles of individuals are closely related to socio-demographic factors, that different styles influence listeners' impressions of speakers, and that even subtle variations in courtroom speaking styles can influence jurors' reactions to testimony as well as to the language of attorneys and judges (Conley, O'Barr, and Lind 1978). Since then, there has been much research on the effects of powerful versus powerless language, male versus female patterns, and so on.

Attention must be paid to such differences in ordinary language use by those who seek to improve adequate comprehension of instructions by jurors, usually laypeople with no legal training and hence with little or no knowledge about the semantics, syntax, and adequacy requirements of legal language.

I have in the past, using examples from Judge Inman (see above), suggested that narrative examples can assist in explaining to jurors difficult concepts such as *proximate cause*. Such examples can be helpful to jurors in that they provide real-world situations. I now suggest that they can also be helpful because of their brief departure from the usually very formal style of jury instructions. They provide narratives with which many jurors will, I think, find it easy to identify, because of the specifics of the narratives but also because storytelling is a very natural discourse technique for many lay jurors. I conclude with the following example, discussed at length in Dumas (2000) with respect to its help in providing real-world situations.

## Proximate Cause

Some of these legal concepts or principles can be difficult for laypersons to understand. I hope this example will illustrate for you a practical example of proximate cause: It is negligence for a driver to drive a car that has bald, or slick, tires. If that automobile with bald tires slams into the rear of a car because the driver could not stop due to a combination of slick tires and wet pavement, then the negligence of the driver in driving with bald tires would be a proximate cause of the accident.

It is possible for a person to be negligent without that negligence being a proximate cause of the accident. If the driver of that car with bald tires is stopped for a red light and is struck in the rear by another car, obviously the bald tires had nothing to do with the accident. In other words, the driver's negligence in driving a car with bald tires was not a proximate cause of that accident.

To find a party to be "at fault," you must find that party was negligent and that the negligence was a proximate cause of the injury or damage for which a claim was made. You must then determine the percentage of fault of each party whom you have determined is at fault.

I expect to continue exploring the usefulness of such examples because of the narrative format—as a way to improve jury instruction comprehensibility by making use of a discourse style that jurors are familiar with and frequently use.

## References

Charrow, Robert P., and Veda R. Charrow (1979) Making Legal Language Understandable: A Psycholinguistic Study of Jury Instructions. *Columbia Law Review* 79: 1306–1374.

Conley, John M., William M. O'Barr, and E. Allan Lind (1978) The Power of Language: Presentational Style in the Courtroom. *Duke Law Journal* 78: 1375–1399.

Dann, B. Michael (1993) "Learning Lessons" and "Speaking Rights": Creating Educated and Democratic Juries. *Indiana Law Journal* 68: 1229–1279.

Dann, B. Michael and George Logan, III (1986) Jury Reform: The Arizona Experience. *Judicature* 79: 280–288.

Dumas, Bethany K. 2000. Jury Trials: Lay Jurors, Pattern Jury Instructions, and Comprehension Issues. *Tennessee Law Review* 67: 701–742.

Dumas, Bethany K. (2012) Teaching Students Who Are Native Speakers of Stigmatized Regional/Social Dialects of American English. Legal Writing Institute Conference, Southern University Law Center, Baton Rouge, LA, December 7.

Tiersma, Peter M. (1999) *Legal Language.* Chicago: University of Chicago Press.

Tiersma, Peter M. (2001) The Rocky Road to Legal Reform: Improving the Language of Jury Instructions. *Brooklyn Law Review* 66: 1081–1118.

Tiersma, Peter M. (2006) Communicating with Juries: How to Draft More Understandable Jury Instructions, National Center for State Courts, Williamsburg, VA [originally published in *The Scribes Journal of Legal Writing* 10: 1–54 (2005–2006)].

# 48

# Authority and Accommodation

JUDICIAL RESPONSES TO JURORS' QUESTIONS

Chris Heffer

In his seminal article "The Rocky Road to Legal Reform: Improving the Language of Jury Instructions," Peter Tiersma (2001) cites an English case from 1314 in which jurors were asked to decide whether land was "free alms" or "lay fee." Presented with this arcane legal terminology, the jury complained, "We are not men of law," to which the judge replied "Say what you feel." Tiersma points out that here lies the nub of the problem with jury instruction: despite usually having no legal training, jurors need to be instructed in the law so that they can avoid "precisely the sort of arbitrary decision making that the rule of law seeks to prevent" (p. 1083). Even in cases where juries favour natural justice over black-letter law, they cannot go beyond (or "nullify") the law without first understanding it. And in death penalty instructions in particular (as discussed in Tiersma's 1999 book, *Legal Language*), understanding the law can be a matter of life and death.

This 1314 exchange between judge and jury illustrates the beginnings of a long history of judges failing to show adequate understanding of the jury's voice in the decision-making process. We would ordinarily construe "we are not men of law" as an indirect request for assistance with the meanings of "free alms" and "lay fee." But the judge ignores the ordinary pragmatics and effectively instructs the jury to put aside the law. Such pragmatic mishearing is endemic in judges' responses to juries and these exchanges help us to understand why the road to legal reform of jury instruction has been so rocky. Furthermore, while jury instruction practices vary enormously across common-law countries (rendering much of the US research on "pattern instructions" considerably less relevant in other legal systems), there is remarkable similarity in some of the ways judges (and high court justices) respond to the jury.

Underlying these exchanges between judge and jury is a tension between authority and accommodation. The judge is the law's authorized voice in court, imparting the authoritative discourse of the law to the jury (Heffer 2013a). Bakhtin notes that authoritative discourse "permits no play with the context framing it, no play with its borders, no gradual and flexible transitions, no spontaneously creative stylizing variants on it" (1981: 343). It thus leads to ritualized formulas in the voicing of instructions, but also to a legal fiction of the "presumption of comprehension" (as noted by Tiersma), since for the "discourse of authority" to remain "legitimate," it is neither necessary nor sufficient for it to be understood (Bourdieu 1991: 113). At the same time, though, the judge is also legally and morally bound to communicate the law to the jury, and effective communication requires converging with, or accommodating to, the discursive practices of the audience. During witness examination and counsel's speeches, lawyers and judges have no trouble explaining technical terms in ordinary language, yet, as Tiersma notes in *Legal Language* (1999: 236), "once the instruction ritual begins, they seem to have forgotten."

Even if one accepts the predominance of authority as the guiding principle in the instructional texts themselves, jurors' questions would seem to demand a move toward accommodation. While the Charrows' first quantitative study of jury comprehension (Charrow and Charrow 1979), and the plethora of studies that followed, have confirmed empirically that jurors tend not to understand pattern legal instructions, this knowledge has always been informally available to judges as a result of juries' frequent requests for clarification. Yet judges' responses to such requests often show no attempt at accommodation. While judges no longer tell jurors to go with their feeling rather than the law, Tiersma notes the judicial practice of insisting that terms with specialist legal meanings or uses are actually "ordinary language" and "understood by jurors."

Judges claim expertise not only in stipulating and interpreting the meaning of legal terms (which no linguist would challenge) but also in determining whether the meaning of an existing term is "legal" or "ordinary." Linguists and psychologists would claim that the evidential warrants for believing that a given term or phrase is ordinary or that jurors will understand it must be found in current usage of the term or in the experimental testing of its comprehension. Judges, though, tend to ignore empirical evidence in favour of the authoritative pronouncements of authorized legal voices. Thus, if the Supreme Court of Georgia asserted in 1980 that *mitigation* "is a word of common meaning and usage" (despite ample evidence to the contrary), then this is so (Tiersma 1995: 13). If Chief Justice Dixon declared in Australia in 1961 that "beyond reasonable doubt is, I think, used by ordinary people and is understood well enough by the average man in the community," then this is good enough to justify ignoring the constant requests for clarification of that phrase by juries (despite Dixon's hedge "I think," or perhaps because of it.) (Heffer 2013a: 214). Just as US judges fail to recognize that the "common meaning" of "aggravating" is not the etymological and legal meaning "making worse" but the more mundane "annoying" (Tiersma 1995: 14), so Australian judges fail to recognize that the ordinary meaning of "reasonable" is "fair, moderate" rather than the "rational" intended in the legal term "beyond reasonable doubt" (Heffer 2013a: 210–11). Furthermore, judges' metalinguistic practices are often inconsistent. After stating that a term has an "ordinary" meaning, they will then offer up definitions from a legal dictionary or encyclopedia (Tiersma 1995: 15) or an historical dictionary (Heffer 2013a: 220).

Rather than concede an often consequential mistake in lexical categorization, judges will often impute ignorance of basic English to the jurors. In the Australian case of *R v. Chatzidimitriou* (2000), the judge, asked by the jury to define "doubt," "reasonable doubt," and "beyond reasonable doubt," responded that these were "very plain English words" that do not require explanation. Refusing to be intimidated (and probably realizing that the judge would be no help), the jury then requested a dictionary (presumably to look up the legal term). Yet the judge, despite the phrasing in the jury's question, argued with counsel that the jurors wanted to look up the ordinary meaning of the words "doubt" and "reasonable," while one of the justices at appeal argued that giving the jury a dictionary "let the jurors do by reading what any competent English teacher might be able to do by recollection" (Heffer 2013a: 220).

In the high-profile English case of *R v. Vasiliki Pryce* (2013), in which the defendant claimed the rare defence of marital coercion, the jury asked the judge a number of questions, including the following:

> You have defined the defence of marital coercion on page 5 of the jury bundle and also explained what does not fall within the definition by way of examples. Please expand on the definition, provide examples of what may fall within the defence, specifically "will was overborne" and does the defence require violence or physical threat?

The question shows both a convergence with legal register and an awareness of deficits in the judge's own instruction (precedent would suggest that he should indeed have given positive as well as negative examples and clarified that the defence did not require violence or physical threat). In his instructions to the jury, the judge had glossed the term "coercion" with the two considerably rarer words "(will) overborne" and "impelled," yet, in a legal ruling on the case, he assisted his fellow legal professionals (but not the jury) by glossing "overborne" and "impelled" with the two very common words "overcome" and "forced" (Heffer 2013b: 17–22). When the jury failed to reach a verdict, the judge described them as showing "absolutely fundamental deficits in understanding," leading to front-page headlines about the stupidity of jurors and the need to disband the jury system.

What we find again and again in these exchanges between judge and jury is a genuine attempt by the lay jury to accommodate to the legal-institutional context, while judges often remain locked into a discourse of authority that prevents them from hearing and actively responding to the voice of the jury. While rewriting archaic and incomprehensible instructional texts will certainly improve comprehension, the gains, as empirical research has shown and Tiersma acknowledges, are ultimately limited. What is required beyond this is for judges and courts of appeal to understand the jurors' perspective: the fact that, without legal training but with combined experience of the world, they have to arrive at a specific decision in a specific case and in accordance with the law. Nelson (2013) found that integration of legal instructions with the evidence in the case, combined with oral narrativization of the instructions themselves (Heffer 2005), led to very significant improvements in comprehension, including a jump from 53 percent to 82 percent for the key instruction on the criminal standard of proof. Perfect comprehension will certainly never be achieved, but pushing beyond the textual barrier towards a focus on the interaction between judge and jury may well help.

## References

Bakhtin, M. (1981) *The Dialogic Imagination*. Austin: University of Texas Press.

Bourdieu, P. (1991) *Language and Symbolic Power*. Cambridge: Polity Press.

Charrow, R. and Charrow, V. (1979) Making Legal Language Understandable: A Psycho linguistic Study of Jury Instructions. *Columbia Law Review* 79. 1306–1374.

Heffer, Chris (2005) *The Language of Jury Trial*. Basingstoke: Palgrave.

Heffer, Chris (2013a) Communication and Magic: Authorized Voice, Legal-Linguistic Habitus, and the Recontextualization of "Beyond Reasonable Doubt." In C. Heffer, F. Rock, and J. M. Conley (eds.) *Legal-Lay Communication: Textual Travels in the Law*. Oxford: Oxford University Press.

Heffer, Chris (2013b) Projecting Voice: Towards an Agentive Understanding of a Critical Capacity. *Working Papers in Language and Literature*. Cardiff: Cardiff University. Available at http://orca.cf.ac.uk/52487/.

Nelson, Sally (2013) *Directing Jurors in England and Wales: The Effect of Narrativization on Comprehension*. PhD Thesis. Cardiff University.

Tiersma, Peter M. (1995) Dictionaries and Death: Do Capital Jurors Understand Mitigation? *Utah Law Review* 1: 1–50.

Tiersma, Peter M. (1999) *Legal Language*. Chicago: University of Chicago Press.

Tiersma, Peter M. (2001) The Rocky Road to Legal Reform: Improving the Language of Jury Instructions. *Brooklyn Law Review* 66: 1081–1118.

# 49

# Jury Instructions Written for Jurors

A PERENNIAL CHALLENGE

## Nancy S. Marder

Over a decade and a half ago, Peter Tiersma identified problems with jury instructions that still remain true today. In *Legal Language* (1999), he described how and why jury instructions are written in a formal language that is difficult for jurors to understand. In "The Rocky Road to Legal Reform: Improving the Language of Jury Instructions" (2001), he elaborated on the problems with pattern jury instructions, but also described steps that California had taken to improve its instructions. Tiersma's discussion of jury instructions in these two pieces invites a re-examination of why these instructions remain so difficult for jurors to comprehend and what can be done about it today. California's revised "plain language" jury instructions—to which Tiersma made significant contributions—show that improvement is possible. California's instructions should serve as a model and inspiration for other states.

In both *Legal Language* and "The Rocky Road," Tiersma identified several features of jury instructions that make them difficult for jurors, untrained in the law, to understand. Jury instructions are typically written in formal language and contain words or phrases that are archaic, technical, or obscure. For example, capital jury instructions rely on technical terms like "aggravation" and "mitigation" (Tiersma 1999). Jurors, accustomed to everyday speech, are unlikely to be familiar with the technical meanings that the law ascribes to these and other words. As Tiersma explained, the law makes use of formality, just as religions do, in order to give authority to its texts. Although the formality of jury instructions might make them sound learned, this formality also stands in the way of easy comprehension. This is a problem in every jury trial, but is particularly significant in capital cases in which the jury has to decide between life or death (Tiersma 2001).

Although Tiersma focused on how the language of jury instructions makes them incomprehensible, I think the way instructions are presented to jurors exacerbates the problem (Marder 2006). Jury instructions are typically delivered by the judge at the end of the trial. The judge reads the instructions slowly and carefully, but usually with little expression. The reading can last for hours depending on the complexity of the case. In many courtrooms where the judge does not give jurors individual written copies of the instructions, jurors must sit and listen, hoping they can remember what they have heard. In other courtrooms, the judge gives all twelve jurors a single written copy of the instructions to share when they begin their deliberations.

Even though educational theory suggests that people have different styles of learning, courts treat jurors as if they all learn in the same way (Dann 1993). Some jurors learn best by reading, others by listening, and some by doing both. Courts could accommodate different learning styles by giving jurors an individual written copy of the instructions so that they can follow the instructions as the judge reads them aloud. They could then write down any points they want to raise during deliberations. An even better approach, which both Tiersma and I have recommended but which few judges follow, is to give jurors the opportunity to ask questions about the instructions before they begin their deliberations (Tiersma 2009; Marder 2009). Judges are reticent to adopt this practice, perhaps because they fear saying something that will lead to reversal. However, if jurors are to understand the instructions, they need answers to their questions. Although they will have the chance to speak to each other during deliberations, they view the judge as the authority on the law.

In *Legal Language* and "The Rocky Road," Tiersma also explained why it is so difficult to change pattern jury instructions even though there are myriad empirical studies showing that jurors have difficulty understanding them. He pointed out that trial judges forget what it is like to be a layperson and to hear legal language without having had any legal training. Trial judges are reluctant to change the language because any change entails risk of reversal on appeal (Wascher 2005). If trial judges adhere to the instruction that has been given in the past and has survived previous appellate scrutiny, then the risk of reversal is small.

Pattern instructions are usually written by committees that consist of lawyers and judges. I serve as the professor/reporter for one of these committees in Illinois. These committees want to do the best job they can, but their members are professionals who are familiar with legal language. They were trained as lawyers, not linguists. As a result, their instructions draw heavily from the language of statutes and case law. They do not want to take unnecessary risks by departing from the language of statutes or case law, even if comprehensibility suffers in the process.

One solution to this problem is for jury instruction committees to make use of outsiders, such as linguists or laypersons, in an effort to ensure that instructions are understandable. However, they may be reluctant to do so for several reasons. First, as committee members have explained to me, they have been appointed to serve on these committees and they feel that writing the instructions is their responsibility. Allowing a linguist or layperson to offer suggestions, even if the committee has ultimate responsibility, is seen as a dereliction of the committee's duty. Second, in states where the committee's work is done behind closed doors, committee members want to make sure that instructions remain confidential until they are released to the public; going outside the committee raises the possibility of loss of confidentiality. Third, the committees strive to write balanced instructions, which do not favor one side or the other. The committees worry that outsiders' suggestions might tip the balance. Ideally, committees would test their instructions before they publish them, but testing is expensive, time consuming, and resource intensive, especially if it entails deliberation to replicate what actual juries do. Thus, jury instruction committees tend not to test their instructions.

Appellate judges are an unlikely source for change in making jury instructions more understandable to jurors. As Tiersma noted, appellate judges are far removed from knowing what laypeople might or might not understand. Moreover, they presume that jurors understand jury instructions (Tiersma 1999). This might be because appellate judges understand the instructions, so they think jurors will understand them too. This also might be because they worry about all the other cases that were decided using the same instructions and are concerned that these cases might be affected if the instructions were changed. Appellate judges face an additional hurdle in understanding the plight of jurors. Appellate judges have the luxury of carefully parsing the written language of the instructions, and they assume that jurors can do this as well. However, jurors are not lawyers and sometimes they are not even given a written copy of the instructions. It is hard to undertake a careful reading of the instructions when the judge simply reads them aloud.

If all who are involved—trial judges, appellate judges, and jury instruction committees—are unlikely to make jury instructions more understandable for jurors, how will change come about? Tiersma's experience on the task force in California that created new plain language instructions from scratch suggests one avenue for reform. After the O. J. Simpson criminal trial in California, a Blue Ribbon Commission on Jury System Improvement was created. The commission recommended that new task forces draft plain language instructions. One task force focused on criminal instructions and the other focused on civil instructions. The civil and criminal task forces' work was much harder and took much longer than expected, but they created instructions that are easier for jurors to understand. Every year, students in my Jury course vote on which California instructions they find more understandable—the plain language instructions or the earlier pattern instructions—and every year, they choose the plain language instructions. Other states do not have to start from scratch. They can learn from California's experience, and work from California's jury instructions, which are available online.

Improvements in a state's pattern jury instructions will come about when leaders in that state's judiciary insist upon reform (Marder 2006). In states where the chief justice of the state supreme court has given a mandate to jury instruction committees to rewrite their instructions and make them understandable, these committees have taken their task seriously. Arizona, for example, has rewritten its jury instructions and geared them for a sixth-grade reading level. Although some lawyers prefer to preserve jury instructions as sacred texts, jurors appreciate plain language instructions. They want to do a good job, and are frustrated when they are not given the tools, such as understandable jury instructions, with which to perform their role.

It is more important now than ever before that judges instruct jurors so that they can understand their tasks. In the digital age, some jurors have turned to the Internet and social media to find answers to questions they have about the instructions, as well as other aspects of the trial. At the very least, judges must explain the law to jurors in a way that they can understand, so that jurors will not seek clarification on their own or speculate as to the law. Although some of Tiersma's writings on jury instructions predated Google and Wikipedia, his prescription that judges need to instruct jurors in language that they understand has become even more pressing today than it was over a decade and a half ago.

### References

Dann, B. Michael (1993) "Learning Lessons" and "Speaking Rights": Creating Educated and Democratic Juries. *Indiana Law Journal* 68:1229–1279.

Marder, Nancy S. (2006) Bringing Jury Instructions into the Twenty-First Century. *Notre Dame Law Review* 81:449–511.

Marder, Nancy S. (2009) Jury Reform: The Impossible Dream? *Tennessee Journal of Law and Policy* 5:149–183.

Tiersma, Peter M. (1999) *Legal Language*. Chicago: University of Chicago Press.

Tiersma, Peter (2001) The Rocky Road to Legal Reform: Improving the Language of Jury Instructions. *Brooklyn Law Review* 66:1079–1118.

Tiersma, Peter (2009) Asking Jurors to Do the Impossible. *Tennessee Journal of Law and Policy* 5:105–147.

Wascher, James D. (2005) The Long March Toward Plain English Jury Instructions. *Chicago Bar Association Record* Feb./Mar.:50–54.

# BIBLIOGRAPHY OF PETER TIERSMA'S WORK

## Books and Monographs

(2012) (with Lawrence Solan) *The Oxford Handbook of Language and Law*. New York: Oxford University Press.

(2010) *Parchment, Paper, Pixels: Law and the Technologies of Communication*. Chicago: University of Chicago Press.

(2006) *Communicating with Juries: How to Draft More Understandable Jury Instructions*. Williamsburg, Va.: National Center for State Courts.

(2005) (with Lawrence Solan) *Speaking of Crime: The Language of Criminal Justice*. Chicago: University of Chicago Press.

(1999) *Legal Language*. Chicago: University of Chicago Press.

(1985) *Frisian Reference Grammar*. Dordrecht: Foris Publications.

(1985) *Language-Based Humor in the Marx Brothers Films*. Bloomington, Ind.: Indiana University Linguistics Club.

## Articles

(2012) A History of Languages of the Law, *Oxford Handbook of Language and Law*. Oxford: Oxford University Press, 13–26.

(2012) Language Policy in the United States, *Oxford Handbook of Language and Law*. Oxford: Oxford University Press, 248–267.

(2012) (with Lawrence Solan) The Language of Crime, *Oxford Handbook of Language and Law*. Oxford: Oxford University Press, 340–353.

(2011) The Rule of Text: Is It Possible to Govern Using Only Text?, *NYU Journal of Law and Liberty* 6:268–287.

(2010) Redrafting California's Jury Instructions, in Malcolm Coulthard and Alison Johnson (eds), *The Routledge Handbook of Forensic Linguistics*. London: Routledge, 251–264.

(2009) Asking Jurors to Do the Impossible, *Tennessee Journal of Law and Policy* 5:105–147.

(2008) What Is Language and Law? And Does Anyone Care?, in Frances Olsen, Alexander Lorz, and Dieter Stein (eds), *Law and Language: Theory and Society*. Düsseldorf: Düsseldorf University Press.

(2008) (with Matthew Curtis) Testing the Comprehension of Jury Instructions: California's Old and New Instructions on Circumstantial Evidence, *Journal of Court Innovation* 1:231–261.

(2008) The Nature of Legal Language, in John Gibbons and M. Teresa Turell (eds), *Dimensions of Forensic Linguistics*. Amsterdam: John Benjamins Publishing, 7–25.

(2008) Writing, Text, and the Law, in Charles Bazerman (ed.), *Handbook of Research on Writing*. New York: Lawrence Erlbaum, 129–141.

(2007) The Language of Consent in Rape Law, in Janet Cotterill (ed.), *The Language of Sexual Crime*. Houndmills: Palgrave, 83–103.

(2007) The Textualization of Precedent, *Notre Dame Law Review* 82:1187–1278.

(2006) Some Myths About Legal Language, *Journal of Law, Culture and Humanities* 2:9–50.

(2005–2006) Communicating with Juries: How to Draft More Understandable Jury Instructions, *Scribes Journal of Legal Writing* 10:1–54.

(2006) The Language of Legal Texts, in Keith Brown (ed.), *Encyclopedia of Language and Linguistics* (2nd ed). Oxford: Elsevier, 6:549–556.

(2005) (with Lawrence Solan) La Lingüística Forense en los Tribunales Norteamericanos, in M. Teresa Turell (ed.) *Lingüística Forense, Lengua y Derecho: Conceptos, Métodos y Aplicaciones* (Maria Angeles Orts, Trans.). Barcelona: Institut Universitari de Lingüística Aplicada Universitat Pompeu Fabra, 147–168.

(2005) The New Black's, *Journal of Legal Education* 55:386–400.

(2005) Language Wars: Truce Accepted (with Conditions), *Green Bag* (2nd ed.) 8:281–290.

(2005) Categorical Lists in the Law, in Vijay K. Bhatia, Jan Engberg, Maurizio Gotti, and Dorothee Heller (eds), *Vagueness in Normative Texts*. Bern: Peter Lang, 109–130.

(2004) (with Lawrence Solan) Cops and Robbers: Selective Literalism in American Criminal Law, *Law and Society Review* 38:229–265.

(2004) Did Clinton Lie? Defining "Sexual Relations," *Chicago Kent Law Review* 79:927–958.

(2003) Jury Questions: An Update to Kalven and Zeisel, *Criminal Law Bulletin* 39:10–32.

(2003) (with Lawrence Solan) Hearing Voices: Speaker Identification in American Courts, *Hastings Law Journal* 54:373–435.

(2003) (with Lawrence Solan) Falling on Deaf Ears: Scientists Say That Earwitnesses are Unreliable. Why Aren't Courts Listening?, *Legal Affairs*, 71.

(2003) From Speech to Writing: Textualization and Its Consequences, in Marlyn Robinson (ed.), *Language and the Law: Proceedings of a Conference*. Buffalo: Hein and Co., 349–365.

(2002) The Language and Law of Product Warnings, in Janet Cotterill (ed.), *Language in the Legal Process*. New York: Palgrave Macmillan, 54–71.

(2002) (with Lawrence Solan) The Linguist on the Witness Stand: Forensic Linguistics in American Courts, *Language* 88:221–239.

(2001) A Message in a Bottle: Text, Autonomy, and Statutory Interpretation, *Tulane Law Review* 76:431–483.

(2001) Textualizing the Law, *Forensic Linguistics* 8(2):73–92.

(2001) The Rocky Road to Legal Reform: Improving the Language of Jury Instructions, *Brooklyn Law Review* 66:1081–1119.

(2001) A Missed Opportunity: United States Supreme Court Upholds a Convoluted Death Penalty Instruction, *Clarity* 46:20–23.

(1999) Jury Instructions in the New Millennium, *Court Review* 36:28.

(1995) The Language of Silence, *Rutgers Law Review* 48:1–99.

(1995) The Ambiguity of Interpretation: Distinguishing Interpretation from Construction, *Washington Law Quarterly* 73:1095–1101.

(1995) Dictionaries and Death: Do Capital Jurors Understand Mitigation?, *Utah Law Review* 1:1–49.

(1993) Reforming the Language of Jury Instructions, *Hofstra Law Review* 22:37–78.

(1993) Nonverbal Communication and the Freedom of "Speech," *Wisconsin Law Review* 1993:1525–1569.

(1993) The Judge as Linguist, *Loyola of Los Angeles Law Review* 27:269–284.

(1993) Linguistic Issues in the Law, *Language: Journal of the Linguistic Society of America* 69:113–137.

(1992) Reassessing Unilateral Contracts, *U.C. Davis Law Review* 26:1–86.

(1990) The Language of Perjury: "Literal Truth," Ambiguity and the False Statement Requirement, *Southern California Law Review* 63:373–431.

(1988) Rites of Passage: Legal Ritual in Roman Law and Anthropological Analogues, *Journal of Legal History* 9:1–25.

(1987) The Language of Defamation, *Texas Law Review* 66:303–350.

(1986) The Language of Offer and Acceptance: Speech Acts and the Question of Intent, *California Law Review* 74:189–232.

### Articles in Linguistics

(1994) (with Jarich Hoekstra) Frisian, in Johan van der Auwera and Ekkehard König (eds), *The Germanic Languages*. London: Routledge, 505–531.

(1993) Lokale Markeardens yn it Frysk, *Tydskrift foar Fryske Taalkunde* 8:110–114.

(1986) Language Change in a Bilingual Community: Some Frisian Data, in J. van Oosten and J. P. Snapper (eds), *In: Dutch Linguistics at Berkeley: Papers Presented at the Dutch Linguistics Colloquium at the University of California, Berkeley*. Berkeley: Dutch Studies Program, 45–66.

(1986) Comments on the Development of Breaking, *Us Wurk* 35:1–11.

(1983) The Nature of Phonological Representation: Evidence from Breaking in Frisian, *Journal of Linguistics* 19:59–78.

(1982) Local and General Markedness, *Language* 58:832–849.

(1980) (with Tseard de Graaf) Some Phonetic Aspects of Breaking in West Frisian, *Phonetica* 37:109–120.

(1980) Some Theoretical Implications of Stem Alternations in Dutch Diminutives and Plurals in W. Zonneveld (ed.), *In Studies in Dutch Phonology*. The Hague: Martinus Nijhoff, 247–263.

(1980) Phonological Opacity and the Notion of Contrast, in W. Zonneveld (ed.), in *Linguistics in The Netherlands 1977–1979*, Dordrecht: Foris, 466–483.

(1978) Bidirectional Leveling as Evidence for Relational Rules, *Lingua* 45:65–77.

(1975) The Nature of *f* and *v* in Frisian and Marathi, *Journal of Phonetics* 3:17–23.

# NAME INDEX

# SUBJECT INDEX